Presen[illegible]nd Place

Also by Jeremy Hooker

from Shearsman Books

Upstate: A North American Journal
Openings: A European Journal
Diary of a Stroke
Ancestral Lines
Word and Stone
The Art of Seeing
Selected Poems 1965–2018
The Release
Addiction: A Love Story
Preludes
With a Stranger's Eyes

from other publishers

Poetry *(Selected volumes)*
Solent Shore
Englishman's Road
A View from the Source
Master of the Leaping Figures
Their Silence a Language (with Lee Grandjean)
Our Lady of Europe
Adamah
Arnolds Wood
The Cut of the Light: Poems 1965–2005
Scattered Light
Under the Quarry Wood

Prose
Welsh Journal

Criticism
Poetry of Place
The Presence of the Past: Essays on Modern British and American Poetry
Writers in a Landscape
Imagining Wales: A View of Modern Welsh Writing in English
Ditch Vision

As editor:
Frances Bellerby: *Selected Stories*
Alun Lewis: *Selected Poems* (with Gweno Lewis)
At Home on Earth: A New Selection of the Later Writings of Richard Jefferies
Alun Lewis: *Inwards Where All the Battle Is: Writings from India*
Mapping Golgotha: A Selection of Wilfred Owen's Letters and Poems
Edward Thomas: *The Ship of Swallows*

Presence and Place

Jeremy Hooker
&
Lee Grandjean

Shearsman Books

First published in the United Kingdom in 2025 by
Shearsman Books Ltd
PO Box 4239
Swindon
SN3 9FN

Shearsman Books Ltd Registered Office
30–31 St. James Place, Mangotsfield, Bristol BS16 9JB
(this address not for correspondence)

www.shearsman.com

EU AUTHORISED REPRESENTATIVE:
Lightning Source France
1 Av. Johannes Gutenberg, 78310 Maurepas, France
Email: compliance@lightningsource.fr

ISBN 978-1-84861-971-5

Presence and Place

March 1981

Winchester

I have no record of the date when I first met Lee Grandjean but I remember the occasion well. It was towards the beginning of my period as creative writing fellow at Winchester School of Art and I had introduced myself to the students by giving a reading of my poetry. At the end of the reading, to my astonishment, a man in a white boiler suit stood up and clapped. Nervous on this occasion, my first thought was that this was intended as satire. It was, in fact, appreciation, and this was my first encounter with Lee Grandjean, who, at that time, held a sculpture fellowship at the School of Art. We talked after the reading and it wasn't long before he was showing me the sculpture he was at work on. Thus began a creative relationship that has been, and continues to be, immensely important to both of us.

24 March

Lee came back last night, after we'd had a couple of drinks at The King Alfred, and we took Sue out for a curry. Then for another drink at The Royal Oak, where a group was playing traditional jazz. Talking with him and looking with him at his sculpture have been the most valuable and enjoyable experiences of this term. Lee feels the "necessity of 'going back' in order to find one's present", and is in conflict with the dominant art 'community' prevailing now. My feeling is that it's difficult to make anything real if we're not part of a community. Of course, it isn't a question of simply going back, of a naïve or even sophisticated imitation of earlier forms, themselves an expression of cultural & spiritual movements that no longer prevail.

What are we with no community validating our images to do?

Lee has gone through the process of breaking down that modern art has increasingly come to be, and many artists exploiting it are content that it should be. He has come to the end of a dominant mode of abstraction, which has become limited, and returned to the human figure, and to the task of making images with sculptural integrity, which belong in a common world to which they 'speak'. He is seeking to find his own forms. Easier, he knows, to come back to the task than to fulfil it!

I like his recent work in particular, his family of large, wooden 'container' shapes, which, like ship and womb, hold, carry, and sustain. We hearten and stimulate each other, even though, when excited by sculptures or paintings, I often feel that I'd rather give up words, and start at the beginning with a stick to carve or a sketch pad! Not that I don't know the beginning is where I have to start with words too.

12 May

Full May. "And they sit outside at 'The Travellers Rest'." The King Alfred, actually, with Lee. Walking back beside the canal we see two water voles swimming across to converge under the father bank, and wrestle in the water – mating or fighting? – one biting the other's neck. Such effortless power of growth in horse chestnuts with masses of candles lifted shelf above leafy shelf.

Later we took Sue for a meal at Alresford and sat by the pond with a drink. Here ducks were mating, though it looked like an act of violence, the belaboured, pecked female uttering squawks like noises of pain & terror. At long last, barely audible far off across the pond, an unmistakable vibrant note heard under the water-birds, my first cuckoo.

The day ending with perfect company could not have been fuller.

At Ovington
for Lee Grandjean, sculptor

You would make a form
that contains, which your hand moulds
as we talk, creating a body
between us, in the air. Below
the broad full river glides
hypnotically, silver,
green and dark. Here wind
meets light and water,
and the current at each instant
finds its bed, erupting
over shoals of weed, sliding
through a lucid gravel run,
continually making
and unmaking lines,
as in my mind I catch

and loose its images,
and about our heads
swifts hawking for mayfly
unerringly, explosively, glide.
I would let all go again,
saying – it is perfect without us,
but we meet here, we share
words and your hand shaping
the flow, the brute
and graceful wings.
And our feet beat solidly on the bridge.

31 July–2 August

A family weekend with Lee & Kate at their home, Moor Farm, near Reepham in Norfolk. Today I'm stiff, after cricket on the sands at Holkham – sea far off & broad wet sands reflecting a blue sky – and on their lawn. Last night, a big sickle moon, like part of a wheel's silver rim. Cornfields, pale yellow, ranks of big spiky ears against Moor Farm's red brick & gentle wave motion of pantiles. In a garden corner, partly surrounded by sycamore & ash, and with a screen of willow-herb, a small, peaty pond. The surrounding country has a strong but quite regular swell, and there are no other houses nearby, but, at some distance, three church towers.

I associate a feeling of release mainly with Lee's big, red brick, tiled barn which he uses for his studio, and with the monumental forms he's currently working on. High above his head the strong adze-marked roof beams; below, sections of a huge elm in various stages of being worked, a powerful limestone father & child nearing completion, wood chippings, sketches on the walls, and his tools on a bench – claw & gouge, chisel, mallet, club hammer, bolster, point.

Moor Farm with its family life is a wonderful place, and a place for Lee's work to develop in; a home and garden waiting to be inhabited by his forms, which belong as much as the fragments of Tudor wall paintings discovered in Lee and Kate's bedroom, and the marks of many labouring generations in buildings & fields. Now he's working ten hours a day preparing for an exhibition at Yorkshire Sculpture Park, Bretton Hall in the autumn. I came back brown and aching, wanting to work, and seeing the figures framed in the barn.

10–11 June 1982

In London, where Lee teaches 3 days each week. After an hour in Dillons, I met him on the Waterloo Steps at 6, and after a drink by the river – high, with a swell, glittering in full sunlight – we walked across the bridge and in and out of the Inns of Court, stopping for another drink at The Cheshire Cheese. Still a feeling of Dickens's London and even Dr Johnson's in this intimate area of courts & alleys. Walked on past St Paul's, the Barbican, Smithfield, and through Clerkenwell to end the evening with an Italian meal in Holborn. Taxi to his mother's home in Fulham.

Next morning, we took the train to Wimbledon and spent the day in the Art School. Great torsos of beech & elm, blocks of yellow limestone in the sculpture area: solid reassuring materials. Here I met Michael Penny, Ken Turnell, and, later, Glynn Williams. After lunch in a Wimbledon pub I went with Ken, Michael and Lee to an exhibition of students' sculpture in Cannizaro Park near the Common. There were some fine things here, Glynn's 'Rising, Holding, Protecting', Michael's 'Walnuts', and Lee's 'Angry Man'. I like the frank way in which the sculptors talked about each other's work, looking at it closely – not for the first time, of course – and being openly and constructively critical. They have strong, shared beliefs about what's going on in sculpture today and are critical of mannerisms and literalism. They obviously benefit from their mutual support, as well as being strong individually.

To Soho with Lee in the evening, where we had a meal in a delightfully rowdy Greek restaurant in Charlotte Street. Then a late walk: Soho, Piccadilly, Trafalgar Square. I was blistered, footsore, pounding the pavements but continually learning something of London in Lee's company. Earlier he had pointed out where Marx had lodged. Now we passed Churchill's wartime bunker, the texture of its ivy-clad walls apparent even in the dark; statues; a son of one of the Georges on a towering column; the wide expanse of Horseguards with a solitary policeman keeping watch in the middle, and then the Clubs & Ministries. The latter were overwhelming, rising over us with formal grandeur. I felt minute in the shadow of their forbidding cliff-faces, and totally insignificant in the presence of their power. My mind went back to the feeling of doing important things, of making a world, that I'd had at the Art School. Now we all seemed a speck of life, of no account to these huge forms and the powers they represent. Here were the irresistible imperatives of State. When we got back to Fulham, Avril (Lee's mother) told us how she'd felt the challenge of these buildings when marching down their echoing canyons in the '30s, shouting slogans against non-intervention in Spain.

20–21 October

Met Lee on the Waterloo Steps late in the afternoon, and we walked across the bridge in drizzling rain. Grey light gives a fitting, dramatic atmosphere to the city, a swirl of cloud round St Paul's, all the great buildings lightly shrouded, Nelson on his column a leaden black, making our heads spin giddily for a moment as we look up where he soars, the lights of Piccadilly gaudier than usual in the wet dusk; and again, for a moment at Trafalgar Square and along the crowded streets, pictures of other times flashed on my inner eye – omnibuses, crowds wild with excitement at Victory.

I went feeling strained and found Lee also rather low; which lifted me in the effort to be cheering. We talked over a pint in the Coal Hole. On then to Blond's in Sackville Street, for the private view of Glynn Williams's recent carvings. His 'Shout' dominates the room, a woman with a dead child in her arms, head thrown back, the circle and gaping hole of her wide-open mouth echoed by the lines cut round it in her carved face. Like the stretched gap of a dead fish, I kept thinking; but because Glynn has caught in her mouth the extreme protest of all creatures against unbearable pain. The private viewers milled around, gossiping, and it seemed to me 'Shout' silenced us all, filling the room with a presence that brushed us aside.

4 June 1983

To Margam for the opening of the Sculpture Park. My invitation came from Lee and I walked round the park with him and Kate and their boys. A fascinating place: landscaped parkland & gardens with rhododendrons & azaleas below high rocky bluffs; ruins of the Cistercian abbey; the burnt-out shell of the great mock-Jacobean house; the fine 18th century orangery. The smoking steel works of Port Talbot came into view as we climbed through oak & beech woods and through heather & bracken on the open hillside onto high bare moorland, the channel and the English coast beyond, and Gower cliffs to the west. It rained as we walked on the top, and the day was close. Glynn was there, and I saw 'Shout' and other works by him in the open. Lee's 'Falling Figure' & 'Head of Stas' also impressed me, as did a magnificent Frink head. But there was much that was only whimsical, or a formal game, clichés of contemporary sculpture, which looked especially vacuous against the medieval ruins and the modern industrial forms.

29 July

At Reepham, with Mieke.

The sculptor's house. Here in particular I notice forms: the shipshape red roof of house & barn, with tiles like waves; globular poppy seed-heads; the field track sweeping down to the house in its hollow; fields of pinnacle corn, fields of sugar beet; sculptures in the garden and sculptures and drawings in the barn-studio. Everywhere the presence of things made or being made. And the weather is hot, with blue sky & a few brushstrokes of white cloud. High summer in deep country.

Waking in the night, I felt that I could see time passing. The garden and fields were an eerie grey with the looming, darker masses of trees and shrubs, high up a waning moon. In my mind, I am in the garden, and Mieke is lying close by. Kate is playing the piano indoors and Lee is in the studio working with a kango power hammer and chisel on a block of stone. Two of the four brown hens are pecking under the apple tree, which is full of sparrows chirping loudly.

26 February 1984

Morning. A walk with Lee and the boys near Blickling Hall. At the back of the Hall, the lake with geese on its banks, glinting coldly below us. A view of the Hall from the front, the beautiful, arrogant Jacobean dark red brickwork, deep set between broad yew hedges. On the site of the house where Anne Boleyn is said to have been born and spent her childhood. Lee and I walked back quickly along the road to fetch the car, and we completed a good morning with a first-class meal in a warm and friendly pub.

In the evening, Kate returned from a night supporting the women at Greenham Common. Apparently, every doctor in the country has received a letter from the government asking them to make provision for the possible event of nuclear war. How soon the unthinkable has come to be thought and talked about. As I sit here in the kitchen at Moor Farm, writing or looking out at the pond or across the lawn where a moorhen is feeding, I can hardly believe that this is the same world as that in which the threat exists; but I know it is.

This morning, Lee produced a copy of the book which shaped my imagination: *Britain's Story Told in Pictures*, which begins with a cave man chipping flint & a sabre-toothed tiger, and ends with the Whitehall Cenotaph and a 'modern' (c.1914–18) British submarine. (This, perhaps, is an earlier edition, since I remember a Spitfire & searchlights.) Mother bought me a copy in Woolworth's in Fareham when I was about 5, and though I haven't seen a copy for more than thirty years, the images have often come back to me.

How often is a woman walking with a child aware of what she represents? The image, as I saw it this morning, as I passed one, then another, woman holding a child by the hand, reaches beyond words. I was more than usually sensitive, I suppose, from seeing my children, but also by the intensity of Kate's feeling for her children, and also because being with Lee always intensifies my grasp of images. A woman and a child are a reality before they are an image; the image doesn't invent them, but points to something immeasurably deep and powerful. But to shape the image so as to invoke the reality would be worth the effort of a lifetime to achieve once or twice.

15 May

Lee, in a letter: 'I always wonder whether or not there is achievement in what I do, for in my study of the past I place myself and see my crudity. Ah we live in crude times. So many more machines and so much less order – moral order, spirit order. More intricate knowledge of parts and less of any concept of whole. Which is no kind of wisdom at all.'

23 July

At Reepham, after Mieke has returned to Holland, I'm alone for the first time in a month, and lie in bed with rain pattering on the window and a storm booming a few miles off and coming closer. Today, Peter Fuller, the art critic, and his girlfriend, Stephanie, soon to be his wife, came to look at Lee's work. He seemed very self-involved and showed no interest in talking to me. Sarah Tombs, a young graduate from Wimbledon, is here too, and has been working on a large piece of elm. It's a delight to see her serious, enthusiastic concentration in her work, as it is to see Lee's. Tonight, Kate, Lee and I sat talking in the firelight (it's cold here in the evenings), as lightning pulsed and flickered in the night-sky visible through the windows on either side.

24 July

Dawn. Bluetits chirping in the eaves. Quarter of a waxing moon.

Kate pointed out to me graffiti scratched in the bricks of the house: names, initials and dates, the earliest surviving from the beginning of the nineteenth century. Moor Farm is much older; the land is like a great, still pool of time. It gives a sense of enclosure, where time has gathered in great depth, accumulating in the earth itself, which generations have laboured over season after season. The new wheat looks very ancient, and here I feel the touch and shaping of many hands. This, perhaps, is why seeing a sculptor at work here is profoundly satisfying. Lee's works in the barn and garden feel completely at home. He too is working because he needs to, and working with nature to create new forms of human truths. Thus, his 'Woman pointing', first started in a Yorkshire Sculpture residency, is a strong image of the threat hanging over all of us – everywhere the morning sky of Hiroshima – and a form containing woman's powerful meaning. Although he feels that he has never belonged in any place, I feel that in such images he is making something essential from being here.

Later.
We worked all morning in and around the barn studio, clearing out chippings, using the gantry to lift sculptures, and trussing them securely to the car roof-rack for the journey to London for a summer exhibition. 'Scallops of the Gouge' (as I call it) is a figure some two feet high carved from *lignum vitae*, black-green and harder than some stones, 'almost flint-like'. Still rough, scalloped where it will be polished, and only partially defined, but already with a strong presence. 'Pathos': Lee cuts down to release the naked emotion in the human figure – anger, grief, pathos, etc. – but always in sculptural terms.

He spoke about the widespread misunderstandings of 'organic form' and we looked closely at a hogweed growing close to the barn. 'Structure in nature is very clear; sculpture should aspire to three-dimensional clarity.' There's nothing loose or vague in nature, but in everything a structure of different relationships between part and part. The ribbed column of the hogweed stem has the strength and structure necessary to bear the branches which in turn are constructed so as to bear the slender, rayed branches from which the umbels grow.

The sculptural 'equivalents' he used – 'ribbed columns', 'spanning', 'vaulting' – connected the necessary relationship between structure and function in the plant; and the 'exaggeration' he favours and practices in sculpture is not surreal – a making of absurd connections between part and part – but coherent in terms of the proportions and dynamism of the particular work. An example of his concern for sculptural integrity was his worry in case his use of objects – nails, a bolt, a piece of iron chain – which had been in some old gate posts, was merely mannered. (I thought the result in each case effective.) 'Clarity' – his primary value – is evidently the result of a coherent and integrated structure. It follows that the artist will learn nothing of value by imitating nature's appearances, but can learn much by close examination of actual processes of growth and structures of natural forms; but again, not to copy them, but to understand their principles relative to his own art.

The African master blocked out the original form, achieving its proportions and dynamics, and the apprentice 'finished' the work. The Western apprentice blocked out the form, and the master achieved its finish. Hence the value of expert representation in the latter tradition, and the value placed on the underlying principle of form in the other. Lee works from the core, with a sense of the whole and the relationship of part to part forming it, which determine the surface.

After lunch I visited Cawston church; which I found a place of impressive fragments: hammerbeam roof, wooden angels with outstretched goose wings high up, the Speed the Plow carved inscription, a head of the Green Man. But it was barnlike, empty, so that the words standing out on the altar cloth – All in Christ shall be made alive – were little more than words. Once it would have been intimate, communal, a house of pictures & images, and worshippers would have been part of a living body. Now, it is a kind of museum for the visitor; and a museum might be equally fit for solitary prayer.

10/11 April 1985

Late afternoon as the Tate was about to close, I met Lee and we looked at Picasso's 'Weeping Woman'. We then went by the river for a drink in a pub at Cheyne Walk, near Carlyle Mansions. Coming out, we saw Concorde beginning to climb over the city, sun shining on the fancy struts & icing sugar paintwork of the Albert Bridge, and drove through Chelsea to his mother's house in Fulham. After a meal with Avril, an evening of good talk & drinking in a pub crowded with young people near Parson's Green.

Next morning, in rain, Lee took me to see his first major one-man show at Blond Fine Art in Princes Street. Here, looking at the five large carvings, the smaller carvings and the reliefs and paintings, I remembered the words from the Apocrypha which he had quoted to me in a recent letter (and which went as an impulse into my 'Master of the Leaping Figures'): 'To the universe belongs the dancer' (from the foreword to Elaine Pagel's book, *The Gnostic Gospels*).

Now, there was time for me to look again and again at each work, to feel the presence of each and to take in the 'world' which all together make. This is strong work which deserves a wider audience.

'Willow' (elmwood), the feminine form in contrast to the masculine forms of the other large carvings. 'The Figure and the Tree' (elmwood), 'Under a dark sky' (walnut), a carved head with the shadow of a hand painted on it, expressive of anxiety and a shout of protest. In this and in much of the work, tensions: power/vulnerability, shelter/exposure, terror/ecstasy. In several the raised arm becomes the dark threatening cloud, which expresses his constant awareness of danger, 'the last blast of light'. The photograph from Hiroshima of the shadow on a wall of a man on a ladder has made a deep impression on him. Yet his power comes in part from his combination of this awareness with dynamic natural rhythms, the 'earth dance', or from the tension between these primal emotions. 'Figure, two blues' (oak). 'Pond, Willow, Spire' (elmwood). Several reliefs ('Secret', 'Sky and Earth', 'Three blues') suggested to me Stations of the Cross. I don't think this was intended, and wondered whether this, and other suggestions & echoes, were merely my irrelevant importations. 'The Bow Flown Away with the Arrow', a relief whose original impulse was our experience of the swifts on the bridge at Ovington, as it was of my poem. Lee expresses the space between human being and bird, the impossibility of the two being joined, and sadness at this. 'Cold Mirror' (limewood), the one carving which does not reflect nature (though it does reflect the human figure) but which has the double image that recurs as a motif in the paintings.

The exhibition is in its last week and so far, nothing has been sold except a painting which his father-in-law has bought. We were in the gallery a long time, during which one man came in who was looking for the children's book illustrations on the wall in one room, and two women asking for directions to the shop selling school uniforms that used to be where the gallery now is. Finally, a man came in and arranged to display one of the large sculptures in his garden and two of the smaller carvings in his house at St John's Wood, for a private exhibition. This may lead to a sale, and was, from that point of view, the only hopeful sign during the whole exhibition.

Early July

In East Anglia, mountainous, green hedgerows: grass, fern, elder, cow parsley, masses of creamy pink & white dog roses – the best year of the wild rose I can remember. After the flatness of Holland, the English countryside, with dead elms in the hedgerows, is immediately irregular and various, a place of corners, hills & hollow, mysterious, with dynamic, broken rhythms. On the narrow road out of Norwich, uncut roadsides looked like green mountains.

At Corpusty, an abandoned church on a hilltop. Belfry boarded up, windows closed with sheets of corrugated iron, pantiles slipping and a mouldering stone porch. Tombstones sunk to their heads & shoulders in nettles, grass & fern. Near the gate, In Sweet Memory of Dawn. Beloved daughter. Aged 8 months. There were red flowers & dried grasses by her stone. She would have been twenty-one this year.

In Lee's studio. Paintings & sculptures of faces looking up fearfully, fingers pointing. Room in shadow, but here & there, from gaps in the roof, a brilliant spot of light on the floor. Halves of a swallow's empty egg under the nest high on the wall above the paintings. A set of elmwood heads and one in walnut wood, all staring up. A painted relief cut in an old gate; Christ suggested by a Velázquez Flagellation. Figures painted on the bottom of what was once a solicitor's desk. The large sculptures from the show were there too, all a family of image, a growing body of work – which Lee was pleased that I said. He is more strained than I have seen him before, and has only recently won temporary relief from financial difficulties.

Lee is asking how to express things through figures, but beyond appearances and naturalism. The body is a medium for expressing emotion, felt physically. He wants to hang on to the subject while transforming it into another reality. I saw the influence of Picasso in the staring faces, and Lee said that he was always 'hitting up' against Picasso in what he was attempting to do. For Lee, Picasso is *the* artist of the twentieth century – from cubism to abstract expressionism – who liberates subject with new transformations. 'Being born in mid 20th century (in 1949')', he says, 'I can only hope to understand last half of this century but find enough to be of value for all the futures.'

Hot days. Digging, sweating, weeding an overgrown strawberry bed near the sculpture of fox and goose. Looking up, eyes cleansed by sweat, I see the trees & woods as a depth of blue shadow, and the sharp-angled red-tiled roof and barn. Malevich, the white cat (the other, grey cat is called Gris), lies beside me in the shade of raspberries. White cat, pink nose, pink flesh of ears showing through fur, eyes like transparent pebbles. She catches a vole and brings it to show me.

Chickens, ducks & ducklings. Moorhens & baby rabbits on the lawn. Partridges & lapwings with their chicks in the fields. A hare like a small deer.

Sweet dawn. The word 'ancient': light shining on dust & spiderwebs in window panes, a thick hawthorn hedge outside, and a glimpse of wheatfields & woodland beyond it. Gold dust motes. Red & blue lupins, moorhens in the grass. Saxthorpe, Edgefield, Corpusty, Baconthorpe, Little London. Church towers, all with an air of abandonment, standing apart, the few unbroken strands lying slack on the surrounding landscape. Yet I would re-enter the pattern, come back to wood & earth & stone. But even if I could it would be no good breathing a finished air. What George Oppen says about one's generation is true: that we know it by its confusion and wounds, and if we do not find it, we are lost, abandoned to irrelevance. Lee and a few friends, known & unknown, are my generation.

A walk to Holkham beach with Mieke & Elin, Lee & the boys. Down a long track (Lady Ann's Drive) between fields, through a pinewood, passing close to the Queen's lodge. When we got to the beach, it began to rain. Thunder & lightning. Lee at once directed us to make a shelter of driftwood planks, fish boxes, a plastic sheet in the dunes, and arranged and built most of it himself. This kept the rain off us, and we huddled together in high good spirits under the roof while the storm came close and moved away. Then, in a fresher air, we played rounders on the sand, and the sea began to come in.

At evening, the distant sea, where the sun caught it, flickered like flames. Then mist, the sun over the sea a red-gold ball, glimpsed between pines, and we walked back, past musty elderflowers, hay, and cow parsley smelling strongly after the rain. From a field edge hidden in mist: Cuckoo! Cuckoo! So, I wasn't to miss it this year after all.

On the way back we stopped for a drink at an old pub, Lord Nelson, at Burnham Thorpe, and sat outside with our drinks at the edge of the playing field, looking across at the church where Nelson's father had been vicar. In the mist, this looked flat, like a cut-out. It was a haunted place beside a small stream in misty evening light, with swallows skimming over the green, and as Lee told his boys the stories – telescope to the blind eye, and so on – I could feel something of the sea's pull for the boy, as if it were actually plucking at the still earth around us.

14 October

A beautiful autumn morning walking and driving with Lee along the Embankment, the river in Monet light, a faint, misty blue. New gold leaf shining on the face of scaffolded Big Ben. Statues: Cromwell, Churchill's turned back, Epstein's Smuts, a dark, striding figure with a gull perched on his head. Through the East End. Whitechapel. A new mosque, sweat shops. Jack the ripper's hunting ground at Spitalfields (Brick Lane, Fournier Street). The Blind Beggar and the Krays' territory. Along the Mile End Road, past Queen Mary College, where I went for an interview years ago. To Bow, where we called at a wax factory to get some wax for Lee to use in modelling. On the way back we visited the house which is being renovated for Avril's friend, Henry, who had sold his rubber plantation to the Malaysian government. This is a large, solid 18th century house, formerly owned by a family of Huguenot weavers. This also gives some sense of the city: to walk on wood floors, up the stairs, in & out of spacious, airy rooms, thinking of the world this was, one house among others in a narrow street, stone walls of demolished houses on the other side. Hawksmoor's beautiful Christ Church stands on the corner, and there were groups of policemen in the area, waiting for the arrival of a Bangladeshi religious leader. Other fleeting images as we drove away: old, grey-bearded Bengalis, a sprawling middle-aged man in the car alongside us, pushing out his false teeth with his tongue. Whitechapel to Wapping, where we parked the car and walked by the demolished docks towards the grand medieval fantasy of Tower Bridge & the Tower. Lunch at the Dickens Inn by St Katherine's Dock, with a distant view of Scott's Discovery & some beautifully painted London barges. From there I went alone by tube to Russell Square and walked to Dillon's, then back via Waterloo to Winchester.

22 July 1986

Train to Norwich, where Kate met me at the station and we drove to Moor Farm. Walked with Lee up the track by barley fields, between banks of midsummer flowers, and round the garden, the mock-gothic front of Booton church across the fields, and several of his sculptures standing up in clearings in the wild meadow alive with butterflies & moths. He showed me his latest work and work-in-progress in the barn-studio, which has had some improvements. Two of his pieces in public places have been vandalized this year – one he no longer cared about much, and was glad of the insurance money, the other ('Father and Child', a Hemel

Hempstead school commission) he has here and is replacing the broken stone head, knocked off with a sledgehammer. In recent works, especially in a dancer, the sinuous, dynamic movements are even more marked, and in some there is a tension, or balance, between the gravity of mass and the leap or flight of movement. A major current preoccupation is the imagery of angels (in part, a development from his bird imagery), and the model of the Islington Angel, presently being cast, suggests how fine the finished work will be. Before a late supper, we played a long game of cricket with Guy & Louis between apple trees on the lawn.

23 July

Rain after drought; a surprisingly cold day, like autumn. In dry intervals, I weeded a border beside the house, while Lee worked on 'Sundance' – a work in stone commissioned for Fournier Street – outside the studio. Grey sky, darker grey jets flying low overhead, splitting the silence.

To Heydon with Lee for a drink in the evening. We discussed the idea of collaborating on a work.

24 July

This morning I cycled over to Salle to look closely at the church. Outside: two angels censing on either side of the door, bodies & upper parts of the wings with scales representing armour, but making them appear like mermaids. Wings ending in points, like fern. A woodhouse with club held across his chest over the north porch, which had a dead Christmas tree on a bed of fox-red needles, under a roof boss of the Last Judgement. Inside, light & space lifting the spirit with the pointed arches, windows, and high roof. Simultaneously, a familiar musty smell keeping the spirit earthbound. Silence, except for the clock ticking in the tower: heavy monotonous footsteps at my back. The fury of the iconoclasts was soon apparent in empty niches, broken statues, disfigured carvings, missing brasses leaving the outlines of medieval figures set in the floor. In this vast, almost bare shell, perhaps only the wooden angels under the roof remember a lost meaning.

The slender, high, pinnacle tower commands a wide countryside of cornland and beet fields; fine, stylized angels stand on the parapets on either side of the roof. Today, it was like an island in a sea of cloud, with gulfs of blue sky, and tidal waves of cumulus. Wind streamed through grass growing over the graves. Inside, tall pew ends catching my sight were momentarily like the large congregation that once filled it. But it was quite empty, all the power raised on the backs of the great flocks of sheep gone into the ground.

Cycling back, I saw the physical unity of the area, formed partly by the church towers, partly by the land's contours in relation to the sky, and partly by the red-brick farmhouses, several of them gabled in the Dutch fashion. I thought of the things I had seen, and especially of the angels, which are alive on the roof of Salle, and of the relation between these and Lee at work on *his* angels, struggling both for true meaning and recognition in a world that cares little for such things, or for the individual effort in their making. And I thought, as I am thinking now, about how we might work together, on what subject or idea, not whether it would be possible, since we have a fundamental imaginative sympathy, and often seem to be working in our different arts for the same thing.

Later

The curves of the land, dark, wooded hollows scooped out of cornland, clouds. Man-made shapes in relation to these: church towers, pinnacles, red roof keel, pantile waves. Angels in wood or stone, still in flight, visible bodies of invisible being: survivors on the wreck of the church, or a new creation. Jets splitting the silence, cancelling the groundwork of local meanings, their rumble against the mallet blows of the sculptor chiselling wood, making a boat image containing two figures.

Curves of the landscape and in the corn, like a child's lettering or the outlines of a hill-figure cut in chalk.

Lee talking in the studio – a swallow flying to its nest in the roof overhead, nestlings squeaking, over the black-painted bow-and-arrow swift sculpture picked out by light falling from a high window. Smell of wood shavings; soft chips to finger as he talks.

Earth & sky: moments of feeling physically part of the whole, being one with nature instead of separate. The relief called 'Within': a humanistic version of Christ in Glory.

Duality: how make one material speak about two different things? The same material, but different forms, different feelings. New feelings – ancient language. Our world is a dangerous place because the root is lost. We have wealth and technology but are spiritually poverty stricken. The human root: being part of things instead of fighting against them. The figure is a vessel, e.g., 'Hold', made at Winchester, but now a widening seeking out of the root. 'Dante's Barque' (Delacroix); Dante and Virgil. A symbol of existence: the passage through time, through life. The figures will be separate, looking out in different ways – still working at it.

Work more sculptural since the Blond show. Concern more symbolic, instead of with naturalistic detail (will scrape off the black paint on the swift, because too naturalistic. Generally worried that paint might be a substitute for what sculptural form should effect). Work getting thinner, denser, tighter, taut with meaning. Fear and ecstasy are close. *We can destroy everything* – the past as well as the present, culture & everything that has lived, all memory.

In this part of East Anglia, in the connection between earth and sky, one feels drawn out – and so we walk up the track, past ripening blackberries, over the disused railway line, to the curving barley field, the angle of three church towers, the roof & chimney of Moor Farm – red roof keel & smokestack – sinking down into the hollow, a yellowhammer singing its dry song in a hedge, and continue talking about how we might work together.

Angels at Salle

I feel for them:
                                        spirits
bodied in stone, motionless
winged beings the wind abrades,
soldiers standing at their post
on a long-abandoned field.

6 November 1986. London

A bright day, vapour trails high in the blue; below, jet liners, slender and graceful, coming in to land. Plane tree leaves swept into heaps on the pavements, where I walked with Lee to Parson's Green. Down a turning off the New King's Road, in a yard, the workshop of Mr Fiorini, bronze caster. Five or six men & women at work, most of them members of Mr Fiorini's family. Dust & fragments of plaster everywhere, casts, sculptures, including a Henry Moore (Mr Fiorini was his caster), and a figure representing a naked Winston Churchill with a penis befitting a bulldog (apparently the work of an elderly sculptor disgruntled at not winning a commission for a Churchill statue). Mr Fiorini, who has recently cast Lee's Islington Angel, showed us around. A good-humoured, thoughtful man of about sixty, a workman in overalls, he said that he could have made more money at another occupation, retired 'years ago, but the work gets hold of you'. He was driven on, always with the desire to do better, 'to achieve a more perfect colour'. Lee describes him as "a great 'patinator', holding all the secrets".

April 1987
Groningen, the Netherlands

Lee, Kate and the boys stayed with us for a week before Easter and we enjoyed many expeditions.

By Lauersmeer & Waddenzee, for example:

Earth, water, sky. Tall golden feathery reeds; many seabirds – ducks, geese, curlews, oystercatchers, plovers, sheldrake. Church spires, in mist at long intervals on the horizon far inland, both emphasize the space and give it a human dimension. Lambs skipping in the fields. Several windmills working, including *De Vier Winden*, where we stopped *and* heard it rumbling as the green-painted sails went round.

On the way to Westernieland, deep in the country, a heronry of about fifteen nests in trees beside an isolated farm, birds at the nests or slowly, gravely, flying to or from them, grey in grey sky. Back from an excursion over the border into Germany, we visited the monastery at Ter Apel, a medieval, brick building in woodland. It is a museum now, but was formerly 'Domum Novae Lucis', House of the New Light, situated on a sandtongue (to quote the visitors' leaflet) surrounded by a wild peat moor.

Over the border into Germany, to Haren, a small town which was almost completely asleep at lunchtime, as if everything had been shut against our coming.

Into Drenthe, to Anloo on the Hondsrug, on a day of fresh breeze & heaped, white cloud. Dark brown peaty rolling ploughland and a walk through woods to a hunebed, where the boys stalked us. Stopping by the church, cloud coming up behind the building could be seen through the windows, which included that beautiful, green-tinted, Puritan light. Only suppose *there never was another light*, only the light of the sun, and of the human mind, self-illuminated, with never a gleam of supernatural light.

Lee's greatest fear is that he should die without fully expressing the artistic truth that he has in him to express, that he should fall short of achieving his ambition. I understand the fear, but no one is more likely to succeed, since he has the gift and the energy and the will. He talked about the completeness of Gaudier's work; his own work is not complete in that sense; he is working through and working towards, creating good works & images in the process, but with much still to clarify and achieve. We talked about our work together, too. I understand better what he has in mind now, though at present I have a clearer idea of what he might do with my images, based on notes taken while walking in the New Forest, than of what I might do with his response to them. Still, I think the collaboration has considerable possibilities for both of us. Certainly, his works make me want to write.

Of all the people I know, Lee has at once the strongest sense of present artistic need and the greatest sense of tradition. He told me about a History of Art which he has long liked to read. On the front inside cover it has a chart of sculpture in the ancient world, long lines representing the thousands of years of Egyptian sculpture, etc; on the back inside cover the chart representing modern movements has many short, broken lines, Impressionism, Expressionism, Cubism, etc. He simply doesn't believe in the break between charts. What they taught him is that the tradition is continuous. As he says, "our small lives merge into a greater whole. An emphasis on 'the moment' is pathetic." He is a workman, a sculptor, in the tradition designated by lines at the front of the book.

If I could learn enough about sculpture, I would like one day to write a book about Lee's work and ideas. In the meantime, though, he gives me the greatest encouragement to do my own work, and we have work to do together.

10 July

Lee met me at Norwich station and we drove back to Moor Farm. Heavy grey cloud, midsummer smells & dusty roadsides. Green barley round the house & garden. I was too tired on arrival to take in much of what Lee told me about his work on our project. He had just taken delivery of a load of very heavy African wood (iroko) for his 'Peterborough Arch' sculpture, and the long blocks, together with a big elm torso (perhaps for 'Naked Man'), filled the barn studio. Tired, I walked up the track to where the three church towers can be seen. As always, a sense of loss, more, perhaps, than a sense of exclusion. I want to avoid mere nostalgia for an idea of the past, a mythical Middle Ages, or Age of Faith, as I want also to avoid mere churchiness, that mainly aesthetic feeling for old religious buildings which is a substitute for thinking about religious questions.

11 July

Morning: walking alone into the barn, in shadow with oval spots of light on floor & timbers from shafts between loose tiles in the high roof, where, with flashes of white, whirring wings, a swallow flew back and forth looking for a way out. Looking in half-light over the baulks of timber to the far wall opposite the windows, I was startled to see three wooden uprights (for 'Parable' I learned later) leaning against the wall, and had for a moment a strong sense of having stepped into the workshop of a maker of crosses. Later, walking with Lee to the field wild with long grass, nettles, purple vetch, where his 'Angel' (small head bowed, long, curved, graceful arms reaching up) stands echoing the vertical lines of Booton's twin towers across the valley, he talked to me about what the cross means to him. He is not a Christian, but for him the Cross is an axis, a juncture of powerful relationships (between vertical and horizon, the human stance between sky and earth, between life and death). He asks 'what is whole?' and seeks 'to recover nature in us'. In his Peterborough arch, the entrance or opening and the thing that opens are one. We talked about awe, and how in England one has to struggle with guilt and embarrassment in being serious about such things.

Lee showed me the first stages of sculptures ('Deepening half-light, listening' & 'Bolder Fountain') belonging to our project. As we stood in the yard looking at these, a white dove fluttered down and clung to my notebook, and we later rescued a half-naked, fleshy baby dove from Malevich, the white cat. When I looked through Lee's notes on 'Their Silence a Language', copying out what I felt I might use, I kept reading 'half-light' as 'half-flight'.

Later in the morning we drove with Louis to North Walsham, where Lee returned some lifting equipment he had hired to the workshop. On the way back, we stopped at Salle Moor Farm and picked strawberries, a little way past the high pinnacle church tower.

Jazz in Reepham Square in the evening, a Norwich youth orchestra, dressed in purple & black, playing to raise money for a local leisure centre. We joined the crowd and stood around listening and drinking beer.

12 July

A day of cricket, picnicking, lazing in the garden.

After dark, Lee and I walked on the track through the fields to the Cawston – Reepham road, and the white cat followed us all the way there and back. Cloud hid all but a glimmer of the cap of the full moon, in a sky faintly lit with neon towards Norwich. Only a few house lights, set far apart. (By day from this path a fourth church tower is just visible far to the east, and the land in which the farm is folded rolls gently to some distance on every side.) I asked Lee about his beginnings as a sculptor. As a boy in Peckham Rye, he always had a stone in his pocket and would endlessly pick at and clean it, and, like most boys, he would usually kick a stone when out walking, but, more obsessively than most, trying not to lose it. Aged 5 to 8, in Bucharest, he was out with street kids all day roaming the city, while his parents were busy with Cominform work. He was always alone (inwardly, if not in fact), and when he came to England, he felt foreign, like his name, as if he didn't belong anywhere. I think he has that sense still, in spite of Moor Farm, and of London, although he has found belonging in making art.

My mother had spoken to me of the inner core of aloneness that each person has. Lee's loneliness as an artist is different; he is driven in his work in a way that I can understand. Now, walking on the stony path in the dark, smelling strong midsummer night scents of corn and bean fields and elder flowers, he talked about the difficulty of work (he has a phenomenal amount to do on public sculptures, as well as work including ours) and the tension between what art demands and the call on his unselfishness as a family man. We talked about the fullness of life, and the joy & privilege of working.

13 July

Cycled alone in the morning to Cawston church (St Agnes). Looking up at an angel poised like a diver at the end of a beam of the wooden roof I distinctly had the illusion that its outstretched wing feathers moved! And was that a Sheela na Gig holding her vagina open suspended from the central beam? The guide book records a Green Man among 'old gods' carved on the roof.

Afternoon.

Helped Lee & the driver unload more off-cuts of iroko wood from the lorry. He has enough now for a gallery of reliefs. Later he drove me and Louis into Norwich, where we had a drink by the river before I caught the train.

23 March 1988

'Sculpture is the daughter of light,' Fenosa was fond of saying, quoting Picasso to his wife Nicole: 'in good sculpture, light has to flow in, as though you've just poured the water from the carafe into the glass.' 'Painting too, 'Nicole objected. 'No,' said Fenosa. 'Painting can be a fluke. Sculpture depends on a civilisation. To live, it needs a whole society: the labourer, the mason, the joiner, the mayor, the vicar, the poet...'

From the obituary of Appeles Fenosa, Catalan sculptor, died 25 March, 1988

1–7 August, at Moor Farm

'The landscape thinks in me, and I am its consciousness.'

—Paul Cézanne

"He remained a loner in the midst of a region where every stone, every tree, every brook was familiar to him since his youth. He never grew tired of its colours and harmonious shapes, its light and distant vistas dominated by Mont Sainte Victoire. 'For me,' he wrote to a friend, 'what is there left to do ... only to sing small; and were it not that I am deeply in love with the *configuration* of my country, I should not be here'."

John Rewald, in *Cézanne, The Late Work*

To begin with, perhaps because emotionally tired and still dejected, I saw little, but enjoyed games of scrabble at night and cricket in the nets on the lawn, which left me aching, and, initially, more miserable at not being able to bowl as I could when young. Not really looking at anything, I was only half seeing some of Lee's older sculptures in the yard & garden. Then all changed on the third morning when I looked with Lee at the new work in the galleries (whitewashed rooms converted from part of the barn), saw them, and saw again the earlier related sculptures – the body of work which he is constantly developing and refining.

'Balance': a large work, stained blue-green, one 'pillar' angular, fragmented, chunky, the other rounded, tree-like, emerging from a bulbous root, or egg, with flame-like forms around the 'trunk'. What I saw first in the figure spanning the pillars (close to the old roof beam) was a suggestion of the crucified Christ, strongly present in the raised 'arms' and bowed 'head'. (This sculpture, bought by Christchurch Museum, Ipswich, was subsequently destroyed. Left outside, it rotted.) Later, looking more closely and talking with Lee, I saw in this work and in others, such as 'From the City', images of Lee's life between country and city, not of his alone, but of the human situation between nature and the man-made world. He works of course from felt, physical experience: coming from Moor Farm to Liverpool Street, walking on pavements, between buildings, hard things with sharp edges; *seeing a tree against a building,* 'an entwining plant around a metal railing'. He seeks a balance, the truth of the experience of the contradictions. He remembers images of total destruction. He was brought up on London bomb-sites, made camps in them, played on broken rubble, but didn't think of them as bomb-sites (the word was synonymous with 'playground'). He saw plants creeping over broken walls: 'the things that survive are greater than us'.

Where in another work I see Christ descending from the cross Lee sees poignancy, vulnerability, the embodied emotion. He is wary of too many words. He will talk about 'the stretch and tension of being within a space, of living', of 'sprung tight forms', of 'a tenuous thing becoming itself from a flat thing,' and of 'a coming from, stepping down from', 'ascending, like a breath coming out'. He will not deny what I say about the figure of Christ (but as a figure that spans and joins earth and sky, or nature and the man-made, not as the Saviour nailed to the cross), or about flame or dance or angel, but he talks from a sculptor's experience, from the way in which his imagination penetrates reality. Consequently, these great motifs are realized in the work, and are progressively clarified, so that the tradition lives now – for example, what we see is the form of the cross coming alive with meaning (new and old), not a copy of an Old Master image, nor an imposition of an idea on the form. The initial inspiration is mainly formal: he feels many meanings in the relationships between the forms. I think that what happens is that as he works at the relationships the meanings become both clearer and deeper, and are there for us to see, rather than for him to talk about.

Lee can talk about meanings, but he thinks, feels, sees as a sculptor in terms of materials and formal relationships and embodied emotions, not in concept of, say, 'dancer' or 'angel'. Consequently, he has carved some of the great angels of our time. He is 'making religious work without being too conscious of it', and 'using symbols without being mannered'. This is what he says and I can see that it is true. He is a religious artist of great power and delicacy, at once boldly imaginative and sensitively refined, a workman and a poet in wood and stone. And, because most people in the 'art world' now feel threatened by the meanings, which, being quasi-religious, strike at the roots of the self-contained ego, they do not see the forms that embody them, or see them as if they were only forms, and invent descriptions that belittle the whole work.

For his reliefs, 'The Call', 'Entrance', and 'Praise, Awe, Despair', he is using old gates, which give 'a sense of ancient place', and are 'staves on which to hang notes'.

In the yard, there are two blocks of French Lepine stone (like a fine Portland, he tells me, probably from the same bed as Portland stone, in south-west France, but cleaner to carve). The blocks of white stone ring when we knock on them. They are the material from which he will carve his public sculpture for John Bright Street, Birmingham. In the barn studio, there are several wooden sculptures in progress. He works on several simultaneously, 'keeping them fresh'. 'From' (which we hope to buy) resonates with the meanings the word has come to have for me, yet is subtly other, too, in a way that makes me want to reach deeper.

EXTRACTS FROM 'FROM'

His body holds fast
to the earth. Yet he is, too,
a bow bent to shoot,

and the soul's arrow
drawn back, alive to his touch
in every feather.
*
He is always that
which he is about to be.
Now as he emerges

From the wood, he is
the tree walking, the passage
that will be his way.

Between earth and sky
his body stretches. He strides out,
and earth underfoot

thrusts and pulls. His flanks
are downland curved on the sky.
He is a flame also –

elmwood flickering,
blazing through trunk and limb,
burning in the mind

of the maker carving
him, consuming dead wood,
shaping him anew.

'By bringing forth thingliness, sculpture also brings forth the earth as a place where our bodies can resonate to the rhythm of things. In the origin of sculpture is its purpose: to return us to the home, to the mystery, we so often run away from and yet never quite leave.'

F. David Martin, *Sculpture and Enlivened Space*

I mentioned Martin's book to Lee and told him something of its tenets, which are indebted to Heidegger ('Touched by presence, the ancient name of Being'). I found things to learn from and things to question in it. Should I lend it to Lee? It seemed to me a book he didn't need to read, since he practises the important truth it enunciates.

Next morning, I was still dejected as I walked alone up the track from the farm. Then it was *presence* that took me out of the thought: Salle, the pinnacle tower appearing over the treetops; then Cawston tower; next Booton's, and the figure, including the barn and house roofs of Moor Farm, was completely visible. The things with presence, the ancient churches, do not immediately speak their meaning – the crucified Saviour – but speak now of another order, stone-built, situating in place something beyond place, linking earth and sky – that ideology, in modern critical terms, but what an idea!

Christianity gained worldly power (what god was worshipped here?) but contained its opposite. Now (a jet trainer crossing, lights flashing under grey cloud), all we have are worldly powers, glass and steel, naked with purpose or concealing it. Here, a rising breeze ripples leaves of sugar beet, yellowhammer's dry-throated song, small in the midsummer silence, a cock crowing at a distant farm. What I wanted to say was something about my sense of the broken figure that the churches and their dead symbols formed, and the powers that actually rule the world, and Lee's sculptures, which relate to the other presence, but reach out to new meaning, to embody the human, enlivening the place. The thought would not come clear, and was perhaps darkened by the solemnity of personal dejection, though I know that the solitary artist works with joy, and lives to struggle. I leave the thought as it was: dark, at the place on the track where the ancient buildings broke in on me, and formed a figure I can't interpret, not alone, but with my friend's sculpture, and with the powers that would negate both these and his work.

In the afternoon we all went for a walk at Mannington Hall, around the flint and brick manor house, in the rose garden, and round the estate on a carefully prepared walk. Again, my enjoyment was tinged with cynicism at being treated to a tour of a great open-air museum. Yet this isn't quite fair. The truth is also that I am restive at being a member of the public with governed access to the country, and covet a freedom which few can exercise.

On Friday Mieke and I drove to Peterborough, with the main aim of seeing Lee's' Peterborough Arch' sculptures, commissioned by the Development Corporation, for which he chose the site outside the city, in line with the cathedral, and at a distance from it, beside water and on a hill. 'Peterborough Arch' is a magnificent entrance to the city, striking even when seen fleetingly from the adjacent dual carriageway, but very impressive when seen close to. 'Second Entrance', with two joined figures back-to-back, shows how rich in meaning the 'language' of images Lee has developed is. In fact, the two figures are the same figure, at different moments in time: in Lee's terms, 'becoming more full through witnessing an experience'. His symbolism harmonizes with, and renews, important elements in the Christian tradition, but is also other, not tied to the religious meanings, such as man as a spirit at war with his body and with nature, which we in the West have emphasized. We had an unhappy experience of Peterborough, finding the few people we spoke to unfriendly. We were both on edge, which prompted my first thought on seeing the arch: how long before it is vandalized? There was an evangelist in front of the busy shopping precinct shouting about the soul. The cathedral spoke with some eloquence a language of stone, which I increasingly find a dead language, concerned with medieval political power. It was the sculptures that awakened in me a living religious sense.

The day was hot, sultry, with tarnished-silver thunderclouds, unpleasant on the busy roads across the Fens. The evening too was warm, as we all walked about in Norwich before going for a meal in a stuffy Indian restaurant.

Saturday morning: cloudless sky, sun on gravel, between shadows of apple trees on the lawn: midsummer as we dream of it, as it has rarely been this year. Summer of the 'pinnacle corn', of shadow blue as sea water lapping a distant wood across heat-hazy wheat, of bearded, purple thistles, and cumulus of hedge parsley & hemlock. Summer when the dust lies light. It was still and hot when Lee drove us to Holkham. Half way down the track to the beach, before the pine woods which open on dunes (with a few nude, older men wandering there like survivors of a Stone Age tribe) and the sea, we came on a party of birdwatchers all intently peering through sophisticated telescopes, camera lenses and binoculars across a marshy field in which some water-birds were swimming on a pond. Fortunately standing apart from the group, we convinced ourselves that we could see a large bird like an eagle sitting on a fence on the far side of the marsh. Shortly afterwards, Mieke asked one of the birdwatchers what they were looking at, and he told her they were looking *for* a rare sandpiper. On closer observation our 'eagle' was revealed as a sheet of plastic draped over a post.

16 May 1989

In a letter from Lee:

"I am near, very near being able to work from the 'motive' around me in Moor Farm: of trees and the vast range of growing living structure. I feel I may, now, be able to see beyond their surface. I know that's all I have to *see* and all I want to *see* but I need to feel beneath it, to get a sense of the whole. I have to use their 'within'; and see and draw *it* through the surface and what exists between the surface and me, and, further, within me. To hold the subject's inner rhythm. Content in the imaginative object is that inner rhythm. Felt, experienced through presence."

New Year's Eve. At Moor Farm.

At night, before the boys' bedtime, Lee lit a bonfire of thorn, holly cuttings, and the large torso of an early elmwood piece, 'Witness'. The holly crackled and whistled and hissed, tongues of flames and streams of sparks shot up into the darkness, and Lee and the boys lit fireworks, which were left over from November 5th. We roasted ourselves by the fire, pushing cuttings from the outside into the blazing core as it burned up, and stayed out until almost all of it was consumed. Later, indoors by a log fire, we saw in the new year with wine and champagne.

1 January 1990

Looked with Lee at his recent sculpture and took notes as he talked.

His sculpture carries ideas expressed in forms. The difficulty today, he says, is 'reading' sculpture, i.e., so that people know how to, and really look at it, and in consequence Minimalism gets loaded with extraneous ideas. The previous evening, we had talked about the work of Richard Long and, in particular, Andy Goldsworthy. Lee is trying to do something quite different, and is careful to say that his attitude towards their work, which is quizzical and sceptical rather than hostile, is coloured by the fact that it is lauded as *the* new sculpture, while his is dismissed as 'old-fashioned' in comparison. What should be talked about is what is *there*, in the work, which holds the meaning. But what gets talked about in contemporary sculpture is the ideas surrounding it. It is clear to me that Lee's ideas about nature and our relationship to it are at least as interesting as any other contemporary sculptor's, but the work of the fashionable invites discussion about its ideological context while his embodies ideas in sculptural terms. The *presence* of the sculpture makes you feel things through forms.

When he first moved from the city to Reepham, in 1980, he experienced 'moments of incredible existing in the world', and 'of connection to that which is other than human, 'such as he had never felt as much in London – from standing on the land, or walking on the earth, or watching a bird fly and 'feeling a part of this whole thing'. This is the feeling in the early autobiographical figures. For example, being a tree, sharing this existence. Trees are vertical like us, they do not wander over the surface, but are rooted. They are 'more satisfactory beings', like Indian temples carved out of living rock. 'They were what one longed for, an unconscious being in nature'. Later he talked about the influence on him of the landscape round Moor Farm. It is a landscape which gives a sense of being on the top of a great height, not as at Winchester in the bowl of a river valley. It sets the vertical (trees, which mark the edges of fields, church towers, telegraph poles, walls) against the horizontal. *Things reach up in this landscape, but are rooted.*

Sculpture is a struggle for permanence, for outlasting. (I had also just been reading about Paul Nash's identification with Wittenham Clumps, with a natural and man-made work which had existed long before him and would long outlast him. There is, I know, a powerful emotion, which is not exclusive to artists, although they may feel it most intensely, which comes from placing oneself in relation to an awe-inspiring form or process with a span of life much greater than one's own.)

For Lee, the hope of our time is *participation*, with equality of being rather than hierarchy. In his work the arch makes the tree and the figure columns of the same thing. 'An arch is an image of wholeness.' Also, the figure is passing through, but is *for this moment* a part of the column. We looked closely at a number of works, including some belonging to our collaboration, e.g., 'Elusive Spirit 1 & 11, 'Bolder Fountain', 'Naked Man', which is perhaps the finest work he has yet made. He said that in making this, for the first time, he wasn't afraid of referring to Henry Moore. He also confirmed the reference to Michelangelo's Rondanini Pietà, which I saw in it. At the same time, it could be only Lee's work. Sometimes the concept precedes the sculpture, but the sculpture doesn't illustrate the concept. *The idea has to be experienced again in the form of the sculpture.* His drawings discover the energy of things, their rhythms. His sculptures are made from his drawings, but the latter are not like maps which he follows. He is usually working on a number of things at the same time, exploring meanings.

After we had looked at several pieces in which he uses the image of the 'stacked' city – rough-cut blocks one upon another at different angles – he showed me a slide of a stained-glass window in Canterbury Cathedral. This depicts Lot's wife turned to a pillar of salt as she looks back at Sodom and Gomorrah, and standing between the cities and her husband and the others who have escaped. It is a most expressive, beautifully designed work, in which the burning, destroyed cities are imaged by a stack of fragmented buildings. It is, in fact, a Cubist work, non-representational and creating a 'realistic' visionary image. There could scarcely be a better illustration of the claim that Cubism was a *rediscovery* of a way of giving the imagination form. Its dynamic, non-literal arrangement of forms gives the *experience* of the city burning, the flame and collapsing buildings, the horror and relief of those who have escaped.

Lee also referred to the layered, stacked quality of Giotto's cities – he prefers the early Giotto and 'primitive' Italian art to Renaissance painting and yet he showed me Leonardo's drawings of the Deluge, in which the dynamic forms break down his scientific observation.

These illustrations were, for me, a compelling lesson. I know the modernity of Lee's work, partly because I share the experience which it expresses – living with the threat of global destruction, desiring and in part finding a different, more participatory relationship with nature, and between men and women, and between the male and female elements of one's nature – and partly because I apprehend its meaning *in* the work, because it touches me. I know, too, that he is drawing upon, and renewing, artistic and sculptural traditions with a long history, which transcend the usual period and 'movement' labels. But I have seldom if ever seen and touched the connection as I did then, between the living image in the work of the dead master and the image fertile with present significance and malleable in the mind of the artist working now.

Another remarkable thing is the correspondence between his 'Naked Man' and my words and the origin of both images. When we visited the original, in the New Forest in September, it was his first sight of it, yet one would think, from his work, that he had studied it and meditated on it for a long time. But perhaps what I mean is that the sculpture reveals the close affinity between our imaginations, since what I have seen with my own eyes, and – more to the point – imaged in words, he has cut out of the material in sculptural form. At the deepest level, our experiences are similar, and we seek similar meanings, in different arts.

Lee's best creative period to date has been the last ten years. It is his fertility and development that astonishes me: each phase has seen an increase in refinement and in power, while I could not see how he could go beyond what he had already achieved. But he has, while the work remains a body, but a growing body. 'If we could burn like that for ten years!' Lee said, as we stood by the bonfire. God willing, I will have time, and will work hard in the time to come.

from The Naked Man
(With despair, as always at the beginning)

3
To begin, to begin again
to make an opening –

What obstructs us but fear?
We must give what we have to give
body and soul.

You see the large, blind eyes.
He is there, the ancient wounded one
imprisoned at the core.

What emerges when you cut down
stands free of you,
and sets you free.

Late March/Early April

Working on the catalogue for Lee's forthcoming exhibition, 'Their Silence a Language', Christchurch Museum, Ipswich.

What is the unique person? Not only the stories we tell ourselves waking or dreaming, but perhaps the whole, including elements we do not know, and may not want to know. In which case we would not recognize ourselves, unless indeed we intuit what we essentially are, and may know not in a mirror-image but in a symbol.

In Lee's work, for example. He may be concerned with human being rather than the unique person, but he works from his own experience, in which he knows that being. He incorporates in many works the figure of 'essential' man – a bodily image in which we may feel ourselves, the muscular stretch of legs and back and arms, uprightness, held balance. This is not simplified in the manner of a cartoon; it identifies our physical being as we experience it, and our metaphysical situation, between earth and sky, and between separateness and union. Wholeness, for Lee, is participation. I believe that he does, in fact, shape an image that shows we are more than a part of nature. It isn't only that he doesn't deny the city, as poets and artists using a 'natural' language frequently do. He doesn't deny tension either – between the man-made and the organic, between being rooted and reaching up, between life as the tree and life as the dance or flame – but creates a whole that is a held tension, or the union in being of what we with part of ourselves perceive as opposites.

The whole work is a symbol of his experience, or a sculptural image shaped from his experience. Metaphorically speaking, it is a new word added to an ancient language, in the tradition of image-making descending from prehistoric times. This is, also, a language of monsters and angels, of gods and goddesses – a language of human life, and of the forces shaping and defining human life, that tells us more of the story, more than our daily and nightly fables. Yet this is one story, it tells of what we are and what we might be. And if each one of us is unique (and not, as materialists claim, only an historical, cultural construct), personality comprehends more than waking or dream consciousness, and we are other and more creative than we know, with possibilities greater than we are aware of.

30 April

I was shocked to read the news of Peter Fuller's death in the paper this morning. He was a man in the full vigour of his thought. Even to an acquaintance or a stranger, there is something stunning about that fact. Not that anyone is thinking alone, but the strong mind is that which is most inimical to death. In our living we participate in dying, however little at any time we may think or feel it, but thought is a godlike creative activity, which partly shapes and may seem to control the world we live in.

I don't want to philosophise at the man's expense. Today I have remembered the tea party on the lawn at Moor Farm, and that farcical non-meeting of the kind that perhaps only intellectuals can contrive, with Peter Fuller in his self-absorbed flow of talk, and me in my brooding self-protective silence.

Lee remarked wisely on Peter's death: 'When someone dies who had some sense of a great truth, it is the responsibility of those still alive who share that vision to keep seeking it with renewed vigour.'

20 June

A free day yesterday, which felt like a waste, as I went back to my collaboration with Lee but failed to write anything.

Why am I finding my part in this project difficult? It may help if I try to think it through.

I wrote my first notes on the New Forest, consciously seeking to know it better as a ground, sometime between completing *Solent Shore* and moving to Winchester. In my early days at the School of Art I was preparing to write on the subject, researching it further, when the breakdown of my marriage took my mind away from it. True, I had no idea what I was going to do with the material; nor do I now. But I need a kind of 'blindness' – submission to the material before mastery of it, for in a sense it is the material that shapes me. Exploration proceeds by way of what is found.

Certainly, to begin with, I felt the work would be autobiographical, perhaps even confessional. I remember thinking of the title 'The Naked Man' in those terms. But not for long. That isn't my way: it isn't how the ground is in me, or I am in the ground. I don't grow imaginatively by telling stories about myself. I'm a maker, or nothing. It's in and through images and the relationship among images that I learn, in poetry, to think and feel and see.

Now, in the exhibition, 'Their Silence a Language', it is Lee who has made the images. I am not content, unless in a special case, such as 'From', to interpret his sculptural images in words. That would be parasitic, which is the danger of poems 'about' works of art. There may be correspondence, but description is not creation. It may be, though, that his images stand between me and my original words. That certainly wasn't our intention, which was for my Forest notes to help to suggest visual and above all sculptural images and forms, which would then lead me back to the words with a new sense of their potential. In some instances, Lee has even isolated verbal images, thus in a way shaping *poem* as well as drawing and sculpture! My difficulty then is to *use* what he has shown me, re-entering the subject with a supple imagination, shaping as well as being shaped. He has exercised his freedom, partly on the basis of what I have given him. Now it is for me to exercise mine.

What I have gained from the collaboration so far is an enhanced sense of how a sculptor imagines, of the art and its relation to nature, and to his being. It is knowledge I have been drawn to over many years, since long before I met Lee although I have of course learnt most from him. First, perhaps, I received a sense of it from the land, from earthworks – barrows on the chalk, Silbury Hill. I didn't think of it thus as a child, of course; but, like most children, I was a maker of shapes from the dawn of consciousness – indeed, it is because we are makers that consciousness dawns. No doubt it all starts with the mother! I have some dim sense of all that beginning far back, and want to leave it dim, because it is the source of creative energy, which may be used only if not seen, turned into ideas, analysed. Much later I became interested in sculpture, first Henry Moore, and had an idea in Wales, which remained mysterious to me – 'Towards a sculpture in words'. It was an embryonic idea, a bodily sensation together with the words, a feeling of the rocks on Mynydd Bach and of a poetry that somehow corresponded … At any rate, an idea I put aside for later, as I have so many shadowy 'poems'. Throughout, I have known that there is an important correspondence between poetry and sculpture, especially the carver's rather than the modeller' art (though the child is first a modeller). One day I may write about this.

25 July

From Cambridge to Ipswich, Mieke driving, and with Elin, Kim Landers, and Lee. In the evening, I read my poems to a small audience at Christchurch Mansion in the presence of Lee's sculptures and drawings.

There were a few Constables in another room, 'Willy Lott's House', 'The Mill Stream', a fine portrait of his father, and a painting of his father's flower garden. Most of them were badly in need of cleaning, too dark, and poorly hung. Ironically, they lacked all freshness and seemed merely part of the history of the house, like the chopping block in the kitchen or the pewter dishes.

Lee's exhibition has elicited some interest but not much. A number of visitors, presumably non-professional gallery-goers, had written 'Strange' in the comments' column of the visitor's book. This pleased him; it suggested a response to the presence of the work. In his view, it is the emotional content of his sculptures that the art critics shy away from. His work cannot be neatly conceptualized but elicits a strong emotional response – or an embarrassed turning away. I think he is right, only I would add that the appeal of the work is religious, in that he is making new images for our human being and our relation to nature. Interestingly, one man raised a question about my use of 'liturgical' language – he seemed to be referring mainly to 'psalter' – and indicated the relief hung on the wall close to where I was standing, which he saw as a crucifixion. In fact, it was not. It is evident that, for some, any reference to or echo of traditional Christian iconography is an obstacle to their perception of the work. I have complained sometimes about people simply not listening to my poems, and I know how Lee feels when people, including other artists and critics, don't bother to look at his work.

From my Text accompanying Lee's exhibition, *Their Silence a Language*, at Christchurch Mansion, Ipswich, 16 June to 29 July 1990

Sculpture, more than any other art, affects us physically, and does not let us forget mind and body are inseparable. Imagination, it reminds us, is rooted in sensation, and grows within the world, which it is capable of transforming. This is implied, I think, by Lee Grandjean when he says he attempts 'to speak through PRESENCE: to hold my imagination in a still, silent object'. Take, for example, the figure based on the human body which is one of his primary motifs. The figure is shaped differently, with a greater or lesser degree of abstraction, according to the rhythms of the work of which it is part, but all its embodiments belong to a distinctive family of images, which are expressively elongated, taut, disproportioned. … They are born from the human being's fundamental physical sensations, in which we experience our existence – stretching with taut muscles, standing upright, balancing, being rooted to the earth yet at the same time capable of movement, of reaching up and stretching out. … The figure's presence is the form it gives to human experience, especially (but not exclusively) male human experience. Such sculptural form demands the language of encounter: we 'meet' it, it is 'other', and thus subtly makes us more aware of our humanity.

Sculpture, like the human body, is at once a material and spiritual phenomenon. Thus presence, in Lee Grandjean's work, is both physical and metaphysical. His figure exists between earth and sky, is simultaneously rooted and tense with the effort to ascend; it stands alone, but in relation to other figures, other images; it is a part which belongs to a whole. The sculptures are not inanimate things, but consist of arrested dynamic rhythms; their forms give a new, dynamic life to matter; they actively hold their stillness, speak their silence.

…

Grandjean is an artist like Blake, who reworks archetypal images in terms of his apprehension of life in the present, and in order to express and explore new meanings. Grandjean, like Blake, responds to the giant forms which haunt Gothic art, and for him, too, Nature is a whirlwind of energy, a channel of imagination, which courses like fire through vegetable forms and leaves them, like the burning bush, unconsumed.

…

During the past decade Lee Grandjean's images have developed considerably in authority, becoming more powerful, more dynamic, and at the same time clearer, sharper. There is no doubt that his move from London to East Anglia in 1980 stimulated this development, which resulted in part from his response to the landscape. The country surrounding his home at Moor Farm, Reepham, is undulating, opens here on near fields, there on far distances, and gives one an impression of being on high ground. Evidence of geological processes and marks of historical time reinforce the sense of 'distance', of 'height'. The landscape has, too, distinctive sculptural rhythms. Vertical lines stand out – trees marking the edge of fields, church towers (three are visible from Moor Farm), telegraph poles, roofs, walls – and are set against the horizontal plane. It is a long-settled yet sparsely occupied country, in which one may be solitary but is always standing on well-trodden ground; a country in which things are deep-rooted yet also give an impression of reaching up, and where the church towers emphasise the tension – or, perhaps, the interaction – between strong physical attachment to the earth and desire for transcendence. In country like this, especially after living among crowds and buildings, merely to walk or to stand is to regain the bodily self-knowledge, in relation to earth and sky, that is, often, a source of sculpture as of poetry. … Working at Wimbledon School of Art, Lee Grandjean spends part of each week during term in London, and part at Moor Farm. In consequence, the conflict between urban living and life in the country, that many feel, is accentuated for him. The result, however, is not only conflict, but rather the need to make a coherent whole out of two forms of experience, each stimulating in a different way – for Grandjean is not only aware of the abrasive, jagged edges of the city, but has a Londoner's love and knowledge of it.

26 July

A morning walk with Lee in Cambridge, to the gardens of Christ's College & Milton's mulberry tree, a notable ancient banked up with earth, its sweet red fruit, which we tasted, loved by birds. A garden made for meditation and conversation, bespeaking a high civilized order.

27 July

On the way to Reepham, Mieke and I visited Norwich cathedral in search of images of the Green Man. And found plenty, with the help of an enthusiastic guide, an elderly gentleman who took us to peer at wood carvings under seats and at stonework in the roof of the cloisters. Smiling or scowling, the faces are splendidly bold, with complete confidence in themselves and what they represent, not a trace of humility, not a hint of being overawed, but like the sun inside the building, power undimmed. The guide showed us other works too, notably the wood carving of an owl (symbolizing the Jews) being mobbed by smaller birds, and a wooden armrest depicting a sinner being chewed up by the mouth of hell. By contrast, Mother Julian with her cat, in modern stained glass, lacks conviction.

28 July

At Reepham. In the morning, Mieke and I walked on the disused railway track to Cawston. Time of fruiting: first ripe blackberries, blackthorn laden with purple & greeny blue sloes, crab apples, hips & haws, vivid red & yellow berries on wayfaring trees, rudimentary acorns on oaks. Still one or two wild roses in sheltered places. Feathers & down where a hawk had made its kill.

There is something strangely primitive about Cawston church tower. Kate finds it ugly in its austerity but I don't. It seems to me a *naked* statement of intent. As for the interior, the guidebook can't be bettered: 'Cawston Church lies like a great piece of flotsam washed up on the beach after the tide has gone out …' Seraphim poised with wings spread in the hammer-beam roof, about to dive into emptiness. The tide has gone out, leaving bleached, bare wood, and with it, a way of life, with ploughmen & their families. The altar cloth proclaims that in Christ all are alive, but the statement in which conviction was palpable warns dog owners to prevent their dogs fouling the sacred ground.

Walking back, I had a greater sense of the need of the image-maker now, of the work Lee is doing, for example, making images that incarnate our life, our being, and our need *now*. I even felt that without that work the tradition itself cannot live.

On the way back, a yaffle flew in front of us. Yellowhammers: voice of the dryness & the heat. The horse pond at Moor Farm is drying up.
In the barn: blocks & partially shaped pieces of wood standing or lying on the brick floor. The more shaped, the more they have presence. The unshaped are powerful, but dumb. A sweet smell from piles of sawdust & chips of wood. Into this high space, under cross-beams & rafters, the horse-drawn carts brought hay & corn from the fields. Before that, the woods were felled, the fields cleared, spaces made for the churches – Salle, Cawston, Reepham. The oldest part of Moor Farm was built in 1523, and clay for bricks was dug from what became the horse pond. Inside the barn, a strand of ivy grows up the lintel; outside, ivy is thick on the wall. Against the outside wall facing the house, a fig with ripening fruit. The brickwork feels webbed with age.

Hard-baked rim of earth curved round the field above, the red-brick buildings angular, upright among the curving field rhythms. A straw smell beside the deep lane. A field gate green with lichen, woven with strands of bindweed, permanently stuck open, rusted chain hanging from the post: the way into the fields by the horse pond, standing within its semi-circle of ash trees. Fields of flinty loam. Woods between cornfields solid with shadow, dark green. A line from the field gate to the woods & the church tower, the wooden roof with its angels & green man, stone wildmen & dragons. The near field below the pond is called Hunt's Meadow.

There are signatures & initials on the brickwork of house & barn. We read those we could see as the evening darkened, a few raindrops falling, swallows wheeling overhead. B. L. SEELY N. HARVEY 18 NEALE

09 L. H. (Hunt?) 1904 A. R. ARNOLD 1899. Over the former door, now bricked up: J H 1807 FH 1807. One inscribed in fine longhand script, too worn for the name to be read accurately but the date clear: July 30 1816. Other names: STEARMAN FULLER JAMES. Tally marks. Circles on the barn walls, possibly made with sheep shears.

Easy to think of ourselves too as passing. But that isn't mainly what I see or what I want to say. It is the shapes we make that I think about, and whether we receive them and fulfil them, finding our meaning in terms of what we inherit and where we live, or whether we have to make them, and with what & how.

As we walked back from Cawston, it occurred to me that Christianity is a religion of the rooted, and of those becoming rooted: clearing the woods, settling down in the long agricultural centuries, forming communities and having an intimate understanding of the language Christianity uses, the symbolism of wood and water and blood, of sheep and corn and seeds. A people mobile in modern ways is bombarded with sensations & bodily images, stimulated continually to want what we do not need. The idea is common enough, only there are places where one can feel it, landscapes in which the very feel and look of things bespeaks a great change, like a tide going out and not returning.

24 August. In Frome, Somerset

Climbed Cley Hill with Lee, Kate & the boys on a sticky, hazy morning. 'Like being on a sculpture, walking among big forms.' (Lee) Kestrel circling. Round hay bales strewn like pellets across fields at the foot of the hill; beyond – curtained by the white-out – a meadow with black & white cows no bigger than farmyard toys. In cropped, sprung grass, a few harebells quivering on thread-like stems in the breeze.

23 September

'Elusive Spirit' on the 19th, then two hopeless days, idea after idea stillborn, nothing coming alive in my words. Is the problem with the Forest poems that I am working blind, without one central, quickening idea, and not knowing what I want to say? Lee's work, by contrast, is so strong and confident – the completed work is; I know that he too struggles with chaos.

It is true: I do not know what I have to say. It is the deeper self that I seek to liberate, in the connections made when word and image and rhythm release a life that is not mine alone, but in which I participate.

But failure breeds doubt that erodes everything, and leaves me with the shallowest most negative self-consciousness.

20 October

At the Beaux Arts Gallery in Bath for a preview of an exhibition of works chosen by Peter Fuller. Lee and Kate were there. He was represented by three bronzes including 'From' and 'Tree Arch'. Glynn Williams greeted me with the remark that I have put on weight since we last met. True; and he is a stout fellow himself, a block of a man, as befits the master stone-carver that he is. I love the combination of strength and tenderness in his sculptures; and told him so and he was pleased. Also met Linda Saunders again. She asked me to write for *Modern Painters*.

We said hullo to Stephanie Fuller, who had organized the exhibition. She remembered our meeting at Moor Farm, which had occurred just before she and Peter were married. Lee pointed out to me a small bronze head of a child, 'Gabriel', which she was exhibiting. It had Peter's features and was the head of their unborn son, also killed in the accident.

Peter Fuller's *Theoria*, which I have read recently, is a good book, strongly and clearly argued. I doubt, though, that there can be a natural theology without God, or that nature can continue to bear spiritual meaning for minds which inhabit a godless universe. Peter Fuller had chosen some impressive paintings for the exhibition: Auerbach, Kossoff, two Maggi Hambling paintings of sunrise on the Orwell estuary, a large, mythological landscape by Arthur Boyd. But there was no British landscape painting that matched the work of earlier painters. Is that because the shingles on Dover Beach are more naked now? Or is it due only to differences between diverse individual talents?

3 February 1991

I don't lack reverence, but creative force, strength to take hold of what is given. This is the crucial difference between Lee and me, as far as work to date on 'Their Silence a Language' is concerned. I have seen and even stated the problem in 'Naked Man'; but I need to solve it in action. Does his power perhaps inhibit me? If so, only superficially. By his friendship and by his example he gives me far more than he may inhibit in me.

Good Friday

Lee and Kate arrived in the evening bringing some of his sculptures, bronzes which he is taking to the Beaux Arts gallery in Bath. The bronzes stood around us on the table as we ate, and tried to think of names for those which he hasn't named yet. He brought me a large wooden sculpture for my 50th birthday, a fine slender yet strong work, which in many ways epitomizes the themes he has been working at through our collaboration and earlier. I called it 'Clearing', which he felt was the right name. He takes great care with titles, some of which are inherent either in the process or the finished object (as with poems), rejecting any that are either self-consciously poetic or literal and limiting, and preferring names that express the sculptural act and at the same time open on meaning, like 'From' or 'Passage'.

30 March

Walked with Lee and Kate and Mieke along the drove road to White Sheet Hill in the afternoon. A dandelion on the verge, fully open in the sun. As we lay on our backs on the escarpment which looks across the valley to Alfred's Tower in the distance, I closed my eyes and felt that my face was like the dandelion's. This is an effect of being on the high chalk places in the sun, where everything seems simplified to elemental experience, in spite of the firing range on one side of the path, or a young man on a motor bike (a shepherd visiting his flock) or a radio-controlled model glider some way off, which Lee thought at first was a heron. Two young children, a girl and her brother, came to talk to us and wouldn't leave us alone, bringing us tiny bleached snail shells and white stones, which litter the hill like fragments of bone. I remembered my own children at their age, their excitement at simple things.

Before reaching the hill-fort we passed a milestone: XXll/ MILES FROM/ SARUM, number partly worn away C?/ FROM LONDON? 1760. In a way, this spoke of a world that seems to have vanished more completely than the worlds inscribed in the barrows and grassy rings.

On the way back we talked about Michelangelo & Leonardo. I was thinking of their apprehension of mystery, that they came to in the work itself – man at his greatest outreach, knowing that reality is beyond him. I think we are always rooted in mystery, that it is our nature to be so, and the true artist always knows it; the ablest artist or poet knows himself the most disabled, not by personal weakness, but in inherent incapacity. That (not always humble) struggle which ensues, for the artist has to reach beyond himself, is what moves me most in the work itself. Lee spoke of Michelangelo, in the 'Rondanini Pietà', breaking down the surface (which he had perfected) to reveal the other, and of Picasso doing the same, in *Les Demoiselles d'Avignon*. I understood better what he had meant on another occasion, when he wrote about not being afraid to break our own taste. We are always at the edge of what we can do, or – looked at another way – what we can do is the surface we have to break down, to get at what is within, what is.

We all stopped to watch a lamb that had lost its mother, its bleating the saddest sound there is. The lamb leapt in the air, ran here and there, joined a ewe with other lambs, jumped away, all the time seeking, seeking. One of the primary sounds. How easily we lose touch with primary realities through use of our intellects; yet something in us still responds to the bleating. And it is still such a blind sound: our intellects should be integral to our human being, not a means of denying it.

Driving back to Horningsham to have a drink at the Bath Arms, we saw the huge sun setting golden. Later, a full orange moon over Longleat. If I could say only one thing, and would die having said nothing if I didn't say it, it would be how lucky I am, from the very beginning, in my family, in my friends, in meeting Mieke at Cambridge, when I might never have met her, in meeting Lee at Winchester, and thus not only gaining a dear friend but being able to work closely with a true artist, and I believe an important one. It may tempt the gods (there is only one, the old lady said) to speak thus, but it would be infinitely worse not to say it.

18 May

At the private view of Lee's exhibition at the Beaux Arts Gallery in Bath. Bill Crozier and Catherine had come up specially from Winchester. What I couldn't help noticing was how few people actually looked at the sculptures, (more looked at another artist's paintings hung on the walls). Every time it surprises and angers me, while with a moment's reflection I would realize that most people go to these private views to see each other, and to be seen.

Bill was amusing about the response to exhibitions in Ireland, where he and Catherine have a house. No one speaks about the paintings afterwards. In a primarily literary culture, what they talk about is whether or not the catalogue is well written.

31 May

After lunch in Cambridge, we drove to Reepham. The fields immediately around Moor Farm are bright yellow with sweet-smelling rape.

1 June
In Norwich, at the King of Hearts, for a 'Poetry Day' organized by Simon Millward. Lee brought several sculptures and placed them in the courtyard. Later in the morning I read poems mainly from our collaboration, alongside another of his figures, which the Arts Centre owns. Christine McNeil, Richard Burns and Pauline Stainer were the other readers, and Richard and I held workshops in the afternoon.

2 June
Sunday morning at Moor Farm before our drive back to Frome after lunch. The gate left standing open: a field gate, just above the pond (which is still almost dry), old, weathered oak with goose grass growing up between the five bars and cleaving to them.

Pastoral

A field gate,
five bars of weathered oak,
goose grass cleaving to them,

a gate stuck open
permanently,
rusted chain hanging.

Once the way
from the fields to the horse pond
in its semi-circle of ash-trees,
from the pond
to woods solid with shadow,
through woods to the church,
stone wildmen and dragons,
to labourers' homes.

You may say it opens on
a world that is dead.
I would reply that,
like the goose grass,
this is where I like to be.

In the barn I looked with Lee at some of his new work, especially the large sculpture, 'Resurrection', for the new church, St Mary's, in Peterborough, and 'Chorus', as well as the fireplace which he has made for the Croziers' house in Ireland. He tells me 'Resurrection' is being very much enjoyed in St Mary's, where a female priest has written to tell him she would use it as a base for her Easter Sermon. Looking at 'Steps: Flames', he quoted 'not love of violence but violent love', from my 'Master of the Leaping Figures'. Tree – flame – creative energy. A possible redemption: the place burst into flames; suddenly the building is alive with energy, a magical place. Lee spoke also of 'the female that is of the flame, beyond the male, but also within him'. The female is linked with the dream – the goddess – 'she is at the place we seek'.

I can imagine 'Resurrection' (now almost complete) becoming an object of pilgrimage, as one of the great works of modern religious art. His aim is to reinvent crucifixion as life rather than agony, as hope. Now, it is suspended on an end wall of the barn, its presence a focus of attention. The crucified, dead Christ is an image of the end, which becomes a hope. Here, something is being born. The arms of the figure make the sections of a grail or cup: a form which accepts. The cross is fracturing and opening; it is riven, like an egg or seed, from which the figure ascends, looking up to and receiving the light. What Lee has sculpted is the hope of the belief.

He doesn't adhere to any particular faith but feels that he can make the form of its hope, or understand the emotion of the belief which is common to all who wonder. He counts himself a wonderer rather than a believer: 'a religious artist without a religion'. He can speak not about God but about the whole. He likes the language of the Tao (as I do). 'I am an atheist,' he says, 'but full of wonder at being.'

I saw a reference to the horns of the altar in the upraised arms of the figure. This was not intended, and indeed he knew nothing of the ancient image. One conscious influence was the shaped cross of Cimabue and other early Italian artists. Lee draws freely from medieval art (especially stained glass); he uses and transforms the iconography of the crucifixion. In talking about 'Chorus' he spoke of sculpture having a sound. Volume gives a sense of sound (in African sculptures this is expressed by the size and shapes of the mouths). Raymond Williams on the tragic chorus influenced him in this work. The chorus as a group of dancers; many voices speaking as one; one song sung by many. The sculpture has the form of a hollow tree, containing a space the spectator can look into, but cannot enter. Here, as often, he has created an image which speaks to me of my own deepest concerns – which I might not express in exactly the same terms he uses, but which arise from common feelings and needs.

He has sold 'Chorus' to Harlow Art Trust, housed in St John Community Centre, an old church used as community hall.

23 June

Even an 'edge' can be a comfortable place to be, when an artist inhabits it imaginatively. Perhaps I am learning more about what the edge really is. We secrete the void, Sartre says. I spoke at Norwich of Lee's figures being the opposite of Giacometti's, in the sense that they are figures of relationship.

from **At the Edge**

What is poetry? What is sculpture? Surely, in each case, the imagination is not only a mental faculty, but rooted in the whole body with its connections to the world. Is it possible, though, that sculptor and poet can somehow work together, not in order to illustrate each other's work, but learning from each other how to go further, each in his way? I think of poetry as an art of seeing, an art by which, in my blindness, I learn to see. As a poet I work at the edge of sight, which is the edge of meaning and of language. It is the edge between the little I know and what may be chaos or could be a greater order. Here I waste effort, stumbling in the dark; here, sometimes, I find an opening. This … seems to have something in common with Lee Grandjean's sense, as he begins a new work, that he is cutting into the void. Looking at his completed sculptures, it is hard for me to realize that he too works in the dark, and always starts at the edge, where he may fail. …

…

Grandjean and I were drawn together partly because we are both image-makers, and both exploratory in our methods and by virtue of our need to discover new possibilities of connection. This is an emotional need, rooted in the artist's being, before it issues in theory, if it ever does. As I apprehend it, the need now is to explore relationships in different spheres and at different levels: between the human and the natural world, body and spirit, the one and the many, man and woman, and between male and female elements in the individual psyche. It is a need arising from the shattering of the human image, the image of man made in the likeness of God, in the aftermath of which explosion we all live. …

During the 1980s, both Lee Grandjean and I were attracted to the tree both as a symbol and a source of imagery. … It was natural, therefore, that when we were ready to collaborate on a project we should have chosen trees and wood.

21 October

Today was the first day of Reading Week so I was able to stay at home and write, adding a prose piece to 'Their Silence a Language' and writing three poems, 'Clearing', 'On the road through the Forest', and 'Red King's Dream'. It happens like this occasionally and I'm glad of it. The 'Forest' book (my collaboration with Lee) is finished now, or very nearly.

13 November

'Their Silence a Language' is in several respects an edge. A Forest edge. A cutting edge. An edge between words and silence. An edge of meaning. The Forest is an actual forest, but also, though rooted in the ground, a forest of symbols and images, where I seek the life in them and explore what they mean. Obviously, the poems couldn't have existed without me. Nor could they have existed without the Forest (and without Lee's drawings and sculptures they would have been different). The poems contain autobiographical elements. More importantly, they construct my vision, by which I see, and by which (if another looks) I reveal. Through making them, I grow in understanding (and light is the edge of dark). Together, Lee and I create 'a place' with many internal connections; but it isn't only self-referential, an aesthetic space centring upon itself. It is open all round, and everywhere an edge (light at the edge of dark, as in an actual forest one comes to a clearing, beyond which the dark begins again. Every end an edge, a new beginning.

6 December

Lectured on Ivor Gurney to my 'Poetry & Place' course, then to Sion Hill where I showed slides of Lee's work, read poems and talked about the collaboration to art students. Afterwards a young red-haired woman student who comes from Lyndhurst told me how wonderfully the poems had evoked the Forest for her.

Later

Bounded by language; but sometimes a hint, a breath, a ray of light, from beyond; in language but from outside – or farther out in a universe of meaning than my mind can reach. This also is what I mean by the edge.

10 January 1992
Lee came to stay overnight, bringing the poems with the images he has drawn in response to them. He laid out the sheets of paper on our sitting room floor and we looked at them closely together.

To me, the images were an unexpected development, in the sense that I had seen the poems in my mind in the conventional format of black words against white paper, and the drawings and photographs on facing pages. What he has done is much more original, and at the same time brings out and reinforces the imaginative unity of the project.

Partly in consequence of his images, I am beginning to see the collaboration as a whole, but my way of thinking about it is still dual. On the one hand, there is the book, and also the exhibition, which I envisage as a beautiful and exciting work of art. On the other, there is the collection of poems, which develops from my earlier sequences and has an independent existence. It is the completeness of this that I doubt. There is of course always the sense of the work that cannot be finished, but only abandoned. But I have, too, an uneasy feeling of something missing: which may be a larger personal element, since so much of my emotional life is bound up with the Forest, or a larger sense of the life and history of the Forest itself, or both.

But the cause of doubt is also a source of hope and of excitement. Language and the world of images contain vastly more than my individual consciousness, which, through writing poetry, opens on to more of that world. There is always more to see, more to say, more to understand, and it is in *shaping* words and images that I release the active principle in language that enables me to see, and say, and understand more.

STEPS

First is the feeling,
which I must trust, moving on –
cut into the void.
*

A passage opens –
that is where the drama is –
out of the covert.
*

To attain a truth,
work fearlessly, for ourselves.
We must break our taste.
*
You dance on the edge
of destruction, you dare see
what will come of it.
*
There is work to do
with fire – simplify the self –
charred and blackened form.
*
You finger the edges,
you execute the instant –
gallows-carpenter.
*
A rooted figure,
bound to earth but gesturing
at the open sky.
*
A human forest –
energy between figures,
linking them and us.
*
You shape the image:
it is a bridge we cross over
to meet in the world.
*
To know oneself shaped,
and work with knowledge of death –
that it may bear fruit.
*
Fern, gorse, pine, slow cloud
moving on – 'voice of the rhythm
which has created the world.
*
One use of space is
for speaking across, another
to deepen silence.

29 January

To London by train on the afternoon of a cold, bright day. Lee met me at Paddington and we set out across London on the tube, but got off at Euston Square when it was announced that King's Cross station was closed due to a fire alarm. Out above the streets the sky was violet – black violet, blue violet, grey violet – the beautiful colours of urban winter nightfall. Walking with Lee, I saw with him the shapes of plane and lime trees, and their shadows, against the edges of buildings, and a street of York paving stones, surfaces worn to the grain by the tread of countless feet. We walked from Camden High Street to Little Venice (boats and canal water visible below us in the dark) and by Regent's Park. Then we climbed Primrose Hill; which was what Lee had brought me this way for, and as we climbed, he told me not to look back until we reached the top. As we neared the top we walked into a strong, cold wind. Then, turning round, what a view of the city at night, all round but especially to the south! First, a scattering of small lights, then black middle distance and behind it, in a wide arc, tall lit buildings, small spires, the shell of St Paul's dome among towering blocks, red lights on the Post office Tower, and, far at the back, a luminous triangle in the sky, which Lee pointed out and told me it was Canary Wharf, now the highest building in London. In the lit windows and over all a greeny-grey phosphorescence, and one sound under all, a persistent hum. Looking down on all the little lights, Lee remarked on all the work, the troubles, the dreams – all that unthinkable activity – going on behind them. The city to him is a great and wonderful place, although he feels, too, the indifference and the violence and the jaggedness (but this, aesthetically, is all a part of its fascination for him); and I share this sense of it; it's a great place that I want to enter, in fact and imaginatively. Here, too, on Primrose Hill, we talked about Frank Auerbach, seeing something of his vision in the line of lights, the shapes and rhythms of trees, the mass of earth and buildings, the dynamic movements and interaction of colours. Lee was in love here; he first lived with Kate in a flat close to the hill – he pointed out the building to me as we descended into the streets, and walked to a pub for a drink.

Afterwards we took a taxi to the house within walking distance of Tufnell Green tube station which Stephen Stuart-Smith has recently bought with his friend Marco Livingstone, who is an art critic. This is a fine, spacious Victorian house, where, after a meal with Stephen and Marco, Lee spread out the sheets of my poems and his images on the living room floor, and we talked until late with Stephen about the order of contents of our book.

When I eventually went to bed my mind was racing, not particularly with ideas and images, but simply racing, like an engine left running, after it has fulfilled its function, and I didn't sleep until about 4. Next morning, after breakfast, I walked with Lee in fog to the underground and so made my way back to Paddington, and eventually to Bath, in fog which shut out all but a margin of visibility, all the way.

9 February

Yesterday morning, in fog, Lee and I set out to drive to South Wales. The fog had cleared from the motorway, and as Lee drove, we discussed the present academic climate, influenced by a world of ideas drawn from Baudrillard and other post-modern thinkers. I know well the certitude of closed minds, conceited in a little knowledge, and , like Lee, I feel the need to be able to define the ground of thought I stand on. So, we talked driving down the motorway and over the Bridge and into Wales, when, as we neared our destination, another reality took over and the ideas we were struggling to counter simply disappeared, like the fog.

We were going to Ebbw Vale, to the site of the Garden Festival, where we were to meet Stephen Pettet-Smith, the Visual Arts and Crafts Coordinator, who had invited us, late in the day, to collaborate on a project on the site. At first, the experience of being shown over the site by him was rather depressing. Pavilions and other bright-coloured modernistic buildings had been put up in the middle of the valley, where the great British Steel Corporation works had formerly stood, and they looked, even from a short distance, like an outpost of Disney World set down frivolously in the midst of a ruined industrial landscape. In fact, work on the festival buildings, and on clearing the site, was still going on, and men wearing hard hats (as we too were required to) were drilling and driving dumper trucks and bulldozers and lorries in and around the area, in which there were also numerous sculptural and artistic projects (a Gorsedd stone circle, a wooden structure like a Chinese arch, willows woven into tent-like structures, platforms, sculpture gardens, objects made of old pit-head winding gear and wheels and cogs, and so on, all of them in areas designated to different themes: 'Land of My Fathers', 'Celebrating Wales', etc. Our purpose, with Stephen as guide, was to find a place for our project. In grassy areas beside the rough track winding steeply up the hillside a shallow soft earth covered iron-hard slag.

It was only after we had got up out of sight of the festival encampment that I came alive to the place and Lee began to see possible sites for a sculpture. Just over the ridge that hid the pavilions below Stephen brought us to a small pond of blue-green water rippling and brimming its banks, which filled the hollow of what had once been an opencast mine. On the other side of a fence alongside the pond three ponies were grazing in a green field and on the far side of the field was a farm, which had been there since before industry came to the valley. Standing by the pond looking back across the valley to the other side we could see several rows of terraces, the last house seeming to end arbitrarily on moorish hillside that swept on up and up high above them to a mountain ridge. Above us, slopes with outcrops of rock, sheep that appeared to be the same greeny grey colour as the thin grass, and rock and quarry faces, rose as steeply to a facing ridge. From here we could see something of where we were – below us, the dead industrial valley (but with the noise of men at work on the festival site), a vast area of heaped – up and partially cleared and levelled slag, and farther up, under the town of Ebbw Vale (invisible from where we were standing), the valley of living industry, with long roofs of the tinplate works and tall, smoking chimneys.

We looked at the trees on the hillside above us – oaks and beeches, standing apart, black against the grey-green slope – but there was also a touch of blue – in the water, in shale, in the slate-roofed terraces in mist. The trees were not big, yet they were gnarled and looked very tough. 'They've fought their way into existence,' Lee said; 'you can see it by their shape'. Near the pond was an old birch, a tree that forked from its trunk and had a great shock of twisting branches, which showed, as in the oaks and beeches, the struggle to grow. An old oak fence post, with strands of rusted wire bitten into it, was stuck in the ground in front of the birch. What could we make in this place? I had been thinking of Waldo Williams's cloud of witnesses, of some form of witness that the trees and the fence post seemed to bear, and of the pond as an eye. It was a place for looking, and I was uneasily aware that we could only look, not knowing the life of the valley as it had been, or the life as it was, but looking with that respect, and imagination, which is the least we owe to people who have borne the passage of a great history in their bodies and minds. Later, feeling the fascination of mountain ridges and views from on high, I thought of Idris Davies's poem *Gwalia Deserta:*

> I stood in the ruins of Dowlais,
> And sighed for the lovers destroyed
> And the landscape of Gwalia stained for all time

> By the bloody hands of progress.
> I saw the ghosts of the slaves of the Successful Century
> Marching on the ridges of the sunset…

And what, now, of the language of socialism which had been spoken in the valleys of South Wales with rare force and meaning, and is still spoken there, but with little power? A political vision was forged here, which achieved, practically, welfare for all, or at least an approximation to that ideal; and is now widely scorned or met with indifference, and can seem as derelict as the industries whose people once sustained it.

In making anything here there is a problem of language, in case one's words are only alien, or too loud, or sentimental. A sculpture might be the shape of witness, and a passage between past and present, standing at an edge between earth and sky, the natural and man-made worlds, and the living and the dead. And it might be the more effective for its silence, or perhaps it might incorporate a few essential words, forged in the fire of the necessity to be simple.

And at the site we have chosen there would be sounds: sounds of the wind 'that pulls the architecture about, that pushes through' (Lee); sounds of the stream running by mossed rock outcrops down the hillside; sounds of the train that will bring visitors to this part of the site, (and once the rails that transformed Britain and joined the world in iron circuits were manufactured here). Thinking of this, Lee remarked that the valley would once have been full of sound: hammering, scream and shout of the rolling mill as it shoved steel through.

'A place for a place,' he said. Steel and coal carried the valley out of itself. People escaped from their work to the tops; men brought their girls up from the valley, and girls brought their men; poets found solitude in which to write their poetry, (as Idris Davies did in his valley). People could come here to get a whole sense of the valley, to see it as a container, as a story.

When we had left Stephen at his office and climbed back up to the site by the pond to look at it again, we saw a buzzard circling high in the sky over the valley, hanging still, floating, gliding, giving us another imaginative perspective. And as the buzzard dropped down, I saw how the great ridge on the other side of the valley fell away towards the valley head. The sky was grey with cloud which now and then disclosed a ghost sun. There were darkenings, sudden falls of light, and as we descended a cold, raw mist began to come up the valley.

Afterwards we had lunch in a pub nearby, in a friendly atmosphere, and heard the soft and musical voices of the people around us.

from Ebbw Vale
for Lee Grandjean
3
What word will you carve
to speak for the dead
and not dishonour them
who forged a new world in the heart?

If there are sounds
they are valley voices,
twined with the turns of the wind
and the falling stream.

When silence fell
on the last hammer-blow,
what remained in the air
but a strand of their song?

13 March
Heard from Lee in the evening: the idiot Committee have rejected our project for Ebbw Vale. Still, I have written the poem, and Lee is at work on his sculpture. What we both regret is not being able to contribute to that particular site. No regrets at not being involved with the Garden Festival.

24 July
To Moor Farm. A long, tiring drive. I was on edge, and Mieke drove a lot of the way and on the busiest roads.

Evening. A blackbird singing from the top of the ash tree by the pond and alongside the old wooden gate fallen to in the field corner. Lee has sited 'Naked Man' in the wild meadow, where it stands out massively among tall, blond grasses. At dusk, rabbits' white tails bobbing under the two broad-spreading apple trees on the lawn.

25 July
Tobacco plants, which remind Lee of his youth in Romania, grow beside

the south-facing wall of the house. Behind them, tall white lilies, and vines, loaded with ripening grapes, against the brick wall. On the other side of the path, lavender and mint alive with butterflies and bees.

Walking alone in the garden, I suddenly saw the trunk of Cawston church tower between trees by the pond and across the fields, and although I knew where it was, it shocked me. It has such primitive power, yet in this ancient landscape – as it feels to me – where for ages people have been close to the earth – and where I feel that we are earth – that is where the Saviour spread out his arms. There it stands, a blunt fact, with a 'sinister' look; but my second thought is of the wooden angels under the roof, and of what might have been, in this country, in ourselves, if there never had been any conversion to Christ, however incomplete.

Tree shadows branch on the surface of the pond, one bent like a bow. Horses were once brought here to drink, waggons to be washed. I lean with Lee and Jock on the old gate. Jock had been working in the garden with a scythe and was now resting with a cup of tea. He is 85; he came from Scotland to Cawston in the 1930s and has worked on the land here ever since. He told us that 100 people used to work in the fields in harvest time, whereas now 6 people work on 3,000 acres. He has a cat that goes with him everywhere. It was a kitten belonging to Lee and Kate, and when they were away one Xmas he looked after it, and then couldn't bear to give it back. He would have cried, he said. In fact , once when Lee opened the back door he was crying. So Lee had to have a meeting with Guy and Louis, who agreed he should keep the cat. (Guy reasonably asked why he couldn't get a cat of his own.) They let him keep it, and now it sleeps on his bed and goes with him on long journeys in his car. Jock told us a little about the past in the area – once a horse that he was in charge of took off with a waggon loaded with sheaves and was pushed into the pond where it had gone to drink – but mostly he wanted to talk about his wonderful cat.

Afterwards Lee and I walked through the wheatfield – sandy loam with flints becoming peaty soil – to the beck, which Kate says is called Eyn Beck, and which runs through the old moor, trailing alders and willow – herb and dark, feather-headed reeds. The water is clear, but brownish from iron deposits, with 'pillows' of green weed; ultimately, it flows into the Wensum. Dry-coloured, white-ochre wheat; a red combine harvester working in far fields. Making a circuit back along the lane, we passed white, stick-like dead elms in the hedge, and small living elms.

Up the track away from the farm, by a barley field eaten back by rabbits at the edge. First ripe blackberries from bushes alongside the abandoned railway track. Yellowhammer repeating its song.

Lee said he was a romantic artist. What is that? One who seeks to give form to feeling. He isn't interested in mathematical ratios; he does not have an objective response to subject. He seeks to give form to experience of what lies under the surface of appearances. He has a feeling for the significance of certain moments, of connectedness, of being one with. But you have to be formally very rigorous if you're going to be a romantic, to deal with feeling. 'By penetrative feeling you're honing down something.' As in the great power of early Romantics (Delacroix, Turner): power, but won by method. But why should your feelings, or anyone's feelings, be important? Because they are part of 'the great sea of feeling'.

As we talked, we looked at channels made by wind currents in the wheat, and saw how they suddenly turned round, in a swirl, with lines of wheat stalks lying head-to-head. Off this track into a sunny woodland edge – Cawston Common? – where, feeding on thistles and valerian, were more butterflies than I have ever seen together – tortoiseshells, red admirals, white and brown butterflies, but mostly peacocks, hundreds of them, bright eyed-wings open on the flowers. They were so intent in their feeding that they scarcely took any notice of us.; if we had wished we could have picked them off the flowers in handfuls. It was amazing.

Evening

Cloud breaking up slowly, drifting apart, blue between. Smell of the earth at dusk, dew rising in grass and wheat. On the track, in the curve of the earth, 'a sense of the whole of it, of great height'. 'Look at the colour': black-green in the silent woods. Just here, Lee says, at the highest part of the track, is a good spot for a sculpture. As we walk back to the house, I ask him if he desires fame. What is fame? All he wants is 'to be recognized as doing work'. Yes.

26 July

The art world in England is like a salon. A small group of people have influence and power; outside this narrow circle of concepts nothing is allowed to emerge. Lee's sense of direction is strong, but I feel that he is turning even more to the house and garden as the *place* of his sculpture. It has long been that, of course; older work has almost disappeared in undergrowth – a big stone hand grasping a chisel under fir trees, a crooked stone arm submerging under nettles, fox and goose sculpture (patched with orange lichen) in long grass. I feel that he is now looking more actively for sites, and envisaging works standing in relation to each other. In a way, the place is perhaps to him just a little what my journal has become to me. It would be misleading to push the analogy too far, and I don't mean that either of us has become more 'private'. It's a matter, rather, of having a place where one can be oneself, when access to a larger world is blocked.

In the barn, 'Stoke Figure', stained brown-red, almost touches the roof. Lee has brought it back from its permanent site to replace parts that have rotted. 'Bolder Fountain' is also waiting to be mended; it was pushed over when at a show in the Minories. This is a fairly common fate of his work on public display. In one corner of the barn, near the door, is a heap of bits of old iron from machinery – wheels, part of a ploughshare, other bits and pieces. Above, hung on the wall, a scythe with a rusted blade. The beauty of its curve is echoed in the roof beams and in sculptures and models of sculptures – outreaching arms, curved uprights, bent-bow shapes.

There is a further development, and a fuller, more complex integration in Lee's new work, much of which is still untitled. There is more construction in some sculptures too, *with* wood fitted into wood. I suggested this was an inevitable development of his combination of organic and man-made forms. He didn't disagree, but said it was also influenced by the size of wood blocks he had to carve. Flame and leaf shapes, steps, up reaching, sinuous figures, arch: all are brought together variously and confidently. They are also elements of a 'language' he has created, or statements or explorations in that language, which is wholly sculptural. 'I'm inventing things more,' he said. 'I'm changing things more.' He's discovering meaning – shapes of his belief – in the making, as distinct from having set ideas.

The built and the growing are, of course, two important elements. He expressed his wonder at the man-made post lintel, simple built thing. In this respect, 'Naked Man' was especially important for him, in the relation between struts and organic form. (This sculpture was sold to Wingfield College, Suffolk.) Now the 'edge' – wall/tree, town/country – is a motif evident in much of his work. He speaks, too, of 'a scouring wind', 'a revealing wind', which is connected with the figure stepping through, in that moment between believing and not believing. He accepted my 'leap of faith' but it wasn't really his language, which is more physical, more felt. As we talked the day, too, was blown through, as clouds were driven over from the west, and the sky cleared.

One of the strongest new works is the Ebbw Vale project – perhaps to be called 'The Witnesses' – in which he has used fire, burning the hollow base – image of a crucible – black. From this rise joined upright forms, stepped (a reminiscence here of stairs exposed in bombed buildings in wartime London) and columnar. The latter broadens at the top to an abstract form of shoulders and head. The sculpture incorporates powerful images: of fiery industrial processes, of climbing up to a higher place, of destruction and survival. In Lee's terms, it is the symbol that is the thing itself, or the signpost that points within itself. Rather than being about witnesses, it is an act of witnessing, like a pulpit. Lee has made it of oak which he has stained with iron sulphides, blackening the wood, as the trees on the mountain at Ebbw Vale had been blackened.

Among cuts of wood, part-worked sculptures and fragments of broken sculptures on the barn floor, part of the torso of 'Angel', which was standing in the wild meadow looking towards the spires of Booton when I first saw it. But nothing is lost here: the destroyed work goes back into the mind that made it, energizing and refining new work. So many works destroyed make 'room' for others.

At dusk, sitting alone on the steps facing the lawn and apple trees, cornfields beyond, I tried to puzzle out the special quality of this place. No need to question a place of friendship where I am put in touch with myself. Nor is there any mystery about its beauty, unless beauty itself is mysterious: red brick Tudor farmhouse, 17th century barn, set in a garden among fields, at once a human centre and with a feeling of being high up, with far views.

No mystery about any of this, yet I feel, too, that I almost touch something else here. Sheer superstition, perhaps. I am superstitious, expecting to see a ghost, wondering about all the generations who have lived and died in the house. Why have they left no sign? But of course, they have; the place speaks of them and shows their hands.

I can't help trying to see behind the visible. But perhaps there is nothing there, only the material world, layer on layer, of which we too are made.

It seems as if there is something old in the light. That is what I see and feel here; which is partly a matter of natural rhythms, day and night, windblown trees opening and closing, sky lowering and lifting, sight drawn out far and returning to the centre, summer and autumn, winter and spring. And always the question whether God exists, and if he does not, what are we? What is anything? That sheer materiality of a flint in sandy loam among cornstalks: nothing but sheer process, sheer matter. But that too is beautiful, and awes me. Perhaps I have to give up the idea of an answer as a sentimental belief. We die and the conversation ends. We are only what we were, which being dead is nothing to us. Maybe that is what the look of the flint means, or the look of Cawston church tower, merely stone shaped as human beings are inclined to shape them. We are beings who tell ourselves stories; the story of God becoming one of us is a great story, which it is ever harder to believe as we lose touch with the cultural conditions in which it was told.

Yet belief in it is possible. As I grow older, my scepticism hardens, but remains sceptical of itself. I cannot close my mind on disbelief, and say that story is finished. I can neither escape the thought-world of my time nor make myself at home within it. And there is, I feel, an opening beyond it here, in Lee's work, in what I share with him. Nature lives in his vision, as it has never ceased to live for me. That is why I can see and feel the earth at Moor Farm. He confirms my sense that nature is not dead, as post-modern ideas assume. How could we be for an instant if nature were dead?

But natural vision is now a problem for an artist in the West. And it is only by being a problem, which the artist struggles with, that it can engender artistic life. Where seeing nature is not a problem the vision is conventional, sentimental, dead. The artist who not only sees nature, but feels nature in and outside himself, also knows the crisis of natural language – which is part of the crisis of all language, all symbols of meaning, which is what the modern predicament is. It is Lee's feeling of the modern – his experience of being alive now – that authenticates his sense of nature. He refuses nostalgia; for him, Moor Farm is not a retreat into the past, a rural idyll, an escape from the city. He brings the city into the country, the country into the city: both are equally part of him. As he is, a man alive to the present, so he feels and sees. If there is continuity between his work and that of the former generations at Moor Farm, as I seem to see in their different 'things', it is because he knows the people of the past as makers, as he too is a maker.

As for his 'romanticism', I would describe it as akin to Turner's or Hardy's, as a feeling for reality which must break through conventional ideas of beauty or of art. In Lee's case, convention means not only what tradition may harden into – a disciple of Henry Moore (or Moore himself) making a 'Moore', Picasso contriving a 'Picasso'; it also means the avant-garde with their narrow range of concepts, which totally blind most artists and critics to art that is really new. Blindness – seeing and feeling within a narrow range of taste, according to fashion – is a condition for success both in artists and in writing about them. I have never believed, and do not believe now, that Lee won't achieve recognition during his lifetime, but I realize that it will take longer than I once thought.

And what has all this got to do with God? What real artistic problem or work of art has not? To sense being as a creature is to feel the question of God. It is as if God asks whether I exist. It is the question at the root of existence. Flint, ear of wheat, tiny scarlet flower at the dusty margin of the field: their very existence is a question about God to the mind. And, really, it is love that asks the question. That I love these things, that life which I share with those I love is so precious, and inconceivable as not existing: that, when I feel it most, becomes the question.

What I am trying to say can be seen in Lee's work. There is the experience of being alive in the body, of breathing and desiring, of rising or standing or stepping out, which is simultaneously the question of meaning. What am I? Am I this body alone? What do I belong to? As the question comes to me, it isn't quite the same question that comes to him, since I am closer to speaking traditional Christian language. But our apprehension of being is close.

He says that 'thankfully, I do not have a God dilemma, but something akin: what have I done – have I made what I am here to make'.

Moor Farm is a place of earth: that may be what is old in the light: all the long generations, and behind them the slow forming through ice and water and geological change. But I also feel it is the edge we are at, where the flame is always new.

20 October

I was with my mother when she died, but did not see the exact moment. It was as though, gradually, life went, collapsing inward, leaving her face twisted; and there was only the clay, which would have chilled me more if I hadn't known it is *our* clay.

It was the next morning that I suddenly saw, in my grief, something different. What I saw and felt, I saw immediately. Unknown to me, Mieke had hung Lee's study for Resurrection', a gouache in black and white, on the wall beside the door, through which I could see the wooden model of the same sculpture hanging on the wall in the passage, as, almost in the same glance, I took in 'From', standing on the windowsill. It seemed there were two or three fractions of seconds: in the first I saw the gouache, in the second the three works of art with the sudden gesture of opening, and in the third the gouache with the opening shining in it. It is hard to put into words, but there was the white spirit breaking out of the black cross that had contained it, and suddenly I was looking at what had happened and seeing the possibility of something different from the living person becoming clay. I don't want to exaggerate this or claim to have seen more than I actually saw. For all in that same instant, or immediately after, I knew that Lee's meaning was not the Christian one; that for him the moment of resurrection was breaking out of an old life into a new, or of participation within this life. The works of art convey a wonderful sense of the risen, but not in terms of the orthodox meaning. But does that matter? It was the white body breaking out of the black containing arms that I saw and felt as spirit. And that is really all I can say about it. I knew I was looking at works of art which my friend had made, not something I could call a divine vision or revelation. But what I saw was an illumination, and I felt a temporary freeing from grief, and even, for a time, something like joy.

1 January 1993

At Moor Farm. Morning. When I drew back the bathroom curtains, a flock of fieldfares, blackbirds and redwings scatter from under the old bramley, where they have been feeding on fallen apples. The big thrushes flock together but also drive one another off the fruit, tails spread and raised and aggressively jerking. A heap of fresh brown soil at the base of the tree shows where rabbits have burrowed among its roots.

Frost lines mark furrows in the land which rises and falls. A light mist hugging the beck delineates the curve of the field. Later, I see Cawston church tower rising vigorously out of the mist. Lapwings, tiny black and white birds, move far out on an undulating ploughed field, beyond which, over pines, the disembodied pinnacles of Salle rise.

Sun brightens as I walk with Lee on the track, mist becomes mistier reflecting the light. Frost pockets mark areas of deeper shadow cast by clumps of grass on the banks. In the meadow, near 'Naked Man', I find a dead rabbit, eye pecked out, fur tousled and patched with frost. Both its back legs and long ears are stretched out, as if it died instantly, in the act of flight.

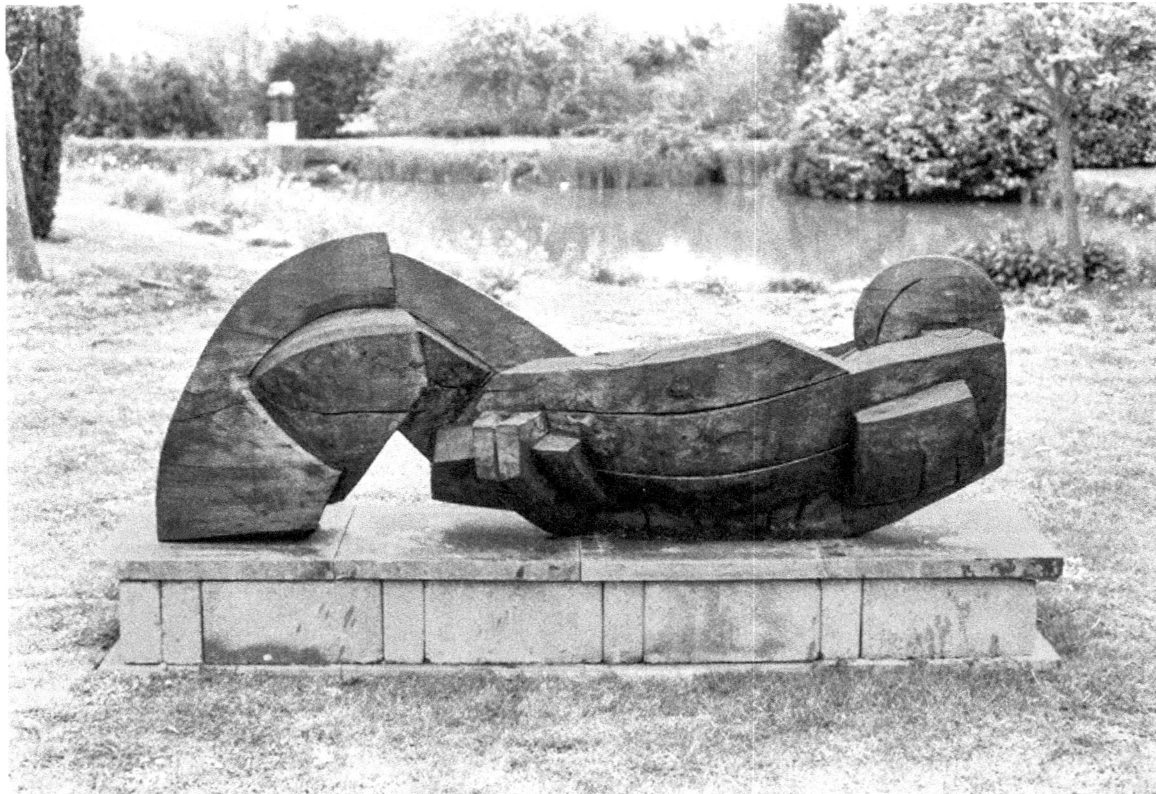

1. *Hold,* elm wood, carved, 1984, 245cm x 86cm x70cm

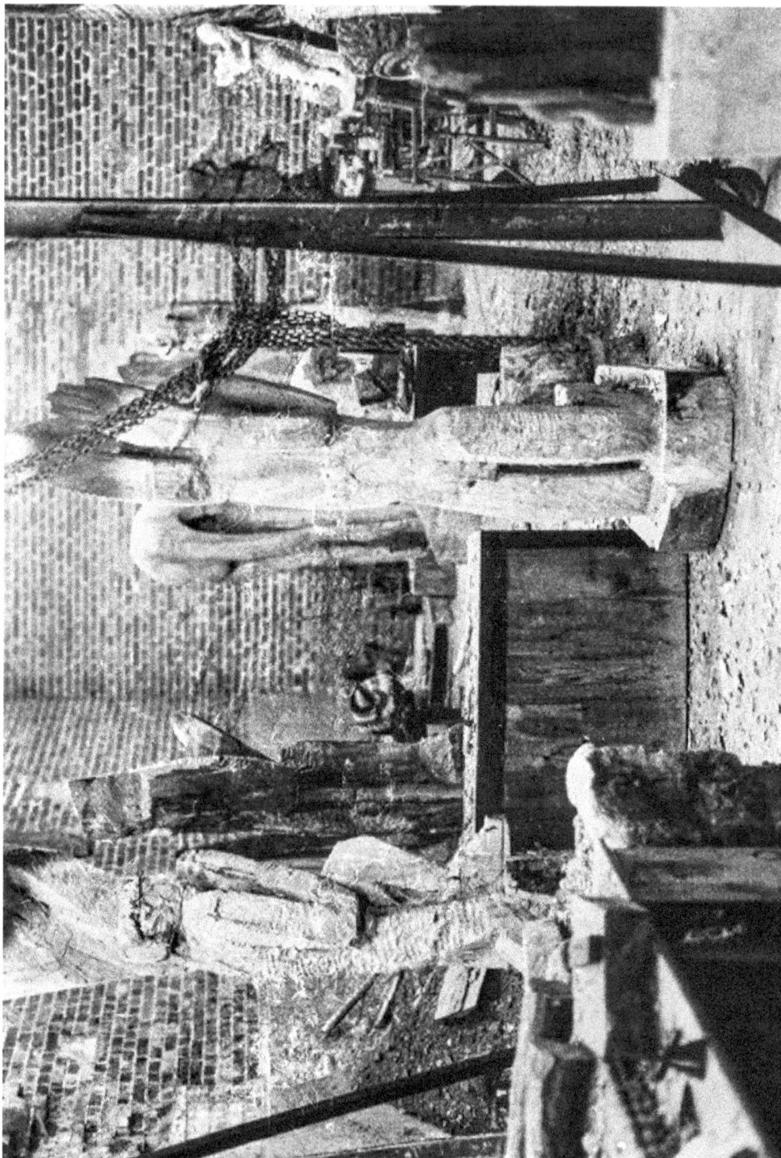

2. Moor Farm, Barn Studio, work in progress, 1985

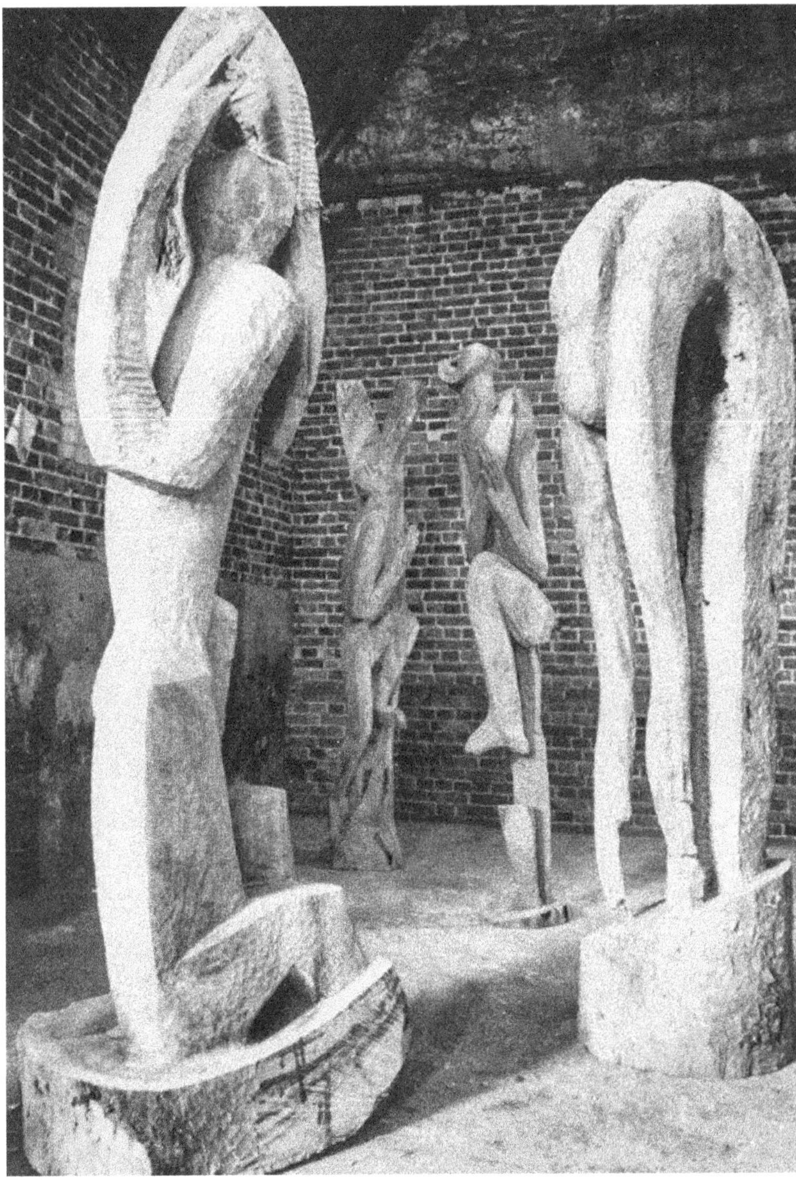

3. Moor Farm, Barn Studio, *Four Figures*, elm wood, carved, 1986

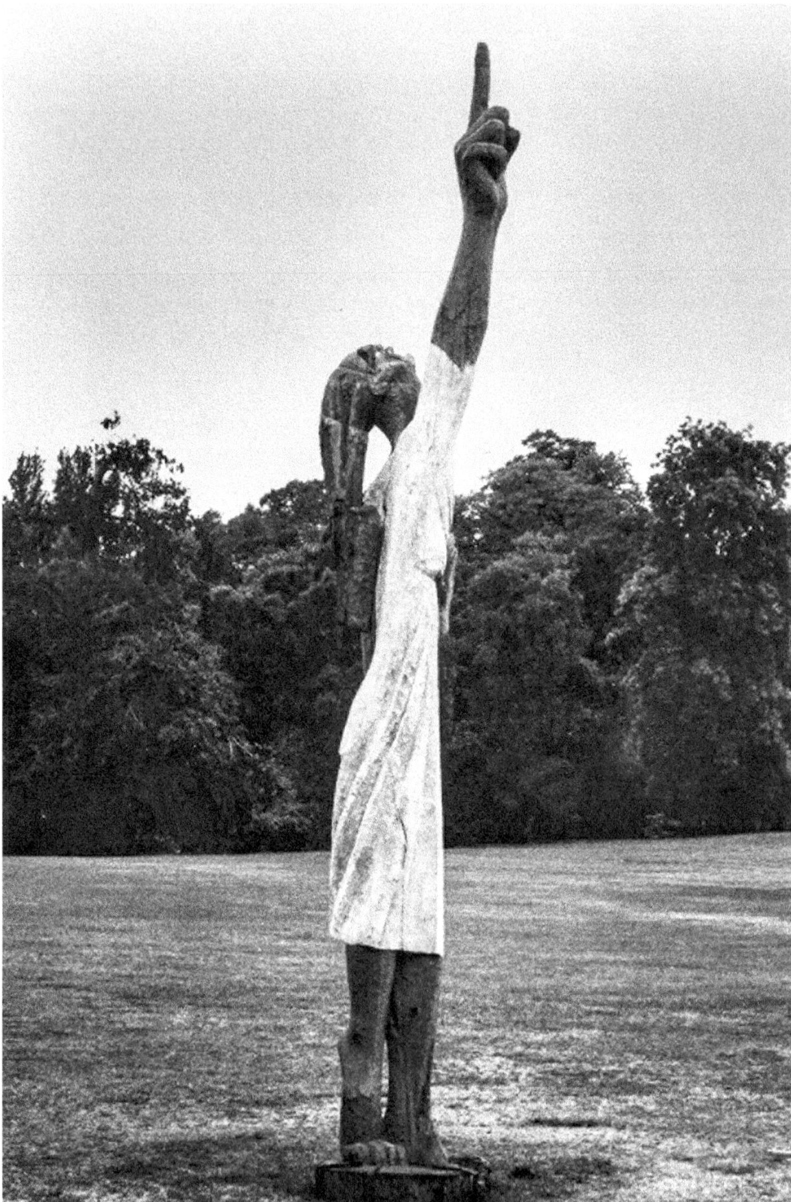

4. *Pointing Woman*, elm wood, carved, Canizzaro Park, 1984

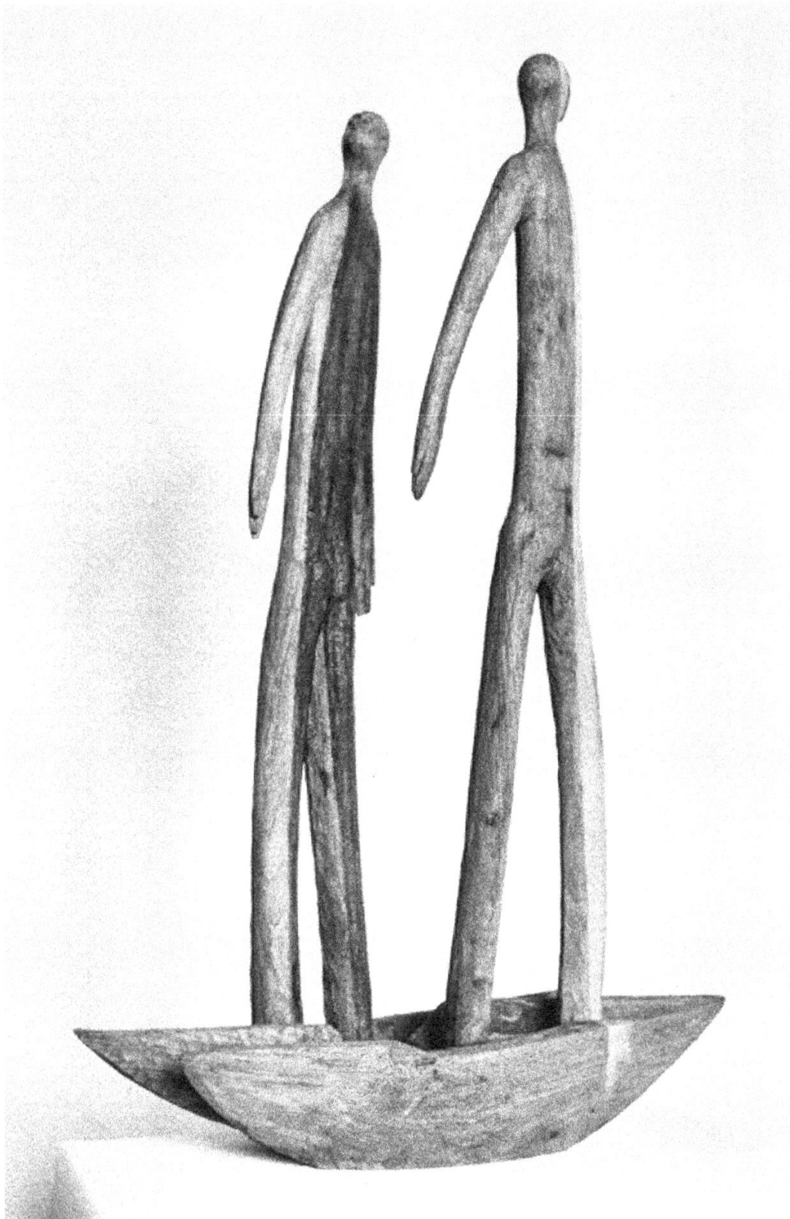

5. *Voyage*, elm wood, carved and constructed, painted, 120cm x 60xcm x 30cm, 1986

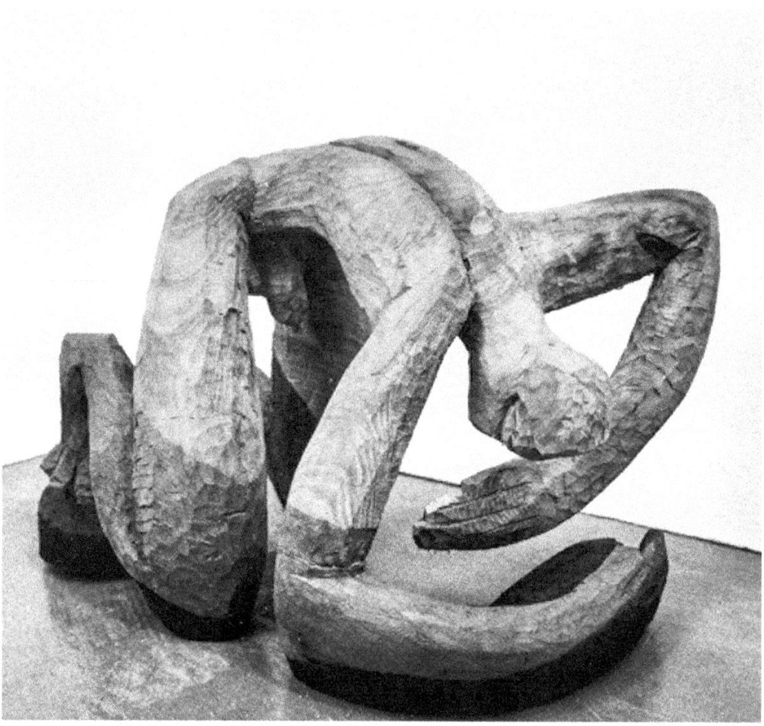

6. *Earth Dance*, elm wood, carved, painted, 1987, now destroyed.

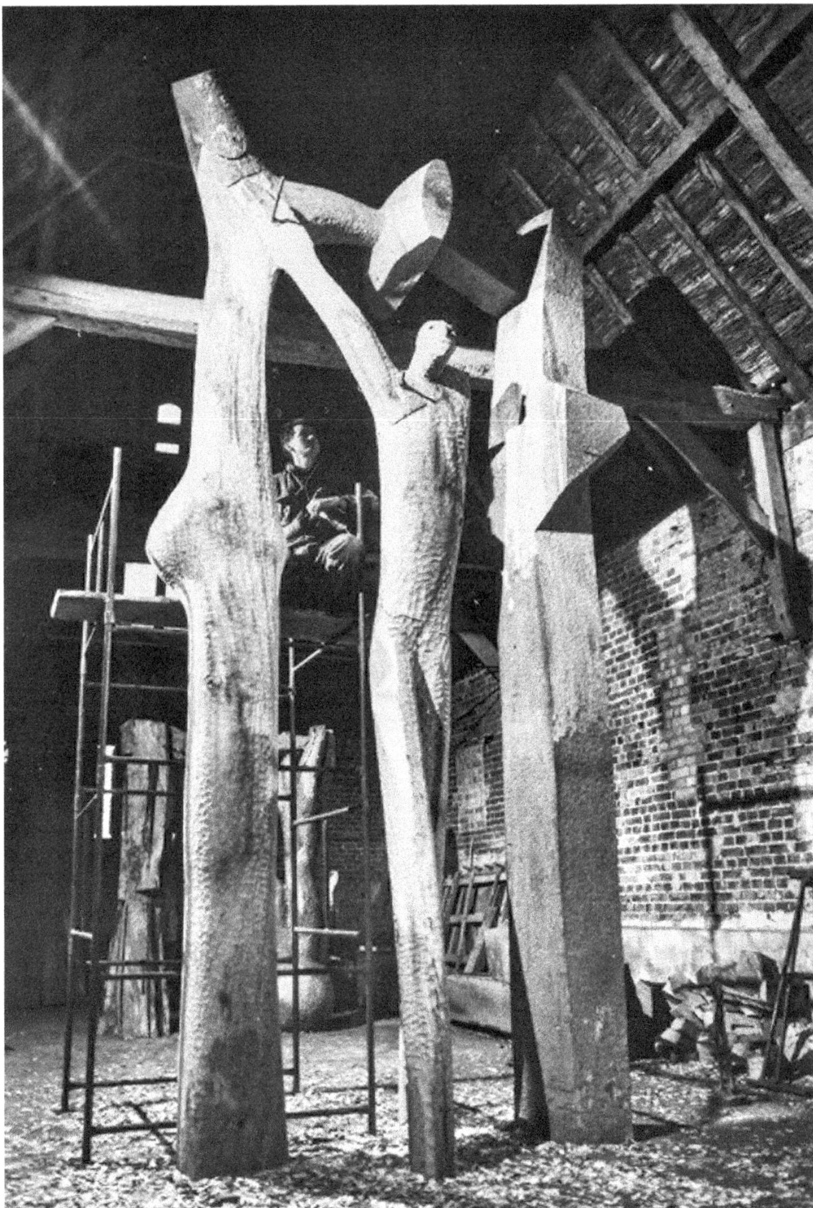

7. Moor Farm, Barn Studio, work in progress, Peterborough Arch,
iroko wood, carved and constructed, 500+cm high,
commissioned by Peterborough Dev. Corp. 1987

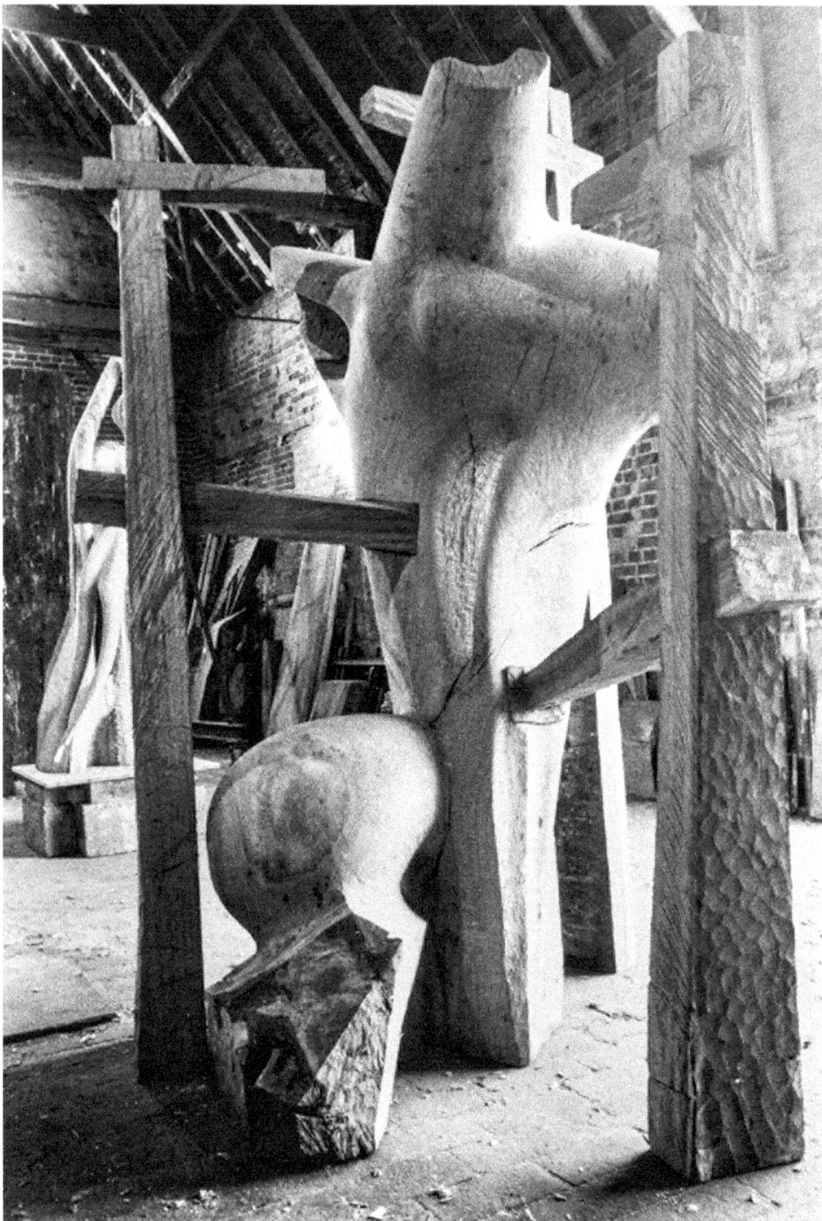

8. *Naked Man*, oak wood and iroko, carved and constructed, 200cm high, 1990

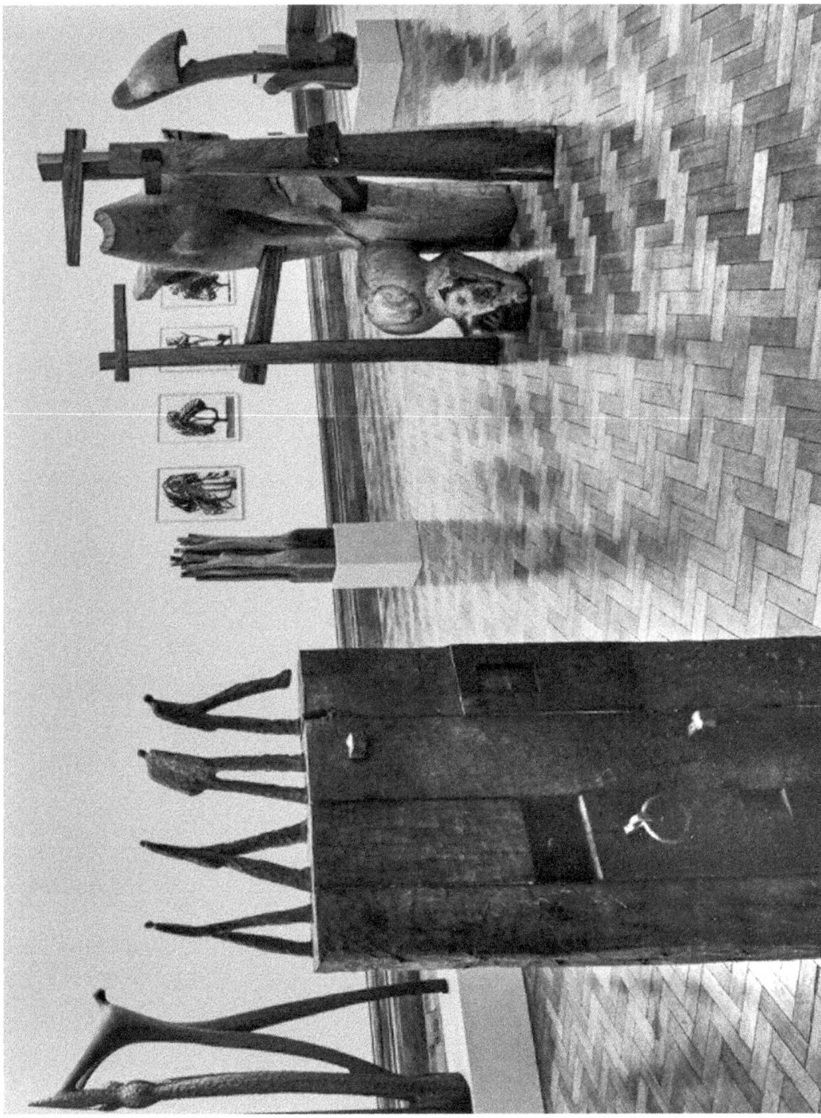

9. Installation, exhibition, *Their Silence a Language*, Christchurch Mansion, Ipswich, 1990

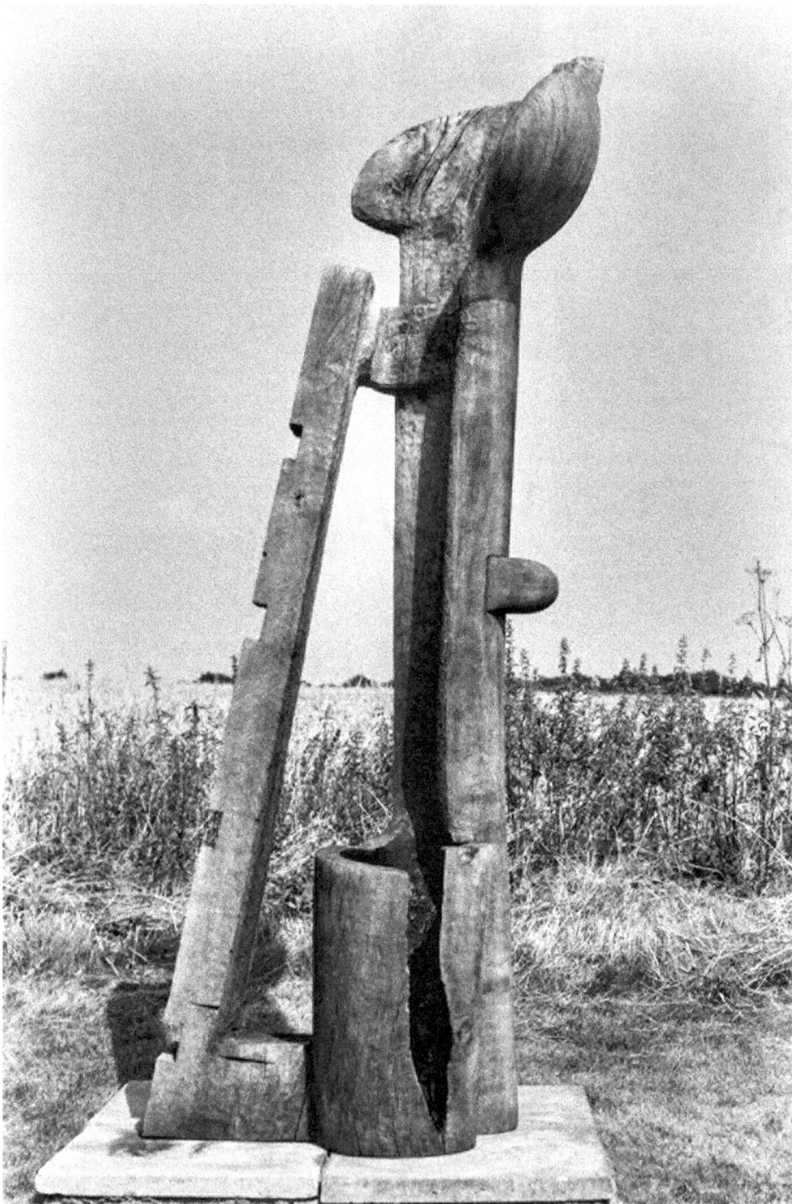

10. *Witness* (sculpture for Ebbw Vale), oak wood, carved, 250cm x 90cm x 70cm,1992

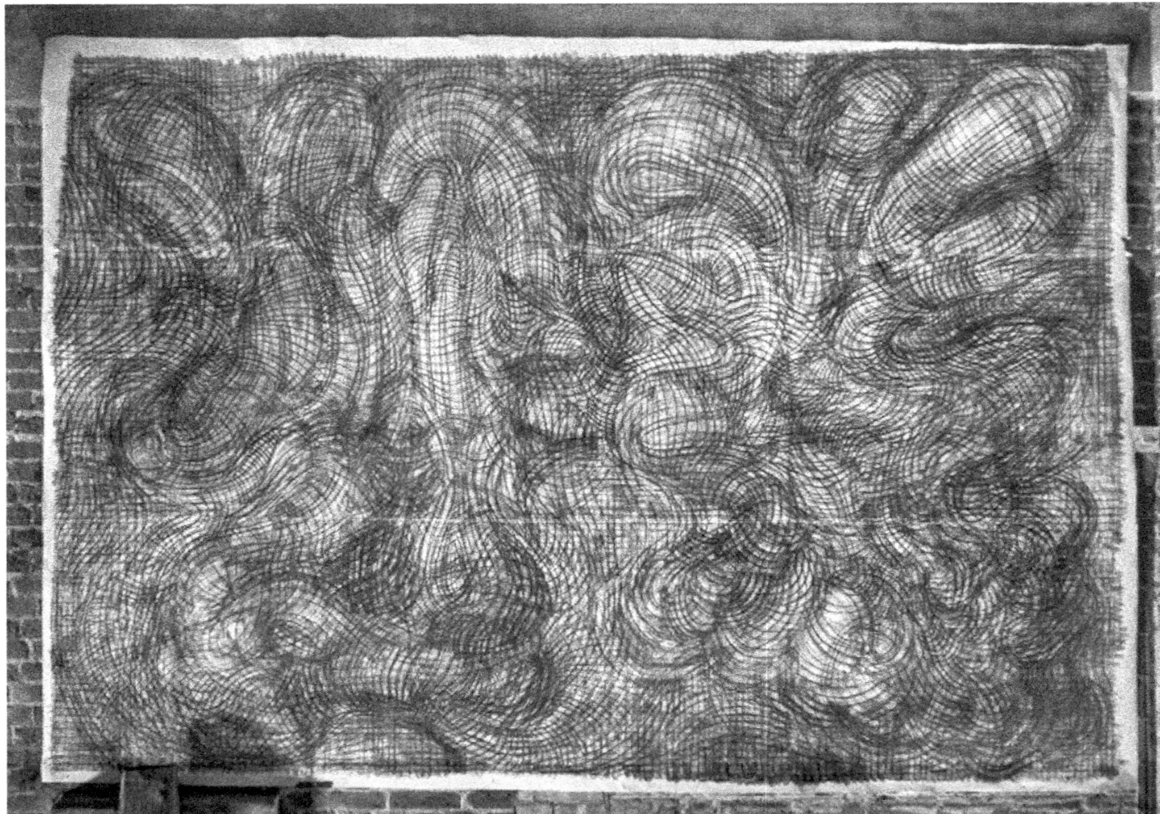

11. *Four Winds*, charcoal on paper, 274cm x 365cm, 1998

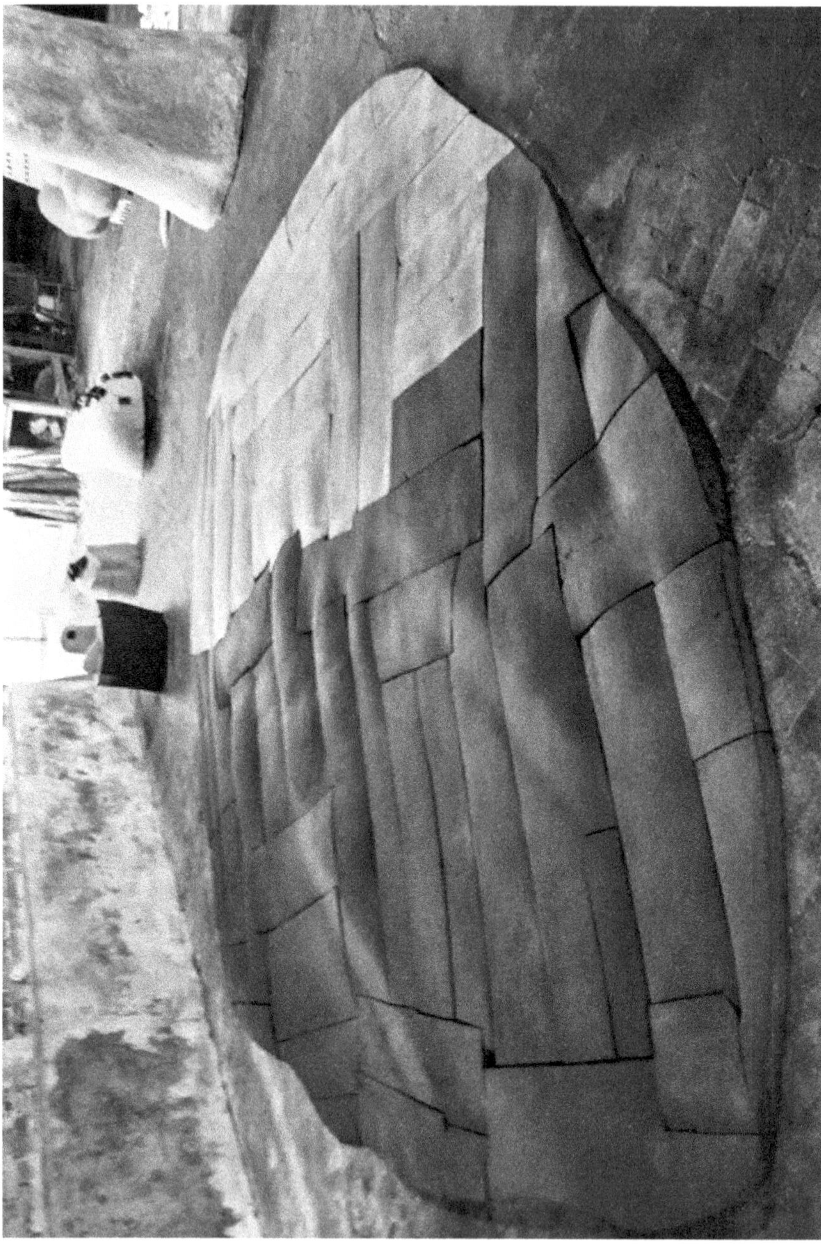

12. Moor Farm, Barn Studio, *Groundwork*, iroko wood with earth and PVA, approx. 450cm diameter (related to *Groundwork* exhibition at Djanogly Gallery, Nottingham, in collaboration with Jeremy Hooker, 1998).

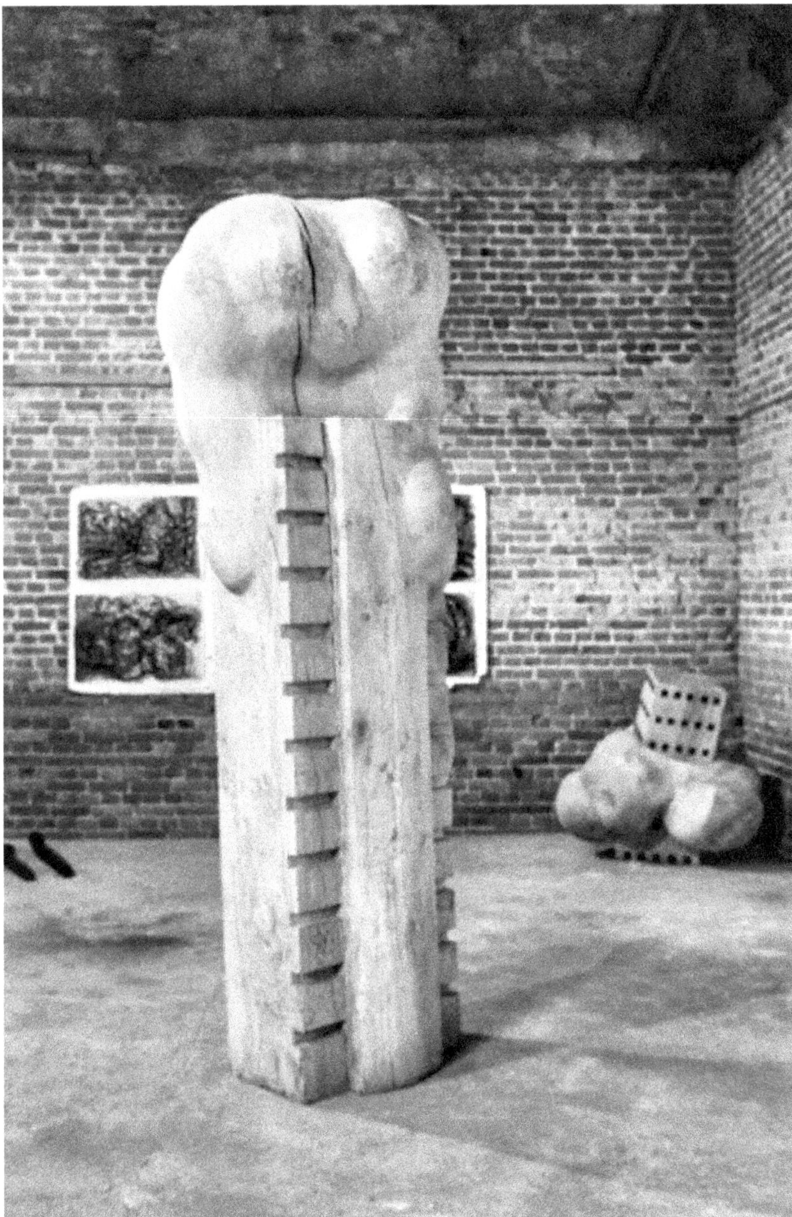

13. Moor Farm, Barn Studio, *Meeting*, oak wood, carved, 250cm high, 1998, (related to *Groundwork* exhibition at Djanogly Gallery, Nottingham, in collaboration with Jeremy Hooker, 1998)

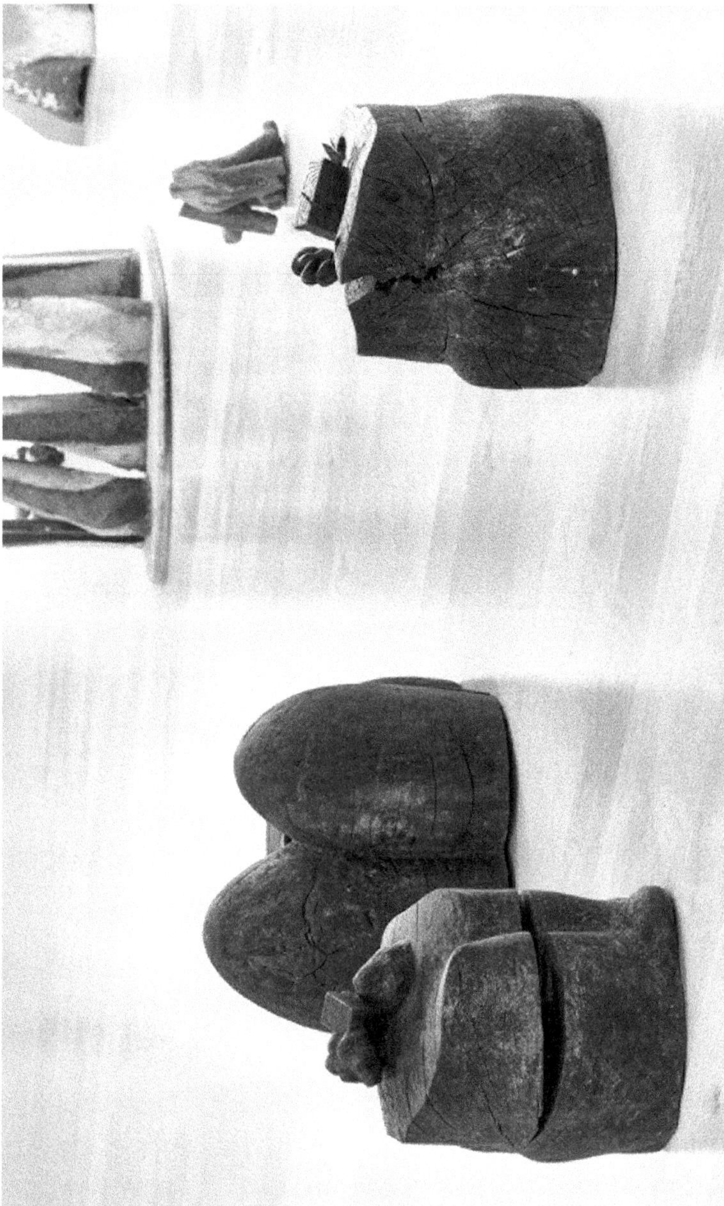

14. *Seeing Things*, Installation View, Grandjean Solo Exhibition, Gibberd Gallery, Harlow Civic Centre, 2023. Photo Credit, Peter Huggins

3 January
Sun bright on a stiff frost, ground hard underfoot, when I walked with Lee through stubble and by the beck, along the abandoned railway line and back across the fields. Now, for the first time, I saw what he sees in the telegraph poles – tall and straight with a cross bar, or two joined together, like long, thin legs. The latter stand for figures; now I saw their influence upon some of his work. They are images of enduring humanity, standing against all that blows, whereas the trees give and flow and bend, their shapes determined by the wind and by their need for light.

This is very much a made landscape. A travel writer recently described Norfolk to Lee, disparagingly, as 'more or less a garden'. And he's right! Lee says. Yet here you can still connect with the elements themselves. You can see how a tree grows, and there's a feeling of openness under the sky. Lee emphasised the importance of the sound of the wind in our ears, the thing that bends trees, and shapes bushes. In this place, he feels himself to be between earth and sky, and the vertical things are part of that feeling.
Later, with Mieke, we looked at his new sculptures. A series of smaller pieces on the theme of 'Edge Between'; some observed, some constructed. Though relatively small, the sculptures convey a sense of largeness: a quality of place, of meeting edges, of crossroads – which way? This way or that way? All embody a moment of transformation. In these and other recent works – the barn is alive with works-in-progress – Lee is using the grain of the wood (oak). He likened the wave-like patterns to Van Gogh's brushstrokes. Here the life in all things, animate and inanimate, is visible. His reading of Primo Levi has had an influence on the recent work, which he calls 'landscape objects'. 'What is there when everything is pared away?' The new sculptures are more abstract, but also sensuous and dramatic, and with what looks to me, at times, like a more explicit sexual energy and symbolism. But, like all his work of recent years, they also develop from what has gone before.

I was relieved at the productivity and the quality of the work: as we had walked round the hard fields, in the cold, bright air, he had talked about doubts and difficulties arising from lack of recognition, and the resulting financial insecurity. Not emphasising these – we talked about other things too, happily and confidently – but revealing the concern.
When will the breakthrough come? How can it come, given the power and vested interests of the existing art world? Cynicism is deeply ingrained in the intellectual life of our time. Not only academics and critics, but many artists and writers seem incapable of seeing and thinking except in strictly

limited ways. There was a passion for renewal – and re-vision – among the early modernists. Now there is a kind of comfortable orthodoxy – or orthodoxies – traditionalist and avant-garde.

25 July

A brief visit from Lee and Kate on a wet Sunday evening.

Lee's new images spread out on the floor. Several sequences, in black and white acrylic, forming a plastic surface on the paper. Images drawn from the Thames, still 'a wild thing', a 'heart of darkness': embankments, openings, a section of the body of water. Images of the land around Moor Farm. Abstracted from Cawston church tower; posts; curves of the fields, but embodying the interaction of natural and man-made energies.

What the images excite in me is the realization that there are other ways than English pastoral of responding creatively to places and to the land. This is what I have been in search of, and now I am particularly receptive to it in Lee's work because I need to renew my sense of touch. Poem and sculpture require in the artist a balance between observation and participation. The observer stands apart from the matter, which the participant is part of, with faculties and senses working together, mind and eye with touch and physical empathy.

The problem with observing is that it may disconnect what is seen. One of Lee's great strengths is that his abstract images powerfully symbolize, and make one feel, conflict and interaction. Thus, an impressionist painting of the landscape around Moor Farm would be very different from his images. The former might please the eye; but the latter involve us, speak to us of our condition, our place between.

2 October

To Taunton with Lee, who had stayed with us overnight.

Starlings whistling high on the perpendicular tower of Westonzoyland church, in which prisoners from Monmouth's army were held after the battle of Sedgemoor. At the battlefield: a churned-up patch of mud near a farm pasture with black & white cattle, willows along a rhine, flat land with distant hills, Quantocks to the west, Mendips in the east. Alders by a wet ditch at the edge. An autumnal wind was blowing among nettles and yellowing leaves, grey cloud breaking to reveal pale blue sky over the Quantocks.

It was a summer's night and dawn when the battle was fought and Monmouth's troops, 'labourers and farmers and small tradesmen of

Somerset and Dorset', were defeated. Inevitably we feel a coldness about the earth and the green, reedy ditches. There's something desolate about what is otherwise an ordinary part of the Levels.

In Taunton we went in search of the Stanwell Gallery, where Lee was to meet the director and look at the space, with a view to holding an exhibition there. At last, he managed to contact her by phone, and we ended the visit successfully with a meeting in the gallery, which is a fine space for an art exhibition in a converted factory.

Lee's tutorial exchange with a student who subsequently left the Royal College and went to Chelsea School of Art:

'Do you ever look at art from the past?'

Long silence. Finally, 'I quite like Cragg's early work'.

26 November

First copy of *Their Silence a Language* in the post from Stephen. As usual, I read obsessively. If only there were another 5 or 6 pieces – the ghost of poems I conceived but did not write shadow the ghosts of white pages. But this isn't my book alone, and, with Lee's work, it is different from what either of us could have done alone.

From ***Their Silence a Language***

Trees, more than any other living thing, have been our servants, but there's nothing domesticated about ancient trees in a wood. I'm tempted to call their silence a kind of language, but know that I'm only attempting to catch the impossible – an unknown mode of being – in words. For although we know what they are, and can analyse all their parts and principles of movement and growth, I always have the feeling that they *look out*, with a 'knowledge' and 'vision' completely different from ours, who look in at them.

1 January 1994

At Moor Farm. A bright, frosty morning. Ice on the pond, which is now, after the winter's heavy rain, full of water again. Shining drops on grass blades in fields. Cloudless overarching blue sky. Cawston church tower standing up out of the land.

For Lee it is all animate. He spoke of 'the pull of the trees at the field's edge'. We walked first in their field, looking at 'Naked Man' & the whorls & spirals in the wood, and at young elms, wreathed in ivy, fallen from the hedgerow, and others still standing but bare of bark and due to fall.

Next, in the river field, a big hare leaped up near us and ran away uphill to the far edge. Another, ears back, jumped up by the river. Then a snipe started up and flew away with rapid corkscrew flight. Then another hare, startling a pheasant close to us.

HARE

Fear of us makes
the heart jump,
the body leap, the long legs
run uphill, and stand –

Absolute hare,
long ears laid back,
long skull, our image
a gleam in dark eyes.

Frost-furred ribbed alder leaves by the river. Grass, thistles, flowering reed-mace in the field left uncultivated, showing again the original moor. In the ploughed field, more hares. As we walked up the next field, suddenly, the pinnacles & tower of Salle church rose out of the ground. 'This is the spot.' Lee was standing a few yards away, from where Salle & Cawston church towers could both be seen (and, behind us, Booton), sun shining on the south flank of Cawston tower, and everything clear and sharp.

Flints among barley stubble. Some yellow rape still in flower. Ice on floodwater reflecting sky, white blue grey, and stubble, poking out of the ice, diminishing where it 'stepped down' into the water.

Afterwards, in the barn, we looked together at Lee's drawings covering one wall and at new sculptures. Some are 'field works', inspired by the fields in which we had just walked: 'East Field', 'South Field Walking'. He said he was now making more use of what he looked at: corners, fence post, telephone pole against tree, slope of land: seeing and feeling what's there, the fixed and the moving. Another sequence is 'River', from looking at the Thames in London: weight of water, ebb & flood of tide, 'a wild thing', powerful, elemental, in the midst of walls, fixings, 'urbanity'. 'Heart', for example: 'thing at the centre.'

In these recent works Lee hasn't abandoned image but is more concerned with the work as object – 'almost whole things', he calls them, 'wholly there, like a child's toy'. He seeks *clarity*.

Initially, the new sculptures, which are smaller (more the size of toys) made less impression on me. It wasn't long, though, as we looked, before I saw and felt the quality of the new work, and the things came alive with presence.

6 January

In London, with Stephen Stuart-Smith, Lee, and Neil Curry. Stephen drove us to Broadcasting House, where we found a restaurant nearby, and, as we lingered over our meal, snow began to fall and we watched it through the windows, falling in heavy flakes and reminding us of London at other times and in other ages. At 10 we met Julian May at Broadcasting House, and later took part in a 'Night Waves' discussion programme about collaboration & image-making, in which the poet-musicians Michael Donaghy & Don Paterson joined us, and Sean Mayne Smith, the photographer, (and Kathleen Jamie in the Edinburgh studio), with Roy Porter putting questions and directing the programme.

Everyone had his or her share of the talk, but I felt that I'd said little of worth (Lee and Neil said more). I did however read most of 'Steps' and the beginning of 'At the Edge', which probably said as much as I could in the circumstances. After the programme we went with Lee to Julian and Sarah's new home in a lovely old cottage terrace near the river – Lee had a sense of a sailor's house about it – in Old Woolwich Road, Greenwich, where we talked until late and stayed the night.

Christmas Eve, in Upstate New York

Letter from Lee:

'It can be liberating moving away from our own place; encouraging universal perspectives and thoughts of wider interconnections within this common moment in western culture. This time of looking back over a thousand years and looking forward to the next.

You are right in this sense of time 'between'. I feel I am trying to understand something about the past five hundred years rather than the last ten.'

'If we dare talk of big ideas,' he says. Why not? This was the voice I wanted to hear – to wake me up to a sense of shared purpose, of creative possibility.

5 August, 1996
Cloudless, or with small clouds driven across the sky by a strong, fresh wind from the south west. Sat out, deliciously cool, under the shade of the apple tree on the lawn, then walked with Lee round the fields, beginning in the set-aside, which in twenty years will be woodland, and is now rich in colours– yellows & blues & rust-red, masses of rosebay-willow-herbs, whose colour, Lee says, is white-violet. Straw bales stacked up in towers on the field beyond the beck, towards Booton. Wheat whitening in the field above the house, fields of barley, fields of oats, sugar beet with a lark singing in the sky above it. Warm, rich meadow smell, which to Lee is a smell of childhood, bringing back a memory from Rumania, in the Carpathians. And as he says it, yes, my senses opening in the present open, also, to the past. Thistledown blown fast about the fields, a light summer snow, or a sudden blizzard. A red combine harvester throwing up dust & chaff as it moves in front of the stump of Cawston church, which stands for times when, seasonally, the country here would have been peopled with workers. But today, except for the driver of the combine, no one, only ourselves walking beside the fields.

Later, in the barn, I looked with Lee at some of the sculptures he is working on, powerful upright forms carved from oak, and a work made from pieces of iroko, which he is covering with earth, and has set out on the ground, like a landscape (and inspired in part by landscape). These are among the works he will contribute to our next collaboration – which I can scarcely think about now. And today I didn't want to try, or to take notes, but only to enjoy looking and touching.

How the red house & tiled roof & barn stand out against the sky, where, late in the afternoon, a faint nimbus of cloud floats high in the blue. Sitting under the apple tree, Lee tells me a little about the therapy he has been having since, last year, he lost confidence and had trouble with his nerves. And now, evidently, he is much better, and has found his direction again, and has time to work. One thing I notice is how he turns away from negative criticism, seeing what other artists are doing, which may or may not interest him, but concentrating on his own work. He eschews as vanity the critical condemnation of certain fashions. I know the temptation of critic as law-giver, but see the wisdom of avoiding bitterness & anger, of saving energy for the work – sculpture or poem – which is one's proper business.

There is also the wisdom of allowing time to sift enduring work from the merely fashionable. As time will anyway.

And if it is one's own that vanishes? Nothing alters the fact that, for oneself, the doing is all that matters.

6 August

I know from my own experience that it is in the self-image, constructed in the distance between oneself and other people, that dangerous illusions can take root. Or a seed falls from the air (T.F. Powys knew this) and from it a fatal madness may grow. But what is the 'air' but an idea of other people's minds and how one is, or should appear, in them? It is confidence by which we sustain ourselves and support one another: confidence founded on a power we have access to – creativity, I would call it – the power which manifests itself differently in individuals, but defines the human, and connects us to each other and, constructively, to the world.

7 August

Through the kitchen window at breakfast, a green woodpecker on the lawn (olive green wing feathers, yellow-green back, red head), intently pecking insects from the ground. Quick nervous alert look round, intent peck.

The front page of the newspaper juxtaposed two stories: that of the abortion to terminate the life of a twin in the womb, because the mother couldn't cope with twins, and the reported discovery that there was life on early Mars – the fossil of a single-celled organism, found in a meteorite in Antarctica. Potentially the most revolutionary discovery ever made, by a species who find it increasingly difficult to live, and to let live.

Looking at the wild field – all the violets & yellows & reds, the white of hogweed, grey-white thistledown – I am suddenly aware that while I am composing aesthetic images, the field is full of alert senses watching, listening, nosing out my presence.

In the barn studio with Lee and M., we look at 'Grounding' (I suggest 'Groundwork', which Lee prefers), and 'Mountain', a work of great force & presence, about my own height, a white form carved from oak, in the shape of a mountain. (This work was subsequently sold to Ringo Starr!) I can't help but see in it the suggestive power of myth: white whale, tusk, cosmogonic birth from the primal waters. Lee spoke of having seen an exhibition of Japanese stones collected because they look like mountains. He mentioned as another influence Gaudier's 'sculptural energy is the mountain'. In all his new work, however, I am aware of new sculptural renderings of his abiding preoccupation with 'the built and the grown', their interactions & rhythmic contrasts, tensions & complementarity.

After lunch we walked round by the road and into the dense, old woods of Booton Common, where we scrambled precariously across the beck on an elastic-branched tree and climbed through nettles and thistles and on a crumbling bank to the edge of the wild field. Startled a tawny owl from its roosting tree at the edge of the wood, and heard its disturbed calls from the interior. Then we sat talking on the seat facing the field, my mind freer of anxieties, able to move among ideas. Afterwards I read poems by Raymond Carver, moving poems from his last book, which only Carver could have written, since it is his way of seeing and feeling, his personality, which shape what in others would be loose, prosaic lines.

from MOOR FARM: SUMMER 1996
August 7

Tools on a bench: claw
gouge chisel mallet
club hammer bolster point

I say them over slowly
Weighing them testing edges.
Adze-marked rafters
and roof beams high
over the work bench,
and in the space where carts
brought in corn and hay
in their seasons,
blocks, unhewn
or partially shaped
standing or lying
on the brick floor.

Not knowing
                    is the way.
So you stand
in front of a block,
chisel in one hand,
mallet in the other

and all around you
is world as it was,
dust of an old image
pulverized.

Under your hand
the block, and you stand
not knowing,
blank to the voice that knows

and make a mark

26 January 1997

The artist Barry Cooper is collaborating with a musician friend who maintains that now, toward the end of the millennium, we have returned to the situation of the first Modernists, the artists and poets and musicians who worked together collaboratively. I am in sympathy with this view. It seems to me that if we refuse the post-modernist notion that there is no 'reality' and persist in believing in the possibility of a greater (not necessarily absolute) wholeness, we, as artists, will be drawn together and, in combining different approaches, seek to create a more integrated work than any one art can produce alone.

I had begun to think of poetry in sculptural terms before I met Lee, and perhaps initially in terms of rock and land. In Lee's sculptural making I sense a way for words – sense, not think; thinking has to come with a feel of process. If not, I am tempted by abstraction, which is more dangerous for me than loss of time and energy spent on critical work. I have to feel my way back from the space of concepts. Here, too, sculpture may help me by its dumb presence, by the touch and feel of mind and hand.

1 February

In recent days I've turned to notes & sketches which Lee sent me while I was working on critical essays. At this early stage of our collaboration on 'Groundwork', or at least the idea of it, shapes move in my mind: Landscape, places, Norfolk, the fields round Moor Farm, London buildings, the Thames. It is a kind of invocation, vague as yet: shapes, energies, masses, textures, rhythms. Nothing as fluent or distinct as reverie or dream. No vivid pictures either, but rather a sense of landmass or dumb object (as in a Grandjean sculpture), and forces under the surface, slow, dark currents. It is mainly Lee's words I have here, some of them forming concepts, some shaping what are almost poems (his secondary gift, undeveloped, springing from sculptural apprehension), and in this I feel how he senses things.

At this stage, I feel stupid, dumb, as if my mind were heavy matter – unfree, unquickened, shackled by my prose consciousness to ideas of what to attempt, and without time to try, and fail, and try again, and perhaps stumble into a course that enlivens words.

Tao, the watercourse way, Heraclitan flux, or blaze. There are ways I come upon in my unknowing, with old words, old ideas, and what they reveal is a world indetermined, unfinished. Tired and empty, I find a block universe, an image-world in which there is nothing new. Without creative daring, that is how it is: dead.

Easter at Moor Farm

A before-dawn drive from Somerset to Norfolk, with the comet going down the sky over Cley Hill, over Stonehenge. Bright dawn reveals frost on meadows beside the motorway and a waning moon.

On the lawn at Moor Farm, a cherry tree massy with blossom, buzzes with bumble bees. In the field, Josh, a young black & white carthorse, comes to me at a trot to receive an apple. There's a multitude of ladybirds on ground elder, nettles, and wild garlic in the garden. Is this a sign that we will have another drought this year? Skylarks are singing, almost out of sight in the sky.

In the barn-studio, Lee talks about his work as we look at it. 'Object sculpture's uniqueness brings the imaginative moment into the real, the idea given form.' "It's the embodiment of feeling into 'thingness' that excites me." 'Wood is a vegetable mass which forever changes. I work with its uncertainty, its fracture and shake; its nature is part of the content of my work: the shaking of any certainty I may be vain enough to try to hold on to.'

"One of my favourite words is 'dumb'. It is the sound of my oak trunks as they roll off the lorry and hit the studio floor. It is the eloquence of the silent object. It is the speaking through being rather than through word. I want to make objects that are eloquent in their dumb presence. That presence which may make a medium of silence: for each work a different kind of silence and in their silence, there may be another kind of meaning. One can perhaps imagine some other hidden visceral organ. An organ of physical empathy with which the imaginative object wishes to engage and that this organ makes possible a kind of **physical** understanding of content.

As Gaston Bachelard says in *The Poetics of Reverie,* 'For things as for souls the mystery is inside'."

(From Lee's talk at Chelsea Arts Club, 23 March)

Peewits tumbling over fields.

Smells of earth and pond water.

The haunting thing in this place of long human occupation is that there are no ghosts. Their absence makes the cut of the present.

NIGHT PIECE

Cut of far roofs, black
against sunset,

owl hoot sounding
the depth of woods:

the present is a blade
you could try with your thumb.

It is a haunting thought
that there are no ghosts,

only this black and shining edge.

Comet, a long tail streaming between constellations – like a beam of powerful torchlight, or a beam shining from a round 'door'.

Looking at magnolia flowers: foxglove-red at base, creamy, shell-like petals. Adjectives are worse than useless – 'curving', 'pointed', 'erect', until there is a sense of potency, a sharing with. TONGUE. Imagination feels into. Language abstracts us from being in our bodies in the world, but can help to put us back in.

Three barn owls hunt moor fields by the alder beck. Float, glide, rapid wingbeats, settle on fence post, body motionless, head turning. On another occasion, as Lee and I walked towards them two 'owls' turned out to be feathery-headed Norfolk reeds. One owl flew towards us, saw us, screeched, swerved. At a nearer view, I saw that the back is mossy brown. Their territory is fields of reed-mace, docks, grasses, brookside fence posts, from which they watch intently. We found an owl pellet, compacted fur full of tiny bones, yellow incisor teeth with which a vole had gnawed. Close by, a fox's broken body, decaying. Hares, sensing us from far off, ran away. Cawston church tower across the fields.

Owl Country

Where the beck trails
alders and dark,
feather-headed reeds,
at the foot of a post,
a pellet,
compacted fur,
yellow teeth
with which a vole
would gnaw
          no more.

Late afternoon. Sunlight falling through elongated windows and shining on facets and curves of lee's new sculptures.

Groundwork: undulating surface of wood and earth-covered wood. Juxtaposed with the mountain form of *Veil.* Mass gathered, mass spread.

Meeting (a massive work about 9 ft tall). Oak (all except *Groundwork,* which is iroko, are made from oak). Here, the 'built' is exploding, as in flames. It incorporates the 'steps' image which represents human ordering, mathematical proportion. Lee is fascinated by nebulae, images, from the Hubble telescope, of places where stars are forming, far out in space, but familiar to us, of the same nature that forms our clouds. In one monolith he brings together turbulence, chaos, complexity. This and other objects are further 'shaken' as the wood dries and splits. He welcomes organic changes as being in the nature of the material to which he has committed himself.

Three *Island* pieces. Visiting Beachy Head, Lee had looked down the chalk and flint cliff, like a section of England, the *thickness* of the island. These pieces are theatrical, a stage for dialogue between 'protagonists' forced together on a limited ground. One of them is called *Where are you going? Don't go.* Images from *The Tempest* are in his mind. I interested him by mentioning the great scene in *King Lear*, in which Edgar persuades his blind father that they have come to a cliff edge, and Gloucester lets himself fall – on the ground at their feet. Later, I read the scene to Lee & Mieke & Kate. The literary references have suggestive power, but I know they are only an element in the sculptures, which are primarily objects, not metaphors or representations which can be 'read'. This is what excites me about them. Listening to Lee talk about his work I feel myself to be in the presence of a great sculptural mind. He conveys the drama and mystery of making, in which imagination as an organ of physical empathy is at work.

He talked further about welcoming 'shakes' occurring in his wood sculptures. He incorporates uncertainty through shaking and splitting in the made object; the riven material, as unstable as Los Angeles on its fault lines. He spoke too of the hole – a form in his new work – as a mystery, and of East Anglian pits and places with a story (for example, of a cart & horse disappearing without trace). In *Buried* (provisional title), one of the most beautiful of the new works, four beehive shapes enclose a cube (an image of houses with many windows, like eyes). I couldn't help seeing in it an image of Jerusalem from rooftops.

During my visit, we went once for a drive to Blickling Hall, glimpsing facets of the handsome red-brick house across water and wondering which of the great trees Anne Boleyn would have known when it was a sapling. But the rest of the time we were content to stay at Moor Farm, walking or sitting in the garden or walking round the fields. Once we talked a little about alchemy (Lee has recently read *The Chymical Wedding*). He said he finds generalised spirituality abhorrent, but values Blake's struggle to be particular. As I have noted before, he now has a wide tolerance of what other artists are doing, but separates object sculpture from a loose notion of 'art'.

I spent some time thinking about ***Quickness.*** As in looking at the magnolia, it seems to me observation can become an idol. Why should seeing be painful (as Richard Jefferies found it) unless we are possessive, wanting to see *all*? By contrast, feeling with, or feeling into, respects being, admits our necessary distance from what we are responding to, together with our senses' relative poverty, and above all recognizes the *thisness* of the other.

The thing to do with verbal images is to make them and let them go, figure and let figure dissolve or mutate (Christopher Middleton). Do not irritably reach after (Keats). Consider Shakespeare's constant restless invention – and mixing – of metaphors to express the quick of different feelings. An art of observation, by contrast, can become fixed in an impulse to possess, and focus on surface areas, since an observer cannot feel into.

from **For Quickness**
It is feeling with, feeling into, that respects the other.
Distance makes this possible. There is no other way of coming close.

1–2 July
Two days with Lee walking in London. This morning I sit down with blistered feet to write up notes.

From Paddington, where he met me off the train, past St Mary's hospital (where his son, Louis, is studying). Ivy against a pub wall. Vertical, edged buildings against cloud: man-made forms against more complex natural forms. Things I would see for myself, with the eyes of an alien which I bring with me on my infrequent city visits, but which I notice more because he is preoccupied by them.

Edgware Road to Liverpool Street on the underground. Jungles of buddleia sprung from brickwork in cuttings; retaining walls of London clay bricks holding the enormous pressure of buildings.

To Broadgate: the new development which Lee thinks of as the world 'after I have gone'. I was reminded of aspects of New York – in Lipchitz's Bellerophon, for example, a large, powerful, tortured figure in bronze, in a space surrounded by turbulent images of buildings mirrored in black glass. Paradoxically (I realize afterwards) the great figure represents a tragic failure of heaven-attempting human pride, in a place that seems entirely human in achievement and sufficiency. Is that the sculptor's ironic comment, or do city-builders need to include it as a kind of lucky charm, as a confession of hubris?

Exchange House: a steel building sprung on a great arch, wind blowing through the space underneath, from which we see an older London of steel bridges over the railway. Nearby we watch work in progress on the steel skeleton of a new building, cranes reaching high into the sky. York stone paving underfoot. A Hawksmoor church in scaffolding. All around buildings that mean business.

Bishopsgate, London Wall, past the Barbican. A city of facades, undercuts. Cheapside. Wren's Mary-Le-Bow. Walbrook. Cornhill, which I wanted to see especially for its association with Langland, in a city which Piers Plowman would have known, utterly different from this one of monumental statuary commemorating wars, commerce, and empire. The Monument (also this city burnt & blitzed & rebuilt).

At St Magnus Martyr, 'splendour of Ionian white and gold', and a fragment of Roman wharf bound against the stone. Then over London Bridge, the brown Thames lapping against similar timbers and ebbing fast.

By Clink Street & old warehouses to The Anchor Bankside, where we had lunch beside the river. Site of the *Marchioness* disaster (Lee talking about someone he knows who survived, going down under the water slowly as though in a dream and coming up a long way upriver). St Paul's dome on the opposite side. Far downriver, light flashing on the pyramid peak of Canary Wharf. Mangy pigeons approached us boldly, eyeing the food on our plates, flying up onto tables as soon as they were vacated.

Time to reflect after the morning's walk. I had come to see the city as a physical entity, and found it, of course, crowded with people. A city of faces, bodies, most of us passing each other indifferently, absorbed in our own thoughts, but carrying on countless impressions. And everywhere desire, sexual invitations, unwanted sexual glances, and desire for fashions (& commodities in shop windows). Inevitably I also feel mortality in the press of humanity & the age of the city, remembering Defoe's *Plague Year*, which concentrates, dramatically, in a brief period, something of our continual dying. But over all human shaping power, human making & unmaking.

Tide ebbing, exposing shores of mud, sand, brick, old wood, iron, plastic – once functional things – the city crumbling back into the river. Walking on past the new Globe, derelict Bankside Power Station, designated to be an addition to the Tate, Blackfriars' Bridge (Shakespeare's & Ben Jonson's London, less in the few buildings remaining than in imagined worlds).

We climbed down steps onto an old causeway. A piece of bladder-wrack on granite sets, ground down, being washed away. Sun gleaming on mud & water. Waterloo Bridge. Verses set in paving stones. Wordsworth's 'Remembrance of Collins': 'Glide gently, thus for ever glide, / O Thames! That other bards may see/ As lovely visions by thy side? As now, fair river! Come to me'. Seeing his state of mind, of course, the poet saw what he wanted it to be; as, later, Eliot saw sleazy sexual obsession, and David Jones saw the main artery of cult & commerce.

Above Westminster Bridge, a cormorant turning in flight, perched on a floating platform. We stepped into Westminster Abbey, briefly, just before it closed. Then, on a rush hour tube (bodies to bodies, thousands of us trying to make room by turning ourselves into things) to the King's Road, where we took a bus to Clapham Junction.

Morning.

To St Mary's, Battersea, a Georgian church of smoky black & yellow brick beside the Thames. It was open, and from the caretaker, an old man who appointed himself our guide, and from the guidebook, we got to know more about the place (which Lee, who works nearby, had visited before, but never when it was open).

'Claims have been made that Julius Caesar's troops waded across at this point rather than higher up the river.' The first church on the site, probably a Saxon one, was built on what 'was originally an island of hard gravel, washed on its north side by the river and surrounded by mile upon mile of reedy marshland'. Here William Blake and Catharine Boucher were married. (Her family, according to the old man, were market gardeners on the productive land by the Thames.) And here, Turner, whose house was on the other side of the river, painted studies of clouds and sunsets over the water. He sat in a chair in the oriel vestry window, a small room that was unlocked for us. There are tower blocks on the opposite side now, luxury developments (Chelsea Marina), Lot's Road Power Station & the remains of heavy industry. Lee remembers when an enormous factory occupied land between the church and the bridge, in the direction of Battersea Power Station, where there is now an estate of luxury flats. (He also recalls, when he was a student, crossing the bridge early one morning and looking up at a house on Cheyne Walk where, in an open upper window, Mick Jagger and Marianne Faithfull were arguing.)

Our guide, who was born in Battersea and had lived there all his life, was full of stories about the church & its history, and about his own life, his two marriages, his daughter's marriage, and burials and christenings. Outside the church we looked over the wall and down on houseboats (Dutch barges), a shingle shore, geese in the water. Airliners quite low overhead were following the river down to Heathrow. (Airliners in the skies over London are part of the life of the city, as much as the ships that used to transport people & goods between the city and the world.) A tug drawing a barge with containers of waste came powering upriver. As we walked back, we saw a heron fly over a building of steel & black glass.

By bus from Battersea to Kensington, upstairs in the front seat, the best place from which to see streets & houses, opening in front of us or swinging round on corners, acacia branches drawn across the window glass. Lee's grandfather, he told me, was a bootmaker, who came from Paris to London (where he settled in Soho) in the 1870s to escape from the Franco-Prussian war. He rowed across the Channel, (which to him would have been La Manche; he refused to learn English).

Arriving before lunch we walked (I shuffled) in Holland Park, seeing a white peacock sitting with bright blue peacocks on a brick wall and visiting the Kyoto Garden, beautifully shaped, with a rhythmic use of rocks & trees, pond & cascade; a place of stillness & contained energy, at once actual & symbolic of a universal balance of forces. Afterwards we walked in the wooded areas, which are surprisingly wild (though managed) for a park in a great city. This was the last walk I intended to take on this occasion, and, late in the afternoon, I took a taxi to Paddington, and so back to Westbury on the train.

from CITY WALKING (I)
for Roy Fisher

As he talks, the empty church
fills silently with shadows.

It is a relief, then,
to walk on the shore
under the churchyard wall,
and look at houseboats, geese
in the water, and watch a tug
powering upriver, drawing
a barge with containers of waste.

At Battersea Bridge,
a heron flies over, mirrored
in a building of steel and black glass.
. . .
The city is also lives we do not lead.

In the Kyoto Garden,
a beautiful woman with red hair
walks elegantly, alone,

and in the time it takes her
to pause on the stone bridge
under the cascade,

we have become lovers, although
she will never know who I am
or how much damage we have caused.

17 August

"Direct carving into a resistant material is analogous to the eye and mind directing their energies into the chaos of the material world in clear lines and formal intersections; to the poet's cutting into time with image and rhythm; it is like the ploughman digging his furrow; it is the imposition of the will of the individual over an epoch, a country or a people; it is like the assertive male possessing a passive female. As in the case of Wyndham Lewis, Pound adopted the 'male' creative principle, believing as he did in the fundamental power of the *logos spermatikos*, or sensual thought." #Richard Humphreys, *Pound's Artists*

Direct carving is certainly analogous to male will In Ezra Pound and Poundians (especially Charles Olson). The analogy, however, is one drawn by the male, and is not the only interpretation of carving, or of relations between sculpture and poetry. For example, it does not apply to Barbara Hepworth's carvings. .Granted the importance of male will in carving, there is also the tenderness of, say, Gaudier-Brzeska's Fawns, which arises from the sculptor's empathy with their sentient being. Pound, by all accounts, was enamoured of an idea of maleness that emphasized will and power. Most Modernists were, and its obverse may be seen in, for example, Eliot's fear of the female, and Joyce's simplification of woman as sexual being. It may have been, ironically, a continuation of Victorian values by other means, together with a modern preoccupation with mechanical energy.

The dangers of idealizing male will are all too evident in Pound's career as a political thinker, and in the attraction of modern male vision generally (e.g., D. H. Lawrence, Henry Williamson, Knut Hamsun, Emil Nolde) to fascism. It is based on a false idea of creativity – which men arrived at responding in confusion to the pressures of their time. Others, who react differently, could seem the confused ones, because out of harmony with the main currents of their time. Hence the supposed eccentricity of John Cowper Powys, a modernist who espoused male submission to Nature conceived as female, and who valued 'female' intelligence both in himself and in women, including writers such as Dorothy Richardson.

It is obvious to us that the Poundian view of carving (as described by Richard Humphreys) was partial. It isn't necessarily the resistance of the material that the sculptor feels. Nor does 'the chaos of the material world' mean today what it meant to Pound. What is most surprising about the description, however, even in relation to the period and the works to which it refers, is the complete absence of any idea of the imagination as – in Lee's words – 'an organ of physical empathy'. It is as if the carver acts only externally on the material world, and as if, by analogy, the male asserts himself over the 'passive female', without any reciprocity in the sexual act, so that neither male or female would be changed, as interaction transforms its participants. The male artist would receive nothing from outside himself, as he imposed his male image on the world.

This is plainly not what happened to Gaudier during his short working life, despite the violence of some of his pronouncements. Did it happen to Pound as a narrowing of vision during the period in which his political obsession became dominant? I suspect it did, though narrowing may also intensify (as in the *Cantos*), and it is in the drama of regret, at least in face of nature, that he made his finest later poetry.

Carving, in Humphrey's description, sounds like an assault upon the material and upon the world. There is truth in that, at the time when artists desiring to make it new, in a bewildering modern world, confronted the resistance of dead traditions. It was only later, perhaps, that 'speaking through being' became important (or important again) as artists felt disconnected, and drained of substance.

9 September

Out of Liverpool Street, crayon shape of Canary Wharf, roof gleaming, to the right. Sky cloudless blue. Purple buddleia fading now, against darkened red brick. Lee met me at Norwich station and we drove to Moor Farm.

For him, it has been a summer of gaining insight into things: images of wholeness and connection, through his reading in the new physics. He has been obsessively drawing 'fields' of looping, interweaving lines, his total involvement with the drawings 'like being part of some elemental sacred dance out of which order emerged'. Probably the closest works to these energy field or 'loop' drawings are Leonardo's black chalk drawings of Deluge and cloudburst. Leonardo drew gods riding on crests of monstrous waves destroying trees and men and horses. He felt the terror of inundations caused by rivers in flood, 'which (he wrote) lay waste the high mountains with their swelling and exalting waves, cast down the strongest banks, tear up the deep-rooted trees, and with ravening waves laden with mud from crossing the ploughed fields, carrying with them the unendurable labours of the wretched weary tillers of the soil, leaving the valleys bare and mean by reason of the poverty which is left there'. Lee's images, however, are not apocalyptic, but images of the whole, self-generating forms emerging out of complexity; images of an underlying energy, felt, for example, in the wind. They are spiritual ideas rooted in looking at the world. (As I looked at the drawings, I could see, through the window, greeny-yellow light on the leaning trunk of the old bramley, and wind in leaves of ash and apple trees.)

Evening.
Bright cleaver edge of half-moon in clear sky, a long-legged hare leaping away into the hedge, and dust smoking over a distant field where a tractor was ploughing. Slender stick bodies and raised arms of hedge parsley, black on bank against the last light in the sky.

10 September
One more day in the sun for tortoiseshell butterflies, alive among numerous dead ones in a window of the side gallery. Outside, swallows were flying back and forth between house and barn, feeding their second brood in a nest in the roof of the shed.

By 'shakes' in wood Lee allows nature to break his images and the uncertainty to become part of the work, or the work to respond to uncertainty.

After Lee had picked her up from the train in Norwich, we spent part of the day with Liz Reintjes, from the Djanogly Gallery in Nottingham, discussing plans for our *Groundwork* exhibition. After lunch, which we ate outside in the hot sun (a plastic bottle of mineral water exploded dramatically and made us wet), Liz and Lee and I sat in his work room and talked about arrangements for the exhibition and catalogue, and afterwards went into the barn-studio to look at work. Liz is pregnant and, unhappily for us, will be leaving the gallery and passing on our project to her successor. This may turn out well, of course, but she is so intelligent about the collaboration and sympathetic towards it and concerned for its best presentation, that I can't help feeling that her leaving will be our loss.

From Lee's notebooks:
He is studying 'the quantum field – the interactive dynamics through which diversified yet consistent order emerges in nature'.

The 'loop' drawings describe 'an energy that is the elemental basis of everything. Out of seeming uncertain chaos a pattern of flow emerges'.

"Life evolves ... on the interface between organism and environment, in a 'sacred dance' generated in the interaction between organisms and the field that embeds them."

Erwin Laszlo citing Brian Goodwin

'I lay on my back on the spread 'groundwork' piece looking up into the vast roof space – 200 years of simple work, stacking hay and thrashing, counting bales. I cut my forms.

Space is a dream'

(Good Friday, 1997)

12 September
Home from college, I write up notes of my visit to Moor Farm, which was important for me and for Lee and for our collaboration. It is remarkable how similar our preoccupations are, and how we make the same 'discoveries' independently – of weather, clouds and wind, for example, as well as of new scientific ideas about fluidity and form. It isn't that I can anticipate what object Lee will make next, any more than he can predict my poems (or I can predict them!); but we find ourselves feeling similar spiritual needs, and drawn to the same ideas, and making – and breaking – images that relate to one another. There are differences between us, of course, especially in our attitudes to traditional Western religion, but even in this sphere there is an underlying energy to which we both respond. On this occasion I also learnt that, since he was a boy, Lee has been anxious about loss. Later, his father's death strongly affected him in this respect, but, from the beginning, he suffered over the idea that anything might be entirely lost. Even if he were cut up into little pieces, he thought, as a boy, something of him would remain. Resistance to loss is, I now see, a spring of his creativity; as I am sure it is of mine too. He is consoled by the idea of connection to the whole.

'A sense of ground being energy.'
Lee Grandjean

'Energy is Eternal Delight.'
William Blake

Since I last saw him, Lee has been reading *Four Quartets*, after buying a copy from a second-hand bookstall at the South Bank during our walk by the Thames. 'They are extraordinarily powerful and very close to the feeling in some of my work here' (July notebook).

17 September

I have a hard wooden table – a good kitchen table – on which to lean my elbows, and, once I have adjusted to the rhythm of the coming term, I should have enough time to write in the months ahead. Other poets may win prizes, and young British artists may appeal to the taste of Charles Saatchi and achieve their ambition of becoming members of the Groucho Club, but I doubt that any other poet is so lucky as to have a close working relationship with a real sculptor and to share a struggle to make images, and a developing vision of nature.

4 April 1998

On trains from Westbury to Norwich. Meditating on the word *haptic*, which I came on in a book about sculpture by Herbert Read.

A form of empathy that takes hold of; internal sensations corresponding to movements 'out there'; a rhythmic sympathy.

April growth, nettles thrusting up, leaves unfolding; *shouldering* downland hill curves. Watching birds flying: we have imagined wings, a bodily feeling of movement up & down. 'Touch' working through language as bodily image.

Fields wet after rain; weight of water in furrows, as earth 'feels' it, heavy and softening. Man as cloud being: day-dreaming, thoughts merge, drift, pull apart. 'Thought' is a word with a word's limitations.

Mind-clouds.
To get hold of
is to break the mind-shell
(ego-fixed, abstracted,
categorized, thought-clouded):

sculptural image
poem as object/song-flow

At Moor farm. Showery. Cold wind & rain, blown cloud. Walked alone up the track, through mud & puddles. Tall hedges green & white alongside the abandoned railway line. Peewit feeding on ploughed field.

5 April

Windy morning. Fine tilth of ploughland. Brown soil; the margin of the field beyond the alder beck darker. Purplish-brown (colour of alder catkins), from peat. Masses of small, smoke-blue ground ivy beside the track from Reepham to Cawston. To the church tower, that is, for me a compelling object: an image which I see as an outsider, but knowing its old meaning within the community. As always, the question: what would we be without it? What are we when it no longer exists, when the network of meanings is broken?

In the barn-studio with Lee, wind blowing hard against the roof, making rattling & squeaking noises in the fabric. My first impression as I step through the door and see his new work set out: fixity and flow; images combining the built and the organic.

'Strange Attractors' (provisional title), a group of three sculptures, three in one. When burnt, black will condense the energies. The work explores the organic. There is a duality in the image: system, geometry, sign/ fluid, open energy. Wood itself is now playing a large part for Lee as a 'vegetable fluid'. Sculpture as 'knots of gathering energy'. Origins of the work in (1) Seeing trees at night in a London Park, the differently folded leaf masses of ash and plane, spot lit by strong light from a building. (2) the liquid movement of wind blowing through barley fields. (3) Thinking about wind, which is only seen when mediated. Its 'shapes' in, for example, whipping up dust. What is this growing thing, this liquid energy?

The 'Four Winds' drawing came first, from the idea of a zeropoint field (Laszlo), field of all possibilities. A drawing that is open for us to make our connections. 'Aerial, a slab sculpture. From aerial view, as in sensations one has from airplane taking off. A burning shadow, which is also a falling figure, Icarus-like.

Two horizontal sculptures. (1) Untitled, island-shape, which uses wood as 'liquid ground', with building images cut down from the wood surface. Centrality for Lee of the *liquidity of wood*, the insight it affords into the movement of everything. Wood is 'liquid made mass'. It grows in movement, in sun, water; moves in decay. (2) 'Whale' (by the pond). 'A sort of living island.' 'Lonely being of the whale – a kind of animal ground.' A protuberance gives it a rolling movement. It carries signs, including the cross. Our 'built images' connect us with the 'other' thing. 'We being part of nature, but separate; our desperate barnacle-like clinging onto the rolling stuff.' 'Precarious living upon the liquid.'

'If it's genuine new ground it's going to be unsteady.'

I feel that in recent poems, in the 'Seven Songs', I have gone farther in making something radically strange. Something I myself have to come to terms with, and which I feel will leave others baffled. It is then that friendly critics may become obstacles, when a poet, tempted to go on producing something he has been praised for, refuses the challenge of moving deeper in/farther out. 'We must break our taste', as Lee once said. As I sit and write at Lee's table in the 'drawing room', I can see clouds being blown over the sky above the old apple tree and hear the *chink, chink* of a small bird. Male chaffinches have been dashing about the house in great excitement and flying against windows. It is that time of year, with nests in hedges that are not full-leaved and do not hide them; when each day the living earth becomes greener, quicker.

Evening.
Wind fallen still, slate-blue clouds round horizons. Walked with Lee in the fields, in wet grass, by the beck. First saw a barn owl on a fence post. Then two owls, blunt-headed, silently covering the ground. Glide, rapid wing-beats, DOWN. Up again and on a post, head moving, looking round intently. We talked and talked, slowly drawing a half circle round the old redbrick buildings set down on higher ground above the moor.

'Each great period of science has led to some model of nature. … What will be the symbol for us? What we have in mind may perhaps be expressed by reference to sculpture, from Indian or pre-Columbian art to our time. In some of the most beautiful manifestations of sculpture, be it the dancing Shiva or in the miniature temple of Guerrero, there appears very clearly the search for a junction between stillness and motion, time arrested and time passing. We believe that this confrontation will give our period its uniqueness.'

Prigogine and Stengers, *Order out of Chaos*

6 April

With Lee in the barn arranging extracts from the poems in relation to the sculptures, nailing them to walls & door, as a model of the exhibition. As we work, it rains; the rain becomes heavy, falling through the roof onto us, onto words, sculptures. When the rain stops, streaks of light enter; there are two patches like white paint on the top of 'Meeting'. Outside the barn hail has gathered in the furrows of an asphaltic roof corrugated like tin, and in a heap on the ground, where it has been funnelled into a corner. Towering white and grey cumulus, pools and lakes of blue sky.

Evening.

By flooded lanes to Blickling where we had a meal at The Buckinghamshire Arms, close to the illuminated Hall. This Norfolk country feels deeply rural now; it must have been another world from the Court in Anne Boleyn's time, although the culture of the Hall would have been much nearer to the Court's than to that of the villages & cottages round about.

7 April

Ground soaked, but no rain at first. I watched a skylark, almost a speck, trembling, floating, in the sky over the barn, filling the upper air with its song. Lee spoke of his hope for the current interest in the organic, in complexity.. He spoke also of his consciousness of a 'phallic element' in his work. This also is an isolating factor, since there is 'a sexless, neutered quality' in a lot of contemporary art. None of what he said surprised me, both because I have similar feelings about the chances for my reputation as a poet, and a similar awareness of sexuality as an element of creative power, and because I am aware of the latter in his sculpture. I was only surprised when he said he could foresee a time when he might stop making sculpture and turn to painting, and when he spoke of his attraction to a scholar's life.

Will the 'Groundwork' exhibition make a difference? We feel confident in it: in the coherence and imaginative depth of the collaboration, and in the strength of the sculptures and the poetry. He pleased me by articulating a sensitive reading of the latter – his support has rarely taken such a detailed form – and I was excited by his perception of 'texts' – key passages and their relation to sculptures. I felt his knowledge of the poems: there's nothing more a poet could ask.

As Mieke is aware, I haven't always put myself forward as equal in my collaborative work with Lee. It's less a matter of feeling, and more a matter of my critical fidelity, my passion to understand the work (whether Lee's or David Jones's or any artist's or writer's that I admire) as fully as possible. A sign of this has been my wish to write a book about Lee's sculpture and drawing. But during this visit I felt differently, not less appreciative, but equal. And this corresponds to my realization that the book, when I write it, will be about our work together, our creative relationship.

Lee's drawings have a rhythmic life that corresponds to the expression of haptic sensations in plastic form. To return to this concept, it seems likely from Herbert Read's use of it to refer to inner bodily sensation, such as swallowing or stretching. What I have in mind is rather a form of empathy, in the way one feels a landscape, for example, with muscular tension corresponding to hill curves and body weight to mass. In this sense, it has a strong sexual element, as people must have felt who raised standing stones or made cup marks in stone. The British poet who comes closest to realizing it is Hopkins with his sense that everything selves, according to an individuating principle which human beings share with the whole of creation. His is a completely incarnational poetic, corresponding to his theology.

A simple way of expressing haptic imagination might be to say that we know the world because we have bodies, so that in this way we know a tree from our feet up, and a bird from tension and freedom in our arms. I am more attracted by this than by JCP's 'becoming' a post or tree stump, because it sympathizes physically with the other's self-being, which Powys risks evacuating to replace with himself.

Lark song

Springing
from clod and flint

rising

invisible

or a black dot
quivering

raining over
and all around

song shower
in April air.

20 August

Train to Nottingham with Mieke for the private view of the *Groundwork* exhibition. Arriving early, we met the exhibition officer, Neil Walker, and were able to look at the work by ourselves and in the company of Glynn Williams who had also arrived early. Lee and Kate joined us a little later, before the main body of visitors arrived.

I had no doubt from the first that this is an impressive exhibition, but initially I found it strange to look at Lee's work in the context of the well-lit, whitewashed rooms, instead of in his barn studio. It was strange also to see the exhibition before it had been *seen*, and had acquired any public life in the response of visitors, and I felt a sharp sense of discrepancy between the work as it exists for the artist and its reception. This combined in my mind with the sense of something hidden or invisible, which I subsequently realized was not only the poetry from which the extracts had been taken, but all that had gone into the collaboration.

Once people began to arrive, and quite a few came during the course of the evening, I was gratified to see that many moved around the rooms looking intently at the sculptures and reading the poem extracts on the walls. I was aware that the exhibition was causing discussions too, and although I didn't actually hear any comments (apart from those made mainly by friends directly to me) the whole atmosphere was one of *interest.*

Stephen Stuart-Smith had come up from London, Kay and Sylvia from Portland, and I was surprised and pleased to meet Ken and Wendy (now Mory) Smith who had travelled down from Bradford and whom I hadn't seen since we were all at Aberystwyth. After the private view, Neil took the four of us, together with several friends, for a meal in a French restaurant, where we enjoyed lively & intelligent talk & good food.

22 August

After a night in a hotel at Beeston, and breakfast with Lee and Kate, we spent most of the day travelling and, after a delay caused by a late connection in Bristol, were tired when we got home.

My hope now is that, for Lee's sake, the exhibition will be well received. Circumstances are against that happening – time of year, distance of the art gallery from London & the critics, not to mention ideological & aesthetic blindness. But there are reasons for hope: it is a good exhibition, with a good catalogue for those who are unable or unwilling to make the journey to Nottingham. I want his work to become more visible, to be seen for what it is. This doesn't mean that I regard my contribution as secondary. At present, there is less of it to be seen. I am proud of my part in the exhibition & in the catalogue, but my work on the project exists as a whole outside it.

I don't think of our collaboration as finishing with *Groundwork*, although I don't know whether there will be other projects in the future. But the imaginative ground between us isn't something that can be completed or exhausted by specific concrete collaborations. This too, I realize, belongs to the *hidden* dimension that I sensed when first looking at the exhibition. It is part of our lives, or something within our lives: a spirit which first drew us together, and has expanded through imaginative embodiments, which don't 'use up' the spiritual bond. Irrespective of whether we work together or not.

from WORKPOINTS

We do not deceive ourselves
that we are survivors
of an Age of Faith

or that searching for ground
is a metaphor
for meaning carried over

or that the blank page
is anything but blank

In millennial light
the ground is unimaginable

In what image can we make a shape?

Friendship, love, the self
gone out from the self

the man who has renounced power
the woman who has assumed it
and let it go

The face in the mirror is no man's –
but someone has wandered out
and stands in front of the block,
someone who is,
you say, a wonderer

8 September

In Nottingham, at the Djanogly gallery, I met David Annwn, and Lee & Kate, and attended Lee's lunchtime talk, when he walked around among his sculptures and discussed them with a group of people. On entering the gallery, I had made the mistake of glancing at comments on the show in the visitor's book, and of course almost the first thing I had seen was a compliment paid to the sculpture followed by: 'the poetry, alas, is sub-Robinson Jeffers'. David quickly pointed out that the 'alas' was a give-away, but it didn't stop me feeling it like a physical blow.

We spent the afternoon together talking, in depth. David has been thinking hard about fundamentals – whether there's anything in which we can trust absolutely – since the death of his parents, and Lee felt that he was emotionally at the edge. The talk despite its seriousness (and why not?) was lively, and often humorous too, and I was delighted by the sympathetic understanding that seemed to come about instantaneously between my friends.

After a quick meal together in a pub, we returned to the gallery in the evening and I gave a poetry reading, drawing on *Groundwork* in particular, and talked, perhaps with special fluency & freedom, around the poems & the collaboration. Afterwards I was approached by several mathematicians who were holding a conference at the university who spoke with excitement about the connections between the terms I had used – *instability, not knowing, uncertainty, edge, making and breaking images* – and the ideas they had been discussing among themselves. Lee joined in the conversation, which was a fascinating exploration of common ground. But we had to disperse all too soon when the gallery closed for the night. We left then, and Kate drove us across the Fens, back to Moor Farm.

from WORKPOINTS

What I want to argue
is that poetry and sculpture
are life sciences.

It is not that we express
some finished
or constructed self.

The point is to step out,
into the space between

9 September. At Moor Farm.
Waking tired after the effort & excitement of yesterday, which I realized was a high point, I felt distress at the probability that the work won't be *seen* – known as a major achievement – as was the case with the previous exhibition, *Their Silence a Language,* now dispersed as though it had never been.

A day of strong winds, but still warm. In the garden: yellow leaves fallen from the birch, moorhens, pheasants, rabbits & a trail of fresh molehills on the lawn, a red admiral feeding on a fallen apple.

Walked with Lee across the field and into the copse that stands between Moor Farm and Cawston. Here, trees grown for timber – ash, birch, oak – spring up tall & slender reaching towards the light. From the edge of the copse the red roofs of Moor Farm seem to emerge from the reddish-brown sandy loam of ploughland.

A storm broke after we had returned to the house, slant rain falling heavily, whitening the world outside. Trees thrashing in wind.

Late afternoon: stormy cloudscape, great shifting mountains of cumulus moving over from the west, grey sheets of cloud, rounded clouds brilliant white in sunlight. Swallows gave the impression of being blown about the sky, but in the side gallery to the barn studio, three dead birds, pied wagtails, heaps of feathers, lay among sculptures. They had flown in through gaps in the roof and battered themselves against windows, but been unable to find a way out. There's something absolute about a feathered death – the stillness, the dishevelled plumage of creatures that, living, are so graceful & agile, so quick, always keeping their distance from human life.

In the studio I looked with Lee at 'Different Grounds – Strange Worlds', a series of pastels covering a large wall, from which he had chosen the best to show at Nottingham. As he told me last time, he is now putting more energy into drawing and painting, and expects to concentrate on this, rather than sculpture, in the future. He is realizing the limitations of carving. My feeling is that he will find new sculptural images in the visual work, as well as pursuing the latter for its own sake.

10 September

Small rabbits on the grass & gravel path immediately outside the kitchen window. A moorhen pecking at an apple under the bramley, from which a yaffle flies away with a laugh.

To Salle church with Lee. Wind visible as currents in graveyard grass. Clouds flowing across the sky, making the tower appear to move. Three old stone figures – two with clubs, like Herakles – standing over the north door. Gargoyles, grimacing, humorously. Angels censing, angels with breastplates standing firm on parapets. Big puffballs in grass among the graves, where one stone was inscribed to the memory of a young writer, Sophie Behrens. Stanley Spencer understood the truth about the dead better than most of us do – that they're people like ourselves.

Joking, Lee spoke seriously about wanting his ashes scattered from a boat on the Thames, but at ebb tide; he doesn't want to 'end up' in Teddington, having struggled to get out of the suburbs!

Inside the church I looked closely at hand-painted pages from a 15th century missal displayed in a glass case. These had been reused as cover for a manorial court roll or book, and had notes, written from the 17th century to the early 19th century, at the bottom & on the sides. One relates to the Mass for the Dead and includes the gradual, sublime words beautifully inscribed: *Requiem Aeternam dona eis Domine, et lux perpetua luceat eis.* Round the pages were notes about workaday transactions, life going on through the years, with the material doings that matter so much to all of us, but, now, without this sublimity.

Other things that caught my eye included stories from Christ's life carved on wooden bosses placed in the chancel roof, and re-painted, stone bosses on the ceiling of a small chapel – among them, several of the Green Man, one with an ape-like face reminiscent of an illustration from an old Darwinian book about the descent of man. Outside, visible through clear glass, where coloured pictures would once have been, leafy branches waving in the wind, sky changing as clouds moved over.

Rain is falling now, and outside, under a grey sky, the light seems to have gathered a dark green from lawn & trees & hedge. There's a heaviness, perhaps of impending storm.

When I speak of the sublimity of the painted missal, I don't mean only its aesthetic beauty and the care that went into its making. These are part of the poetry of meaning: the world that *requires* beauty in the construction of something experienced as divine revelation. And how could we possibly know who experienced it: whether prophetic or poetic minds with particular gifts, or monks following their profession, or farmers & their wives or farm labourers? We don't know what has been experienced here, in this made space, which is emptier now than at any time since the iconoclasts threw down the holy images from their niches. If I am nostalgic, it isn't for the return of a past time, or for a thought-world which I know I could never wholly understand, but rather for an equivalent *making:* the creation of images that carry the meaning of life and death, or that acknowledge, and point to, and have something of the vibrancy of, meaning that will always transcend *all* images. At the same time, I can feel some sympathy for the fury of the old iconoclasts, for whom God could only be obscured, even denied, by images. With that fury spent, and the world of belief largely evacuated, we are left with the responsibility of maintaining such buildings for historic or 'heritage' reasons. As someone had written in the visitor's book at Salle 'Excellent' – a purely aesthetic judgement.

from Groundless she walks

But now her mind is an ice-berg
in a polar sea, mountainous dark
moving under her, bearing her along.

And instantly the image fractures,
and dissolves.

What, then, is possible? She cries
silently, as groundless her footstep
strikes the dusty track.

The child I carry
will crawl into the world.
What ground will he stand on?
What humus, or piece of debris
hurtling from the supernova,
the giant star that once was man?

11 September

Walking up the track with Lee. Blackberries in hedges – the only ones I have tasted this year. We talk about creatures' joy in being, whether the Romantic concept is true. We don't know, of course; but Lee is certain that their life is joy, and fear is instantaneous, not a constant anxious trembling. 'They are just it,' he says, as swallows soar and dive, living their being.

He is thinking about work and speaks, half-jokingly, about making 'something that no one wants'. He would like to give up teaching. This was always a difference between us. 'Am I really helping these people? Don't they want to talk to the latest star?' His role with his students is that of 'fatherly encourager'.

As we walk, we pass into a stench of slurry, spread by a machine we saw departing as we approached, on a field on our left. A jogger who passed us from behind – a retired English teacher, Lee says- now jogs back, and passes us again. Lee has very much enjoyed his time with young artists, and has made many lasting friends. So his fear of 'ending up in the gutter', 'living in a cardboard box', is irrational. He is going through 'quite a fluid time', in different ways – with the boys leaving home, for example, and with Kate about to take a nursing course. We agree that for an artist fluidity is necessary – a kind of creative instability. He has an acute sense that each of us is alone, and has to be self-responsible; that we can't live other people's lives for them.

Afternoon. In Norwich, where I visited the cathedral with Lee. A building of massive simplicity, in which the grooved columns give an added sense of power. We looked at the stained glass of the Erpingham Window (which commemorates Sir Thomas Erpingham who fought at the battle of Agincourt), the figures of beautiful (ultramarine) blue. In the cloister my (everybody's) most familiar Green Man, his watchful face, on a stone-carved roof boss, looking from among gold-painted leaves. Peering closely at a picture of the face, I see that the look is voyeuristic, the leaves attached to cheeks and forehead, rather than springing from the mouth, so that the appearance lacks the force of natural energy that marks the best of his kind.

12 September

My last morning at Moor Farm. I wonder on each occasion whether it will be the *last.* Dew on grass, a few leaves blowing off trees around the lawn, where a baby rabbit is hopping on a path among the shrubs. One of the 'love doves', as Kate calls them, on the barn roof. As I walk across the lawn, a sudden strong smell of horse – Josh, the young carthorse, whose great head & working jaws he had thrust against us as we had leaned on the gate into his field.

A pair of butterflies dance round one another as they fly up into warm autumn sunlight. Shape of the cricket pitch – first year unused – an oblong of mossed-green concrete on the lawn. Nearby, Cawston church tower visible between tree trunks around the pond. The old bramley bowed almost to the ground, as if under the weight of big, hard green apples. Half-moon, colour of small clouds in the sky, but, as Lee points out, geometric.

Lee is periodically 'coming to an edge' in his work – we have to, if we're not to repeat ourselves: if work is genuinely exploratory. But this is also an especially critical time for him and Kate, who is courageously about to embark on a new career, now that Louis and Guy have both left home. He feels more confident, more a sense of achievement, in *Groundwork*, than in anything else he has done. I agree, although I see it as part of a body of work which includes the sculptures that formed *Their Silence a Language* (the exhibition). Having accomplished it he has therefore to go on. The same is true for me.

9 April, 1999

Night drive to Norfolk.

Morning

Walking up the track from Moor Farm in a warm breeze, skylarks singing overhead. When seen, small dark quivering objects against cloud or blue sky. Hawthorn, blackthorn, flowering cherry; a lovely blend of fresh green leaves & white blossoms in hedges. Docks, parsley, hogweed on margins. Green leaves of corn shimmering in fields. One field full of tiny Christmas trees.

Lee, after seeing the Jackson Pollack exhibition in London: 'Art is a beautiful struggle'. Pollack's 'Portrait in a Dream' haunts him. As we walked, and later, in the barn studio, he spoke of his new work as transitional. His new black & white acrylics have something in common with the biomorphic art of Hans Arp & others. But Lee is not aiming at simplification, but to allow greater complexity to emerge. He is interested in cells. We in our time see things that have never been seen before. This is specific to our vision. He spoke of a resuscitation of the organic in new maps of the universe. The new works – paintings, a few small sculptures – are impressive. Once again, they bear a strong, continuous relationship to earlier work, to the loop drawings of *Groundwork* & the dualism of his man-made/organic objects – but one couldn't have anticipated the forms the continuity would take. He sees this as being for him a time of experiment when he is amalgamating ideas drawn from new sciences.

On the track we found a pigeon egg shell with a little yolk inside, probably taken from a nest by a magpie or a jay. In a field a pheasant's wing, feathers scattered around. Partridges & pheasants started up loudly from the moor and a hare sat up alertly and ran off at our approach. Alongside the wood, we saw a wire cage with a magpie trying frantically to get out of it. A bird captured, no doubt, to warn off others from pheasant eggs & chicks in the woods.

10 April

Walked with Lee along the abandoned railway track to Cawston, where, outside the church, we found a memorial to the crew of 'Lucky Strike' & the Emergency Services. The flying fortress had got into difficulties returning from a raid on submarine pens at Kiel, and had crashed on land at Church Farm, narrowly missing the church. Two of the crew had been killed. As we were looking at the memorial a man stopped his mini-van beside us. He was a son of the family at Church Farm and he told us they had paid for the memorial, which had been opened in 1996 by Jack Sasson, who had been Flight Engineer on 'Lucky Strike', and had kept in touch with the family.

Outside the church we looked at the wadwo and the dragon facing each other in the spandrils of the arch above the west door. The wild man (crest of the de la Pole family, Earls of Suffolk) has oak leaves wound about his body & his club, and the dragon is clasped by vines. Inside St Agnes we looked at the hammerbeam roof, where one wooden angel, palms pressed together in prayer, wears a codpiece, and at the painted screen, which depicts St Matthew holding a pair of spectacles to his eyes, and read the ancient inscription to the Plough Gallery: *'God spede the plow and send us all corn enow our purpose for to make;' At crow of cok of the plowlete of Sygate; Be mery and glade wot good ale yis work mad'.* The church guide says there is a pun on Wat Goodale, possibly a Church Warden at the time. Another writer, John Kett, suggests 'that St Agnes was chosen as the Patron Saint of our Church because of the importance of the woollen industry in the parish (AGNUS – A LAMB in Latin).

11 April

Pure dawn, with bright moon in its last quarter going down behind black trees around the horse-pond. Later, walked with Lee into Reepham. Windy, white clouds being drawn across the sky. Wild flowers beside the lane: stitchwort (which my mother called Star of Bethlehem), bugle, garlic mustard, white dead-nettle, smoky-blue ground-ivy & speedwell close to the soil. Came back along the old railway track (now called Marriot's Way), between Salle and Booton churches across fields on either side. Enjoying the freshness of scents and air, we talked about religious belief. Lee asked me why I don't go to church. I admitted the strong attraction it holds for me, perhaps more now, since my Al-Anon meetings, when I feel closer to people (apart from chosen friends) than ever in my life before. But I would need to believe, as distinct from seeing Christianity as 'a great story', and I would feel a hypocrite if I went for reasons of tradition alone, because I like churches, religious language, etc. Lee feels awe at the web of life. He doesn't want the idea of any Creator (a human projection) to interfere with the wholly Other. Something similar occurred among theologians, I suppose, with the Death of God theology. It is interesting, then, to look at some of William Blake's figures (e.g., *The Angel of the Divine Presence clothing Adam and Eve*), in which the traditional God or God-like image, with long white beard & locks, has both power and compassion, and is far from being ridiculous. But I understand that Lee's idea of nature requires him to reject traditional religious ideas as human constructs. He is hostile (as I am) to the concept of human centrality.

From Kett's booklet I had learnt that a name for the beck is Sall Beck, after the sallows which grow with alders alongside it. Looking across the beck, at a ploughed field on the other side, and, beyond the field, a green pasture, which, like Moor Farm, occupies dry higher ground, I had said that it looked like a good site for a Roman villa. Then, in Kett, I read about a farmer who had gone out early one morning in August to inspect his field (which was this one), and looking at the crop due to be harvested, saw a rectangular crop-mark. This disappeared when the grain dried in the sun, but had been so distinctive that the farmer was certain he had seen the outline of a large Roman building. My feeling is that there could have been another on the site on which Moor Farm stands, though it's more likely this area was cleared of woods by Anglo-Saxon farmers. At any rate, I have a strong sense in the place of underlying formations, a crowding of signs of past lives, under surfaces which now seem empty of all but today's agriculture.

Afternoon

To Heydon, where, looking up inside the church, I was startled to see a barn owl perched on the chancel arch. Its eyes seemed to follow me, but we soon realized it was a stuffed owl, placed there, no doubt, to deter bats & mice.

On another shining evening, we walked in the park of Heydon House, under new leaves on horse-chestnut trees unfolding like wings. It was in the pub in this village that, several years ago, Lee and I had first discussed the idea of a collaboration. Our talk then had been quite vague: I seem to remember having had a notion of words cut in stone. It's encouraging now to look back over what we have actually made together. Useful to me, too, when I feel blank, as I did then, initially unable to make a start.

Just before dusk, Mieke and I walked to the boundary between the garden and the moor, where the green track makes for Cawston through the fields, and saw the live barn owl come out of the woods and begin hunting.

Earlier, talking about his father, who was a devout Communist Party official, Lee ascribed the value he places on collaboration to his influence. Lee would much rather say 'we' than 'I'. He always speaks of his father with great affection. When I suggested that such a man would have disappeared in Stalin's purges had he lived in the Soviet Union, Lee said that, alas, this probably wouldn't have been the case, since his father, being a devout believer, always adapted to the Party line.

24 July. In hospital in Bath following a stroke.

Lee visited over the weekend. Blessing of friendship.

He brought photos of his new work – the next step. How often we say the same things in different words, or not quite the same language.

18 September. Old Schoolhouse, Frome, Somerset

Lee arrived at mid-day, bringing photographs of his new work

Charcoal drawings based on tracings of tree shadows, 'like slices of the brain'. Sculptures which began in his thinking as 'stochastic sliced vertical'. Unnamed as yet, these are cellular structures retaining the mass of the oak from which they're carved. They have a sponge-like appearance; one of his students said, 'like the shape of thought'. Another sculptor said he had never seen anything like them – an ambiguous compliment.

Another step. Again, one can see where it comes from, but couldn't have foreseen it from the last step.

In reading David Bohm in particular, Lee has found a source of shared order in scientific writing. In his notebook he writes that so much of aesthetics 'seems concerned with notions of beauty and pleasure which I reject as being too limited, not what I work towards which is shaping states of embodied energy – powerful being'.

'An object is now considered to be more like a pattern of movement than like a solid separate thing that exists autonomously.'

'All has to be understood directly as relationship in undivided movement of the whole. In this movement there is NO THING.'

'We are the earth, because all our substance comes from the earth and goes back to it. It is a mistake to say it is an environment just surrounding us, because that would be like the brain regarding the rest of the body as part of its environment.'

'The whole is not imposed, but is *in* each part and each part is in the whole. That is what I call participation.'

David Bohm, *On Creativity*

At Bratton Camp in the afternoon, equinoctial wind at our backs, then in our faces, as we walked to a seat on the ridge by the White Horse. Hard going for me both ways. Cloud driving over, the whole sky moving, like a smokescreen behind the lowland arable & pasture.

Drove back via Erlestoke & Devizes. Now & later, Lee worried at understanding 'romantic' following John Williams's review of *Groundwork*. Lee feels that he is romantic, but is aware that it is a term of abuse on the current art scene, where it designates a soft-centredness & escapism from which he's keen to distance himself. (Not only because it could be used against him – and is – but because it is most what he wants to avoid.)

What does the word mean, then? The elemental, not the sentimental. Lee strives to get at the core of being – beyond knowledge – beyond ego. He went to live in the country in order to get away from the 'conglomerate ego' of the urban artistic scene, to face living in the world. He asked himself 'what if I was making the first thing?' 'What would you want to body in the world out of your experience?'

He told me that through our first meeting & friendship, I had made him aware of the need for meaning., for *use* of subject. This surprised me, though on reflection I recognized our complementarity. He made me aware of the need to *act:* to work, to make images, instead of exhaustively studying and thinking. We both need to balance study and action. (In recent months, understandably, I have devoted myself entirely to reading and thinking.)

Lee brought a book about Enku, the 17th century Buddhist sculptor-priest, which Roger Ackling had given him. Enku was a contemporary of Basho. In his youth, he had vowed to make 120,000 images. He may have done so, travelling among poor people in the remote mountain regions & fishing villages of Japan, working at speed, with his hatchet & flat file, mainly on cedar wood.

He made images of Buddha, images of Shinto gods, portraits: figures with magical power to protect people from misfortune. His images of Kannon, for example, slender curved finger-like figures, simple as wooden clothes-pegs, but with a grace in shoulder & listening head redolent of wisdom & compassion, or the complex, dynamic figure of thousand-armed, eleven-headed Kannon. Enku devoted thousands of carvings to Kannon. 'With solemn intensity he proceeds to break the traditional concepts. What emerges is a bodhisattva one wants to pick up and hug as a friend. There is an inner glow of genuine compassion, and it is easy to believe that Kannon forewent Nirvana to help humanity.' (Grisha F. Dorzenko)

Yakushi (Healing Buddha). The face is the essence of the benign; one would feel better simply by looking at it. And in this and other images, there is the illusion that the image *looks back,* emitting benevolence, or wrath. This reciprocity is the magic of images. 'The metamorphosis of a chunk of wood into a living, vibrant being' – a being that responds to our response, or causes a response as a god or human being or other creature would. The image with presence speaks to us with embodied being; in its presence we become more alive.

By tradition, Enku died by 'voluntary mummification', buried alive, breathing through a bamboo tube and reciting the sutras, on the banks of the Nagara River.

19 September

Excursion with Lee into the Mendips. At Deer Leap, above Ebor Gorge, we walked on the grass and on the road – for me, slow, difficult progress. Below us, in a broad landscape, drama of light & dark, raincloud & cloud shadow over woods, hills (including Glastonbury Tor) outcropping from the plain, fields a patched, blue-grey shadowy landscape, changing in changing light; dark clouds over whitish-grey clouds, rain. Rough-textured cloud in harmony with the land, swallows skimming dry-stone walls snaking along ridges.

We drove on in rain to Priddy, and then to Ubley Warren, Charterhouse. Gruffy ground: an ancient worked landscape, mined by the Romans & earlier 'groovers'. Gorse & decayed hogweed stalks among hummocks, mounds gouged out, grassy hollows. More like an ancient battlefield than places where actual battles have been fought. A bleakness like the lead mines of Ceredigion but more overgrown. Dark red haws against dark rock.

I waited in the car while Lee explored, rain pouring down, streaming over the windscreen. We should then have stopped at a pub for a meal, but I had become anxious and felt off-colour – partly at the thought of walking with difficulty into a strange place – and we drove home in a downpour.

18 March 2000

'Doesn't all matter, at its innermost particle heart, shake? All movement. That's the creative core, the end, the beginning.' (Lee)

Lee brought photographs of new work with him, including 'Colony 7 'White Trope'. Glynn Williams had seen these as sponge images. Understandable; but visual likeness prevents the objects themselves from being seen. Lee is working now on fluid forms. Not geometrical abstraction but forms responding to complexity on different levels, from cell to nebula.

He also brought several pages of writing – words that he proposes to juxtapose with sculptural images on a web-site. Initially I was moved and impressed by these, but on reflection, and having discussed them with Mieke, I realized that I was responding from within my close involvement with his work and that, for the purpose of a web-site, he would need something less dense, less 'poetic', a more lucid introduction.

Afternoon
On Whitesheet Down in a cold wind. Even quite recently, I doubted that I would come here again, because I couldn't walk up the steep slope and the pot-holed track is dangerous to drive up. But here I was, walking to the Iron Age camp and marvelling at the windswept, frozen-sea shapes of the chalk hills & the view south to the Vale of Blackmore.

19 March
Lee thinks that, physically, I don't push myself enough – he's not wrong – and therefore, following my stroke, have adapted rather comfortably to a sedentary way of life, instead of making myself exercise. Frustrated at our not being able to walk as we used to, he ensured that we made up for it by our walks today. He wants to help me fight the stroke.

First, at Deer Leap, Glastonbury Tor in mist below us. Now, I was able to climb the stone stile and we walked over the hill to a far, dry-stone wall. 'Walking on sculpture' (Lee): outcrops of silver-grey rock, grass smelling of sheep, a scattering of small thorns, larks singing overhead. A smell of nettles ('lemony') in a field corner, a view of a working quarry in the distance, stones from the wall, knocked together, making a resonant sound. Every stone, Lee says, and there are countless numbers of them, in the long walls snaking over the hills, represents a bodily human effort, gathering, lifting, placing.

On the hillside we visited Ramspits, site of a medieval farmstead, which stood in an area once lying on the edge of the Royal Forest of Mendip and may have been abandoned at the time of the Black Death. In front of us an ancient ash, black-budded, riven into three parts, as though it had exploded outwards, but still living. Strip lynchets, rocks & a wooded coombe.

After lunch at the New Inn at Priddy, we drove on ('a round of fiddles playing Bach'), past a copse where wild anemones were in flower, to Charterhouse. Another walk at Ubley Warren, over another stile, on gruffy ground, through a defile between walls of fissured rock. On our last visit, in a downpour, I had sat in the car feeling rather unwell while Lee had discovered the defile that we walked through today.

Back at Priddy, we walked to a group of bowl barrows on the Down. By now, I was almost spent, but managed to walk across the hill field to another group of barrows, where I lay down on the top of the first one we came to, while Lee, almost equally tired, walked on round the group. It seemed to be a good place to talk about the incarnational, a subject Lee instigated as much to take my mind off wanting to drop down, as out of interest. What is it? Can it be manifested in non-Christian art? Yes: where the physical is grounded upon the metaphysical, or where the physical and the metaphysical interact.

The night before, we had talked, with Mieke, about identity. I had spoken about my happiness, which I ascribe to my parents in the first instance, to my childhood and early attachments, which gave me my sense of place. Lee said that he had no such sense of identity, apart from his feeling for London, and being a Londoner. With his father's occupation as a Communist Party official, and family moves from place to place, he always felt an odd one out, and unsettled. As he spoke, I felt that the intensity of his need to 'shape' work relates to his need to make a place for himself in the world.

It is not, perhaps, so different for me. Happiness doesn't obviate the discontent essential to creative work. Also, for many years now, my sense of place has been closely related to a sense of loss, because the very place I carry within me (as part of a personal and ancestral identity) is the one I can never be in, as a man living and working. Even to know my place, I had to go away from it, returning periodically as a visitor, confirming a sense of belonging in poems, which, for the most part, have been valued elsewhere.

As Lee says, the big difference between us is God!

27 May

Lee rang and we had a long talk about the new Tate which he has visited and found enormously impressive, and about hearing Les Murray read at UEA and meeting him afterwards at a book signing. The encounter reflected well on both of them, and made me feel good.

Lee spoke wisely about the fashionable junk (as I would call it) represented alongside important works of art in the new Tate. He feels it necessary to know what is being made, and where it is coming from, partly in order to gain a better understanding of his different way. Self-definition is always partly contrary to or different from, of course. My reaction to fashionable work, whether art or poetry, which I dislike, is much less temperate. In fact, I should understand why some things make me angry. I might learn more about some of my own assumptions.

9 August
When Barry Cooper dropped by in the morning, we talked about Epstein's sculpture, among other things, and Barry (who, like all good artists today, is sometimes tempted to despair) was particularly grateful when I told him about Lee's feeling that working with masculine force (in effect, expressing one's male sexuality and making 'earthy' work, as Mieke says) is totally alien to our contemporary aesthetic fashion-makers, and must isolate the kind of sculptor who follows in the tradition of Epstein. This has nothing to do with 'male' violence or aggression, and neither do I associate it with denial of 'female' being, which is just as much part of one. In my view, the latter was the mistake that modernists made (including Epstein?) in their obsession with mastery & the 'spermatic word'. In fact, leaving aside the potentially misleading language of sexual differences, it is, precisely, earthiness which, today, provokes fear & dislike, & therefore mockery, among aesthetes.

Lee now concentrates on *character* energy which he hopes to be non-gendered. Does human being have distinctively distinguished gender? His interest is in male/female biological life energy As One.

11 August
Westbury to Paddington, where Lee was waiting for me. Taxi to Liverpool Street. From here we walked through Broadgate on a sunny afternoon, past café-bars where many mostly young people, free from office work at the end of the week, were sitting outside with a drink and enjoying themselves. A buzz of excitement & a feeling of relaxation & bright, sexy talk: how different from Eliot's clerks going to work with their eyes before their feet! We had a beer and walked round the area in front of Exchange House and then had a snack at a restaurant on the station. The Norwich train was delayed, and we stood on the platform with nowhere to sit down, no facilities for the disabled that I could see, so that, for a time, I was acutely uncomfortable.

Eventually the train did come in, and when we reached Norwich, Kate was at the station to meet us, and drove us, in the dark, to Moor Farm.

12 August
Mist over the fields at dawn. Later, a sunny day. At the field corner where the gate used to be, opening now on a field of whiskery barley – white, green, yellow, gold – but quite poor on thin, sandy soil. We passed

meadows full of poppies & camomile on the way into Reepham for shopping. Afterwards I walked with Lee round the outside of the garden, past the field where Josh now has the company of a small Shetland pony, Lucy, and they were standing together in the shade of a willow. Tiny stars of scarlet pimpernel in the gravel path.

After lunch I picked plums from a Victoria plum tree alongside the field with the horses in it, reaching down branches laden with fruit, the ripe beside the rotten, with my stick. The first line of a poem I never finished, quoting my father's words, 'June drop from the early Victorias', was in my mind.

Walking with Lee on the path across the fields towards the tower of Cawston church, a pheasant started up from under my feet, and, if it had been possible, I would have jumped out of my skin!

Evening

Yellowish gibbous moon rising into the space between ash-trees by the horse pond: 'round plaintive buttermilk face' (Lee).

13 August

Morning walk with Lee on the stony track, between hogweed on the banks and fields of barley & young Christmas trees, over the abandoned railway line, as far as the road. There were more butterflies here, especially meadow browns, than I have seen since years when I took them for granted. On the way back, we noticed, beside the track, a rabbit that was decomposing, becoming earth. 'Losing its image,' Lee said, and 'becoming thing'.

Late in the day we drove to Wells next-to-the-sea and walked through Corsican pines to the beach, beach huts on stilts & the wide sands, tide out, but turning as we walked to it across a stretch of mud & sand. I threw some water into my face and would have liked to paddle in the sea, but it would have been too much of a palaver to remove my shoes & socks, so I walked back and sat down on a breakwater and watched Lee & Kate, intimate figures, moving together among other couples and groups. All the way from the town to the beach there was a multitude of people, but once on the sands, the sounds were muffled and the space made us small & apart. I found the walk back, up sandhills & over pine roots, quite difficult.

From Wells to Downham Market, where I treated them to a meal (oysters!) at a hotel.

!4 August

An oppressive day, low cloud, stormy atmosphere. Lee at the dentist in the morning, Kate working at the hospital as a student-nurse. I stayed at Moor Farm, writing my journal, reading, the house very quiet.

Into Norwich with Lee after lunch to bring Kate home. Talking with Lee, he often brings a balance to my more extreme views or feeling – cultural pessimism, for example. While I have a way of talking myself into corners, he shows a way out. We see and feel the same things, but his view is more open. There are exceptions, of course.

Evening

Noise of combine harvesters from barley fields on the other side of the abandoned railway track, like tanks.

In the barn-studio looking with Lee at his new work. A black sculpture ('Colony') and a white sculpture ('White Trope'), works embodying 'cellular fluid nebular movement'. Here, 'nothing is hidden/ everything is hidden'. The objects are motionless, but conceived by the mind as constant change. On the wall behind the sculptures, a large 'shadow' drawing, begun as a tracing of leaf & branch shadows under an apple tree on the lawn. Impressions, & at the same time actions of a mind at work, making pictures out of fluid movements. The works are about 'life in its uttermost centre' – 'energy' in micro & macro realities – cells, clouds, nebulae, water. The sculptures & the charcoal drawings can stand alone, but I felt that, together, as a group, they were even more vital. 'Sculptures of the quick,' Lee says, and 'a stream of data'. Asked about the significance of the black & the white, he said his whole project is 'anti-dualistic, mind & body as one'. He is also interested in things travelling at speed – knowledge of the fleeting. He acknowledged affinities between his new sculptures and Hans Arp's biomorphic works.

Other new sculptures include 'Irregular Log', a work which, especially as the wood dries out, defies system, and 'Fresh bread', a number of flat sculptures, like naan breads, which appeal strongly to the senses (including taste), and which are rich in sexual suggestion & other potential images. There's a humour about these, too.

In Norwich cathedral early in the morning, Lee had heard a voice speaking in his head: 'Make your part'. The reference to 'adding a piece to the great chain' (as the cathedral did), he says, was to Ingmar Bergman, one of the many makers that created culture. 'Didn't Eliot call it 'adding to the mountain?'

15 August

Warm, with a light breeze & floating island of cloud. Sitting on the seat under hazels at the bottom of the garden, looking out through hogweed stems & thistles bearded with seed, across the moor & fields (where the Roman villa may have been), at Booton's gothic spires. When Lee joined me and we sat talking, a kestrel flew into view, and, momentarily, completely unaware of us, hovered.

Lunch outdoors in the shade of the bramley, on the shadow of which the drawing is based.

The garden is home to a green woodpecker, which I saw later, and heard as it flew away with a yaffle. As we walked on the path through the fields towards Cawston church tower, a hare ran away from us, ears jumping up out of the barley.

I started talking about the pastness of the past, which I feel here, perhaps more acutely than anywhere else I know. There is an almost-expectation that people who have lived and worked on the farm & in the fields, over the centuries, will appear, going about their labours. Yet one knows they won't; as we too, with all our intense & busy interests, will one day be part of the same absence. Lee spoke of a historical construction he had seen, which showed layers of human settlement & occupation. It made him think, positively, of adding one's own layer. But what (I said) if there is no continuity, which is the assumption, and perhaps the fact, of our time? In his view, 'The very nature of human is passing'. There's something bigger – Nature – than all our constructs. He was brought up to be anti-traditional, going to bed alongside smoke-filled rooms in which his father & other communists were talking about the past as being repressive, and denouncing religion (the opium of the people) for 'ripping off' the workers. This influenced Lee strongly, but from his mother he derived an interest in mystery and the sacred, and his sense that 'Spirituality is the things of nature'. 'Life and creative imagination continue without us,' he says, 'the cosmos evolves.'

At evening I watched for the owl to come out of the dark of the woods. And, suddenly, there it was, close to me – but where had it come from? – flying at head height, turning, diving, rising. I could see its face, its eyes.

Late August, Bank Holiday weekend. At our new home in South Wales

In the morning we walked in Treharris Park, above our house, and along the path above the long-abandoned quarry. Though fenced off and dense with bracken & Himalayan balsam, trees & bushes, the quarry sides could still be seen falling away steeply below us. Above the path, an old farm in the process of being renovated, geese & a fine black cockerel (which I hear from the house). Another row of houses high on the hill, and below, beyond the quarry, a vast expanse of uplands, ending to the south in Myndd Eglwysilan, and clusters of houses, former pit villages, on the sides of the valleys. Some I could name, but most I wasn't sure of, and all this visible from only a short way uphill from where we have come to live.

The following day, Lee took me for a drive onto the moorland above Treharris, on Gelligaer Common, which stretches for miles in all directions, rough, hilly ground, with traces of former industry. Here, we walked to the top of a hill, sheep & cattle around us, a few horses, on ridges, impressively silhouetted against the sky. Also, patches of human squalor, refuse strewn depressingly in wild places. From the Common we drove down to Bedlinog and back to Treharris.

Our outings & walks & talks & above all Lee's company did me good. He was intensely interested in the area and impressed by its mixture of grittiness & beauty. His perception of the kind of place it is, the land forms & materials, the human history & present communities, made me more aware of it, bringing me out of my anxious introspection.

On the final morning of his visit, he showed me slides of his new work: objects cut from polystyrene, a material 'without history', and therefore more appropriate than wood or stone for his present explorations of the cosmic & the microscopic. These struck me as being both beautiful and powerful, perhaps the most immediately aesthetically attractive objects he has made, but also continuous with his earlier work: another step.

17 February 2002

If I've learnt anything it's that there are unknown friends. Nothing could replace my relationship with Lee. What I have learnt with him though is the possibility of creative collaboration, and that one's work can be understood in depth. It isn't necessary to be alone – creative need is shared.

One can doubt this, in isolation or arrogance. When there seems to be no public one can doubt it. Or when the public for poetry seems only to want something else. Confirmation comes not from understanding alone, but from someone else wanting the same thing, with the necessary difference requisite to all creative work.

As Lee makes sculpture, so I write. And that's connected in my mind with the sharing I've always wanted more than anything else, and found initially with a group of friends when I was first discovering books & ideas, first learning to use my mind. My sense of things now is that in writing for oneself, as best one can, one is writing for friends, now and in the future. It isn't necessary to compromise ('we must break our taste'), because that's what the creative mind needs. My ideal, then, is that of two minds, each challenging and enlarging the other. Or, of course, more than two: dialogue between two or many. This is what I have had in recent years with Lee, and, every day, with Mieke, whose quick intelligence has made me go deeper than I could otherwise have done.

16 April

Lee's photographs of his new sculptures and accompanying letter & notes arrived this morning. My overriding impression is that these new works are beautiful: strange-shaped, as elemental forms of life are, and concentrations of light. In the afternoon I started work in response, setting down images/ideas, imaginative-somnambulist, and getting nowhere, but feeling for ways. A provisional title: 'Elusive light'.

17 April

The proofs of *Adamah* arrived today. In college, my first class after the Easter break, I introduced *Groundwork* to a group of creative writing students. One thing about looking over published writing, it reminds one of the time when the page was blank.

from WORKPOINTS

We begin at the end
of the story,
in millennial light.

Overhead on these clear April nights
the Comet's tail streams in the solar wind.

It is as if someone has opened a door
from which a light shines out
across the sky,
and into our minds

illuminating for an instant
images that have made us,
world on shattered world

and all around nebulae
are giving birth to stars.

11 August
A misty early morning following a cloudless evening the day before. After an early breakfast Mieke set out to drive to Harwich and the ferry, for the start of a ten-day visit to the Netherlands. Driving across country yesterday we remembered our first visit to Moor Farm – younger, both of us more mobile, and in love. A wonderful time; and nothing essentially has changed.

Later
Clouded. A walk alone with wet feet in the garden. A rabbit & a moorhen on the lawn. Funnel spiderwebs in the grass. The horse-pond full, lilies on black water. Mock-gothic Booton across the fields, Cawston church tower, along the line of the track. Late summer with a hint of autumn in the fruits, yellow leaves fallen from the birch, spiderwebs, fungi, the stillness – broken violently when, at my appearance at the entrance into the field, a pheasant flies away with loud alarm.

Late afternoon. First view of new work in the barn-studio. My immediate reaction, as at first sight of Gaudí's *Sagrada Familia*, to laugh with delight at the strange & playful forms. These sculptures have a lightness which is only partly to do with the materials – polystyrene & foam filler. They have too a dynamism, a kind of windswept & supersonic quality (appropriate to the imagery of wind-gods) and at the same time they are reminiscent of strange subatomic beings, which we see in enlargements of a water drop. It isn't that Lee is imitating these things, but he is working with a strong sense of the organic, as distinct from the built, which characterized some earlier work. In consequence one is aware of the chemical & the biological in the new forms. He speaks of 'imagining other forms of life' & of 'vortical presences, floating clouds, figures made of complex, fleetingly connected, shifting patterns'. He spoke too of 'a sensing of feeling in the body' – which reminded me of David Bohm and his insights based on interior sensations – and of things that have 'a quality of having grown'.

There's a pile of polystyrene fragments against the wall – debris of the two original blocks – and he makes objects from these: agglomerates of broken pieces, 'part of some greater building whole'. I asked Lee about his response to the objection to his material on ecological grounds. He said he had no answer, but was fascinated by the material with its relative lack of 'history' (though Henry Moore worked with it on *Sheep Piece*), its lightness (full of air bubbles), and granular texture.

As in the photographs, it was also the beauty of these objects that struck me: the integration of colours & shapes, the contrasting shapes within objects, the sense of lightness, as if poised for flight, or caught in flight. One could think of them as the invisible, at macro & micro levels, made visible; and it is hard not to think of something brought into existence as a copy or version of a previously existing thing. But it is more wonderful to realize that these objects did not exist before, but are products of a creative imagination, their lineage discernible in earlier work of the same mind.

Evening
A young rabbit nibbling an apple under the bramley.

12 August
Picking plums from the Victoria, a massive crop, ripe & rotten fruits clustering together.

In late afternoon sun, I sat on the trunk of a fallen tree in the field alongside the pond. A spidery floss of thistle seed taking to the air, leaves seething in a breeze. Cawston church tower a pillar of pale stone, gleaming across the field. The area In front of the set-aside is dense with young trees, hogweed, grasses, sorrel, impossible to see over to the beck now, except from the sloping garden. Tired after recent days, the nerve-shot drive, wondering how to begin 'Elusive Light'. (Lee in the studio cutting pages.)

Talking to Lee, and seeing more sculptures (some from our earlier collaboration) either lying damaged in corners or sinking into the vegetation, my concern focuses upon the need for his work to have a major retrospective exhibition. He concentrates on what he is making now, neglecting earlier work. In one way, this is obviously a good thing, but not for the body of work as a whole, which should be seen. It maddens me to think of work of genius *hidden*, in a culture that concerns itself with every novelty. Lee reminds me that he was having occasional shows, and was teaching, and we were 'taking part'. He says, philosophically, 'We make our work – what happens happens'.

13 August
A day of playing with ideas for poems. In the evening, gleam of a quarter moon between clouds.

14 August
A box containing copies of *Adamah* was delivered in the morning. A beautifully produced book, with Lee's 'Groundwork' cover, well-spaced poems, a good typeface. It arrived while I was at work, sparking ideas. There *may* be something in what I am doing.

Lee took me to lunch with his mother in Aylsham on a hot day. Avril is positive, full of curiosity about ideas; an independent spirit. I gave her a copy of the book.

Once or twice, I've glimpsed the yaffle around the bramley but it hasn't stayed long enough for a clear sighting.

Walking along the track on a cloudless evening we saw four balloons approaching from the direction of Norwich, at first no bigger than soap bubbles, and only just visible. I sounded off about the current 'art scene' & my dream of a truly discerning criticism; unwisely as far as the former is concerned, it does no good and only produces negative vibrations. Sitting on the tree trunk watching for the owl, I saw the balloons passing on the far side of Cawston, the window in the church tower catching the light, as if the church were lit from within, flickering with the sun's changing angle, and going out. The owl did not appear, but a heron surprised me flying along the beck.

15 August
Morning: in the studio, Lee, at my request, talked about & round the sculptures. As a result, I understand better the sequence from drawing to object, and the inspiration he drew from the Greek Tower of the Winds. Drapery in the latter, for instance, stiff but complex, hiding and revealing form. He spoke too of his interest in Bernini & Baroque, influenced by his reading of Gilles Deleuze's *The Fold: Leibniz and the Baroque*, explaining the importance of folding & unfolding. The drawings (including 'Four Winds') developed from randomly placed curves, parallels, a 'flow of process', until other forms emerged. Influence of the crosshatching of foliage & clouds. All the works are about energy, its

forms & manifestations. He had looked at wind patterns in the barley field, patterns revealing the 'order' of the wind in running ripples: an image of energy, movement held and released. Shapes of nebulae, too, and cloud forming, smoke rising, movements caused by a stone thrown in the pond. He saw forms emerging out of movement, in the barley, in the draped Greek figures; one thing emerging out of another. Hence *Violet Changes*, which has behind it different forms in the drawing, and is a unity made out of disparate parts. *In the Bud* the form is fecund, budding, visceral (intestines, fruit), the colour suggested by green & red of fresh apples, and intestinal, menstrual blood. *Fifth Wind*, a transformation of the figure with a pitcher scattering rain. Here, compressed drops, moving into granular linked lumps: 'An event of many things in process'. A visualized portion of part of a continuum, pattern continuing beyond the edge.

'All gathered from the greater energy.' *Scattered Light*. The Greek Wind scatters flowers, which transformed into light. Behind this: drawing, as water with light in it; cellular structures, their variations.

He finds polystyrene good for the making of complex forms, partly because it is light, and with the lightness of another world, 'other worldly'. Reflecting on the work, I can see that its beauty is in part its strangeness. The forms are familiar, but strange also. How explain this? The forms are organic, but not imitations of biomorphic forms, rather, these are sculpted, invented, put together in ways that don't mirror microscopic or macroscopic forms, but suggest (partake of?) the energy animating them. In my own terms (borrowed from Michel Henry), I could say they afford glimpses of the life we never see, and so, while strange and even alien, they are images of the life we too are part of. There's something here beyond the smashing of the Renaissance mirror of Man and Nature. Formally, a development from Cubism, into sensations & ideas of life as we are beginning to understand it now.

Elusive Light

Mind on pathways
through hidden landscapes
imagines the secrets
by which it exists

cloudscape
smoke dance
light
          flickering

Evening
Storm. Heavy rain. Dirty violet, with a patch of greeny blue, ethereal ('El Greco sky'). Bright orange cornfields towards Booton. 'Apples on fire' on the bramley. All evening we were at the edge of the storm, lightning flashing, crashes of thunder. Once, I would have been terrified. Now, though jumpy, I can take in the impressions.

from God's Houses

St Agnes, Cawston

1
A child would see them
fearfully in his mind,
and cry out for light.

He would hear creak
of wooden wings beginning
to move, and see
unforgiving faces
set towards – what?

In the dark they would swoop,
silent as vampire bats.

2
I am not a child now
to be afraid of the dark,
or should not be.

Nor is it fear that draws me
across the fields
to the stone tower
familiar of pheasant and hare

and the white owl
that hunts along the beck.

3
House of carved angels
that stand like trees in wind
on tiptoe at the brink of light,

it is like a stone idol
beckoning,

a blunt statement
that says what it means.

16 August

A lovely fresh blowing air after the storm. Worked on 'Butterfly fantasia' – possibly something there. Picked plums.

What turn of evolution made pheasants announce themselves with such a racket when they fly off in alarm? Walking across the fields and down to the beck – rabbits leaping away, white bob-tails in the air – I frightened the barn owl from its roost in an oak tree over the water. I wonder which of us was more surprised; but only one was delighted. Another roost is on a beam in the open-sided shed by the barn: which is probably why the swallows have abandoned their nest in the shed this year. Took Lee & Kate for a meal in an Indian restaurant in Aylsham in the evening.

17 August

Ideas, *ideas*; but I don't think anything is working yet, or has the seed of life in it. I must remember that I always have to work *through*; that waste & obstruction & mere deadness are part of the process.

Heat fatigue. Barbecue in the garden in the evening. Gibbous moon over a yellow stubble field – possible site of a Roman villa – visible in the gap between trees by the pond, in line with Booton's towers. Moon yellowing, hazy. Afterwards, in the heat & stillness, I barely slept.

18 August

Another oppressive day, with some rain, thunder muttering around. Worked with Kate at putting drafts of poems on her computer and printing them. Something there to work on.

19 August

Lee, in the studio, spoke of 'making an image without material except colour', polystyrene being a 'dematerialized' substance of 'air, chemical bubbles'. His aim is to eradicate our memory of this material & its whiteness: to make 'another identity'. At present he is working on discarded bits, making them into a mass. Nothing of the original blocks is wasted. 'Loaves and fishes', he said, 'the crumbs become bread'. One work-in-progress is made of shards, another of lozenges. The latter is 'molecular'; but he is uneasy with this & other terms, and would rather find different words. His thinking is sculptural, only provisionally verbal. He works with sensations; 'originary' (influenced, here, by Harald Fawkner's account of phenomenology). 'The thought is thing.' Lee recognizes, however, that his new work will be associated with Science Fiction. He says he won't mind. Sci-Fi concerns 'the imagination of the other'; 'the alien'. He's interested in our thinking about this: 'so much like us; another form of us' – which sent me back to Martin Rees:

'Aliens would be made of atoms similar to those we are composed of. And they would realize, as we have done, that these atoms themselves owe their existence to exploding stars. We and the aliens would have a shared affinity with the stars. We would all be stardust – or, more prosaically, the nuclear waste from the fuel that makes stars shine.' *Our Cosmic Habitat*

Later

Worked on 'Barleyfield wind'. Lunch in the garden on a patchily sunny day but afterwards the sky clouded, and, in the evening, rain, and distant mutterings of thunder. By then, Lee had left for several days in London, and Kate didn't return until 11, so I was alone in the house. At first anxious – it was so quiet – looking without success for matches, in case, in a storm, I needed to light a candle! How all one's daylight acceptance of circumstance deserts one – or deserts me – alone as the light fades! This was the person whose mind was entirely absorbed in the process of writing, at the edge of himself, somehow flushed out…

20 August

Worked further on 'Barleyfield Wind', the Actaeon poem & other pieces. In the stubble field on the far side of the abandoned railway track two boys were flying kites, one multicoloured, the other purple, dart-shaped kites, looping and swooping, very fast.

from Barleyfield Wind

It is all imagination:
pooling – running – streaming –
a long, slow surge.
Then, barely a touch,
the whiskered heads
brushed by a breath.
And all the time,
burnishing every grain,
the sun brings to fruition:
a dry, brittle gold.

21 August

Over breakfast, talking about Lee's work, Kate spoke of his 'constant invention': a phrase I shall treasure; it's exactly right. She spoke too of her frustration at his refusal to promote himself, his resistance, even, to sending out photographs of his work (though he does do this). It might have been Mieke talking to me about my unwillingness to make contacts, etc. Well, I don't say the cases are the same, but there are similarities. With Lee, I can see the constant preoccupation with work-in-progress, the very 'invention' Kate spoke of, and the unwillingness to withdraw time & energy from this, which promoting himself would entail. There's pride also, of course, and the sheer resistance – the blindness – of the powers that be to what he is doing.

I understand all this too well. And one day I want to write the book about his work, and our work together. In hospital I felt it was the one book I would regret not having written if I died. And maybe that is still true. But in fact, what takes over is new work – going on rather than looking back, surveying & interpreting work that already exists. Of course, no worthwhile writing is only retrospective; new understanding will always be discovered in looking back. But still, my desire now, like Lee's, is to go on.

Lee says: 'I took up any and every opportunity that was offered. The serious art world does not run on casual approaches. It's always contacts and recommendations'.

A windy day. Great grey & white, bright-edged clouds churning round the sky. Sunlight & shadow. I witnessed a strange event. A magpie & a young green woodpecker were feeding on the lawn, the woodpecker using its head as a hammer to drive its beak into the ground. For a long time, the two birds took no notice of one another. Then I saw they were standing practically beak to beak, the yaffle with its beak open as if being fed, or expecting to be fed. (Kate told me the parent bird had been feeding it in this way.) The action then seemed to turn into a confrontation, with the yaffle backing off, beak still open, but now defensively, the magpie advancing with an aggressive look.

22 August
Worked on the 'Monk Enku' poem. A feeling of old summer light now, sky between banks of cloud a washed-out blue. Yellow stubble fields. Haws in the hedges are all shades between yellowy green and scarlet, but the effect overall is flame. Walked up the track, picking and eating a few blackberries. From the raised causeway of the abandoned railway track, across the fields and over trees, I saw the tower & pinnacles of Salle church.

23 August
Talked with Mieke & Lee about the poems. It looks as though the collection ('Elusive light') is virtually complete. It's almost shaming to look back to my doubts & hesitations, only days ago – but uncertainty is the only way I know.

Another warm day. Cloud building up, grey-blue, livid. Rosebay willow-herb seeds on the air – spiderlike, lighter than snowflakes, but in some places swarming like a light snowfall. One plant has taken root on the chimney of Moor Farm.

25 August
Home, after a night in a hotel in north Oxford to break the journey. This weekend away gave me more than I hoped for. The concentration was fruitful. Lee's new work & his conversation are an implicit influence on the poems I was able to write, especially in terms of imagery of light & lightness, and of energy. I needed to transcend the visual, as opposed to writing the kind of 'grounded' poems inspired partly by other visits to Moor Farm; and although I didn't completely succeed in this, I think I did achieve something new, with quick, evanescent, out-of-the-corner-of-the-eye effects.

Towards the end of our visit Lee received another disappointment, when he learnt that Wilfred Cass won't be showing one of his sculptures at a major exhibition, as he'd been led to believe he would. Outwardly he accepted the blow calmly, but it was clear that he had had to struggle with himself. The problem – exacerbated by his unwillingness to promote himself – is Lee's originality. His work is new, and therefore unfashionable. Yet it is also continuous, in its very newness, with the long tradition of sculptural object-making, and it addresses the present, in response to new knowledge of the universe and our place in it. It is a privilege to be close to this work. Although I am sure he is yet to receive adequate recognition, his work has been seen, but not 'taken up' by critics or curators. There is no clear reason for this. His work may be deemed too complex, not popular, over rich in sentiment and feeling, not 'cool'.

28 July 2003

Sycamore keys lie all over the lane at the entrance to Treharris Park. Their shape – like two arms raised and curving towards each other – has reminded me of something. This morning I remembered what it was: Lee's sculpture, in St Mary's, Peterborough, incorporating imagery of crucifixion & resurrection, in which the arms are raised. For me, it's a wonderful image, though more pagan than Christian. Somewhat like the green cross, perhaps; or the idea of original innocence. But it does depend upon brokenness, as the earth does for seed to grow,

Excursions with Lee

30 July

Abbey Dore. In front of the abbey a field in which three old, arthritic rams were cropping the grass, one of them having to go down on its knees to do so. Nearby, the strong honey smell of a lime tree in blossom.

Inside the abbey, the familiar musty smell & sense of a large, empty space. Here, to me, the strongest human presence is in the bosses fallen, or broken, from the roof, an abbot (possibly St Bernard of Clairvaux) with the Virgin & Child, and especially the golden smiling face of the Green Man. I would come here to see him alone.

Outside, warm grassy smells & smells of sheep & horses. Behind the abbey, an overgrown orchard on the site of the Chapter House, with an old sweet-chestnut covered in small, prickly fruit. Grassy Cloisters with ash, hazel, hawthorn, orange & green cuckoo-pint, rooks in trees over the wall. Blue cranesbill & yellow hawkbit among the graves.

Kilpeck, in view of Hatterall Hill (*Allt-yr-haul*), 'wooded slope of the sun'. Door pillars, interweaving of figures: serpent, animal, human, and foliage & plants. A creative flux, beast tongues, buds, nature springing from human loins, borne on shoulders, each figure at once distinct & part of the one, flowing design.

Walking round the outside, Lee noted that some carvings were by a different, cruder hand. Here, a gallery of the real & imagined, and also a vision to please the Lords of Kilpeck with their hunting interests: hare, dog, deer, falcon, horse, fish, ram, boar. Where we see a poetry of sculpted images, they probably saw the chase, together with grotesques representing temptations & sins.

In Hereford we had lunch at a restaurant that's part of the modern Left Bank Village complex alongside the Wye. Afterwards, in the cathedral, we looked closely at the *Mappa Mundi*, which, with its strange creatures, obviously belongs to the same world as the Kilpeck 'monsters'.

31 July

From roadworks & heaps of chemical & mineral soil on industrial sites at Dowlais to the moorland road from Garlydan to Llangynidr. Outcrop rock weathered, split by ice-knives, quarried, in view of the Black Mountains. Descended to Llangorse Lake, further developed as a leisure centre since my last visit, twenty years ago, but still a largely protected site, crowded with water-birds.

At Llansantfraed church we visited the grave of Henry Vaughan, its position now incongruously indicated by a large sign. But nothing short of restoration & the destruction of the yew could distract from the sanctity of this place, which is deeply inscribed in the words on the tomb. Here we laid a small bunch of wild flowers – self-heal, hawkbit, herb Robert – and fern.

In the evening Lee showed us slides of his new work. The chief of these is 'Socrates', a head 9–10 feet high, constructed on a box which forms part of it. The inspiration for this came from various sources: a book on philosophy which contains images of philosophers including a marble head – wholly conjectural – of Socrates; the image of the thinker, of Socrates as a philosopher 'without text', who exists only through interpretation, as this sculpture does; asteroids, 'lonely fragments', looking like irregularly shaped, smooth potatoes; childhood potato-heads; elephant skin, eyes; Leonardo's grotesque heads; Arcimboldi's. Louis, walking into the barn studio and seeing the sculpture for the first time, at once said, 'Tumour'. This sense of degeneration & 'varicose eruptions' is part of the image, which corresponds to Lee's interests by being powerfully surprising. Mieke found it 'scary'.

Another step, which on reflection one can see as both following a trajectory established by earlier works and embodying a startling newness. Lee spoke of his hatred of polystyrene (the material he is using now), but his liking for its absence of history. For him, it enables free imagining; it releases him from the cultural history compacted in carving. He was making more and more fluid forms in wood, and with this new material he has nothing but the feeling of the image. Wood became for him too 'heavy' – limited and too culturally craft laden.

1 August

After losing our way in Newport and then meandering among Gwent lanes we eventually found Caerwent, originally *Venta Silurum*, market town of the Silures, the tribe which cost the Romans twenty-five years of fighting to pacify – and with whom Henry Vaughan identified himself. Inside the church, a Roman altar-stone with a hollow at the top for the sacrificial fire: 'To the god Mars – Ocelus, Aelius Augustinus, optio, willingly fulfilled his vows. Alongside this, the Paulinus stone, dedicated to the 'Commander of the Second Augustan Legion, [next] proconsul of the province of Gallia Narbonensis, [now] imperial governor of the province of Lugdunensis, by decree of the community of the state of the Silures'. The church is partly dedicated to St Tatheus, an Irishman who founded a monastic settlement at *Venta Silurum*.

Though footweary, I found the village more haunting as we walked around it. It was very quiet; there were few other people about. The carpark was alongside a hummocky pasture with many nettle patches, under which one could imagine layers of past life, Roman & medieval. Nearby, among houses of the modern village, were foundations of Roman houses & shops. From the church we walked to the site of a Romano-Celtic temple – 'exactly which deity was worshipped here is unclear'. It's the same with Mars – Ocelus, a British, possibly a Silurian deity, a mixture or combination of the Celtic & the Roman, but, to us, unknown.

The place is in a flattish, wide bowl with low hills at a distance, easy to defend and prime agricultural land, with the Severn foreshore nearby. 'Roman land': a place with the Roman groundwork still visible, but a 'shaping' mixed with other, older, influences – much of it mysterious as to what the people had actually believed, and over which other ages have passed.

From here we went to Caerleon for lunch, after which we visited the Roman museum and amphitheatre, which was probably a mistake. We had seen enough, and busy Caerleon, with its more developed tourism, was a disappointment after Caerwent. There was a certain charm about a theatre group of young players rehearing a play about Robin Hood in the amphitheatre, but by now I was thoroughly weary.

2 August

Up the steep hill through Bedlinog, where Lee says he hears the sound of men walking, pit-boots on the paving. A warm, breezy afternoon, the finest during his visit. Wisps & fine brushstrokes of cirrus. On the moorland, climbing to the summit of a hill, far views in every direction, Brecon Beacons to the north, Mynydd Eglwysilan behind us and below, and beyond it the faint outline of the English coast. Great spaces of moorland with here & there an industrial installation, an open cast mine, an abandoned quarry, the man-made shape of a slag heap interrupting the natural hilly contours. Hang-gliders far off, wings brightly coloured, one going over at a great height. What a view there must be from up there!

Occasionally a thistledown floats past. Sheep & horses graze on the slopes. There are patches of purple thistles, here & there a tiny 'fist' of red fungus, or moss. No birds until we see a buzzard floating over the more cultivated landscape below us, in the direction of Treharris, and a number of rooks. As we climb back down to the car cumulus is gathering, which brings moving shadows.

3–4 April 2004

Weekend visit from Lee, who looked at the garden to determine the best positions for the two sculptures ('Silver' and 'Company') we are acquiring from him.

Sunday afternoon: up in the wind on the moorland road between Senghenydd and Nelson. Lambs with their mothers in fields behind dry-stone walls. Stiff, ochre-coloured moorland sedge, like bristles on a painter's brush. 'You can feel the scratch of it in the sight.' Hornet-noise of a biker through wind buffeting the sides of the car. At places on the road winding uphill we might be almost anywhere in rural Wales. But, just below, the industrial ruins of Senghenydd, and, from the mountain ridge, mining villages, a scattering of white houses clustered together, in broad, hilly country on all sides. 'Who wouldn't feel a stranger here?' (We had been talking about this with Mieke the previous evening.) 'You'd need to be born out of the rock.' In Senghenydd, a gorse bush ablaze among partially grown-over spoil heaps, fragments of a brick railway bridge and a large, derelict official-looking building with its windows blocked in. Back over the moorland road: 'Not a place of easy living, a place to be held on to through adversity', including the weather.

Later, I said to Lee – not for the first time – 'you could be a poet'. It's the way he uses words – as he says, he has a hatred of received phrases; he wants 'to say it as it's felt'. In consequence he's acutely perceptive, with an original turn that's often profoundly revealing. He helps me to see things in myself and around us in a way that inspires and supports.

21 August
Lee & Guy brought the two sculptures in a hired van and manoeuvred them into their places in our garden.

22 August
On the moorland above Bedlinog. While Lee & Guy walked to the top of a hill, I stayed below watching swallows fluttering or skimming by, close to the ground. Purple thistles, some with down taking to the air. Tiny yellow tormentil among short moor grass. Smells of sunwarmed dried dung & sheep's wool. As I was sitting in the car, a shorn sheep standing on the bank above stared in at me.

At times the passage of time is hard to believe in. It seems only recently that I was at Moor Farm with Mieke and we were walking with Guy, who was then a little boy, on the lane and he fell over, and Mieke ran to pick him up as he began to cry.

20 November
From Lee's lecture, 'Thinking with Stuff', University of East Anglia, September:

'I am forever making associations during the process. Being open to possibility. When I am working I feel a greater access to my stored experience. The mental material of the unconscious.

Process for me becomes a physical working dream, proceeding along a route with generalised conceptual intention but without predesigned formal outcome, the specific outcome and the final detail of finish must be discovered. For me that is the vital authentic energy in a work, it is that which constitutes quality, that which we say *works*.'

No one that I know of is speaking with such authority of the creative process. If only the theorists who dominate our intellectual life had any sense of what is involved in making an imaginative work. It is the difference between speaking from experience, as Lee does, and over-standing, conceptualising at a mental remove, without bodily knowledge or access to the unconscious.

Could any theorist say as Lee does: 'I am incapable of a certain kind of consistency: that of those artists who repeat a format. I am suspicious of it, mistrust it as a symptom of settled laziness and complacency'? A theorist could condemn laziness and complacency, but it would be very difficult for any theorist not only to admit inconsistency, but to realize it as a creative necessity.

Lee speaks of hoping to 'make objects that resonate *with* spirit'. I couldn't better that as a description of a poem which is alive.

20 August

Lee drives us from South Wales to Moor Farm, breaking the journey at Roughwood, the old farmhouse on the edge of the Chilterns, where Kate's mother lives. Here, turning off the motorway on to a green lane, one is at once in the country. The house, with an extension designed by Voysey, stands in seven acres of lawns & gardens, with walnut trees & copper beeches. In some ways, it reminded me of Howard's End, but this country, near to Milton's cottage at Chalfont St Giles, is now, as Lee said, 'pop star country '. In the gardens we heard and saw a green woodpecker, and I thought, as a light aircraft passed overhead, that my brother Dave might have been flying it. We were close to where he had lived, and the aircraft probably came from the airfield at Denham, where Margaret scattered his ashes.

We met Kate and Guy at Roughwood, and, after lunch, with Kate driving, came on to Moor Farm. The route they now take, bypassing Norwich, passes Parson Woodforde's church. In the evening we relished passages from his Diary.

21 August

Clouded over. Fine drizzle. A rabbit, a grey squirrel, and a moorhen on the lawn. A male pheasant on a branch of the bramley. Trees in the 'set-aside' field now hide the slope down to the beck. Walked round the pond – black water cupped in a hollow within a semi-circle of trees – into the field to see Cawston church tower. How nakedly these Norfolk churches stand up out of the land!

With Lee in the barn studio. Stepping over the threshold the immediate impression is of a surrealist's cave of wonders. But Lee is no surrealist. It's the colours and diverse shapes of the sculptures that initially create the impression of a wizard's toys. Use of colour is something he's developed strongly since the time when he was carving wood.

In the barn we looked closely at a new work, made from bits of melted plastic bottles stuck together. This is domed, like a skull or brain, and powerfully suggests a Golgotha, a hill of skulls. This, however, is one suggestion; another is neural pathways; another, cellular, molecular structures. Lee is concerned with 'the energy of complexity', with the rough edges & nodal points of the organic. He makes images, but wants to avoid the fixity that certain names impose – the fixity of familiar suggestions, such as 'brain' or 'hill of skulls'. Eventually I suggested 'Nest', which he felt was better for the complexity of the work.

In the gallery adjoining the barn Lee showed me completed sculptures. These, which have led up to what he is making now, include 'Domestic' – a spiky, uncomfortable piece – and 'Boxer', influenced by Philip Guston's bandaged head. One piece, 'Thus and Otherwise', incorporates a copy of Nabokov's *The Eye.* Most of these sculptures reconstitute objects of everyday use, such as chairs, a mirror, a table, etc. Some embrace ugliness, work against known aesthetics; they are vital, radically different from the pure abstractions of a Caro or Mondrian. He uses paint as material.

Late afternoon, early evening

Cloudless, warm. Picked blackberries with Lee from hedges round the wild field. High grass, hogweed, knapweed, meadowsweet in a moist place near a sallow.

Sitting alone on the seat facing the new woods above the beck, watching a small white moth: whatever happens, best to bless the life that goes on without us.

At dusk we walked up the track. On our right the field has been ploughed, a rich dark brown with a reddish tinge. The land here has a new owner, who is developing it in part for shooting. Now, in failing light, we were aware of a large flock of birds on the ploughed field, which we could just make out as partridges.

22 August

Bright early morning. Two young green woodpeckers eating ants in soil clawed up by rabbits close to the barn. Rapid head movements, up, down, sideways. Alert, sleek young yaffles, colours less pronounced than on adult birds. Lee had an elmwood sculpture that was virtually destroyed by woodpeckers. Of course, he could have prevented it!

It was clouding over as I walked up to the abandoned railway track, where a jogger, a thin man dressed all in white, appeared from one side and disappeared in the other, like a ghost. Behind him, a pair of cyclists restored a sense of solidity to the scene. Now, a silvery rain is falling straight down on garden & trees.

Afternoon

In the barn studio. In making sculpture Lee does not work from a model, but brings underlying patterns (complexity, order/disorder) 'into image'. He favours 'rough-making', as with Guston, work that is at once sophisticated and childish. He speaks of his interest in cartoons, the paring down, the 're-seeing of peripheral things', such as a chair. As in African sculpture, cartoons produce a simplification of the world. He looks for what emerges in the process of making. His interest is in 'making what [he] hasn't seen before'. The work is transformative, reconstitutive. 'Wrongness is interesting.'

A crucial continuity I'm aware of in his work over the years is duality: rough/smooth, controlled/uncontrolled, artificial/organic. Old work (wood-carved) and new work (styrofoam, plastic, discarded domestic object), side by side in the barn, are remarkably different, individual, (not least when brightly painted), yet they also constitute a family of images. (Again, my fear is that, as he goes on, constantly inventive, and some earlier works decay or are destroyed, without a major exhibition drawing upon all his work, the great achievement of continuity & invention won't be seen.) He says some shouldn't be seen, because they are transitions and don't last. They 'have to go, best to go'!

23 August

Another bright morning. Cirrus & blue sky, cumulus at the horizon. Warm smells from hedge-banks & field margins, seeds on a breeze. Walking to the abandoned railway track I can see Cawston church tower, but, from there, Salle is now hidden behind trees.

Afternoon

Church visiting in country close by. St Nicholas, Brandiston, 'no longer needed for regular worship'. A small flint church with a round tower.

In the porch the stone slab of a medieval altar (*mensa*) set in the floor, splashed with bird dung. Inside, a ledger slab with the name *THOMAS* incised in Lombardic lettering. Thought to relate to Thomas Andrew, rector from 1338 to 1349. Most moving, a wall plaque commemorating two sons of a recent rector, Lieutenants killed in 1917 & on 2 November 1918. Outside, dragonflies, and thistledown becoming airborne from a hedge by the graveyard.

The second church we visited, St Faith's, Little Witchingham, was a real surprise, as Lee & Kate told me it would be. Red paint on white walls in the interior reveals itself as fragments of magnificent wall painting. Here are trailing vines, grapes, remains of a painting of George & the Dragon, and, finest of all, fragmentary scenes from the Passion. Most expressive, the Flagellation, in which one guard has his foot raised so as to strike Jesus with more force. But here also is Jesus, with a forked beard, being taken from the cross, against which a figure climbs up on a ladder; a scene of Jesus with Mary Magdalene, with a tree behind her in the garden; and, most complete, a scene of Jesus inviting St Thomas to touch his wounded hands and side.

All are fragmentary, but enough remains to reveal the excellence of the work, 'as good drawing as in early Italian painting', according to Lee. The north wall had been prepared for painting. It's thought the Black Death interrupted this phase of the work.

Outside, on the church wall, there's a memorial, only just discernible, to John Neale. Neale is a name scratched on the brickwork outside at Moor Farm. Kate once visited the church with a friend, and they were trapped inside by a storm wind that rose suddenly, whirling leaves around outside the windows. I thought of American bombers taking off and coming in low to the airfield close to the church, which is now once more productive agricultural land.

from St Faith's, Little Witchingham

Such violent action
drawn with delicacy
and gentleness, so that, almost,
we can see the hand moving with brush
scrolling vine leaves,
rounding a grape, touching in
the forked, red beard.

Nothing is missing
though so much has gone.

Only plague finished the work
leaving life in this empty decommissioned shell.
Soon grass will be at the windows,
leaf shadows move with the vines,
ground elder, nettles, red campion
rise up to bury the nameless stones.

Inside, a quick hand brushes the walls.

24 August

Rain & wind for the last day of my visit. Cold enough for Lee to light a fire in the living room.

Evening drive out of Norfolk. A dramatic sky as we approached Essex – part cloudless, part eggshell blue, part turbulent cloud shot through with sunset colours. Canary Wharf visible far below, London like the gleam of a holy city. Home just before midnight.

23 September, 2006

With Lee, who drove across from Norfolk yesterday, returning with me to Moor Farm. Long delay at the Bridge due to roadworks.

Arrived in the evening. Owl calling in the woods towards Booton. 'Throat-clearing' calls of pheasants settling for the night. Sounds that emphasise deep silence.

24 September

Rabbits & pigeons on the lawn, two rabbits playing, jumping over each other. Green woodpecker in the bramley. Kate gave me a vivid description of the stoat she sees occasionally in the garden. Picked blackberries with Lee from bushes on the field-side of the pond. Trees now hide the beck from view, and maize grown as cover for pheasants obscures the view towards Cawston. In the open-sided shed used as a garage the Ebbw Vale sculpture, streaked white with owl shit. On the rafter a pellet which, broken open, reveals a small skull among other bones. Fig laden with hard, green fruit against the barn-studio wall.

Inside, Lee showed me new work and talked about it. 'Sunset over the Battlefield': a dense cloud-like form bursts through an Ikea-like construction. There's a deliberate reminiscence of Goya's *The Colossus* and my immediate impression was of a symbolic representation of the World Trade Centre. This, however, was not Lee's intention.

Here he is working on the contrast or interaction between the built and the grown, the systematic and the fluid and shifting, which has long preoccupied him. I remember that he was fascinated by contrasts between clouds and flames and explosions – the chaotic, shifting forms – and fixed constructions, such as tall buildings, before 9/11, after which the image of planes flown into the buildings left an indelible impression on our minds. After the event, I recalled his images.

'Yellow Light': a construction of wires through which he has poured paint, black, and, finally, yellow gloss. 'Where are the edges …? Perhaps the yellow is the form and the black is space.'

'Angel': a work made from tiles which composed the old bathroom shower. A strange messenger, a winged, kneeling form. Angular, with silver edges, and a John Lewis chef's knife thrust into it (inspired by a newspaper murder story). This is a singularly bleak piece, without the warmth that, in different ways, usually characterizes his work.

Most impressive, perhaps, an untitled piece which he thinks of as 'Milk and England' (not a Grandjean title, I say, and he agrees). A bulky form, reminiscent of a Moore reclining mother figure (and, I think, a Picasso bull), made of melted plastic milk bottles. This is white, of course, but with red & some blue labels (from Sainsbury's 'British skimmed fresh pasteurized milk'). Impressive here is the balance between the whole image and what one sees, almost simultaneously, as the fragmentation of bone-like, milky pieces. Material and scale both matter in this instance, as distinct from other quite recent work, where image predominates, and indeterminate micro/macro size. There's reminiscence (of the Moore), but not likeness. Lee's concern is with the work itself, not with making a sign of something else. In this & other new work he's using a mix of 'languages'. He's improvising on themes, making discoveries in the process, and reflecting how the mind works, including chance, sudden connections. 'I want to make forms that surprise me.' He has always been excited by painting, and has become a more visual sculptor. This is immediately apparent when one sees the colours of work in the studio, where the floor on which paint has dripped is now like a huge abstract expressionist (stone & brick) canvas.

Late afternoon
In warm sunlight slanting across stubble fields & a soft breeze, I walked alone up the track to the abandoned railway line. The pinnacles of Salle church are no longer visible above trees ahead, but below the tree-line Cawston church tower stands out, pale stone shining.

25 September
On a wet, closed-in morning I made bread with Kate in the kitchen, satisfyingly kneading and pummelling dough.

Later, while Lee was fixing shutters in the study, I read his UEA lecture. Now an annual event, this one is scheduled for the end of the week. Here he is reflecting on the new works I had seen, and now looked at again in slides, so that I was able to take in his thought at leisure.

'I have dedicated my life to something called sculpture but sometimes I feel that making the kind of objects I do, is in some idiosyncratic way an attempt to construct a different kind of painting.

The drip of paint has a life of its own.

The work is an event of meaning not a signpost outside of itself towards the concept.

... all the time whilst working with transformative process one is looking to the work to show you where to go next.

Improvisation on themes is as real to me as a musician.

Central to my continuing to make sculpture is a fascination with the relationship between what is seen and physical sensation, how the mind sees optically then brings into operation those parts of the brain that are active in physical sensation and thereby open up different vocabularies of meaning.

My work abounds with the systematic other being messed about by some chaotic other.

Of the Eagle Nebula, he says: 'We are part of a material ground that ranges from subatomic particles to neurones and nebulae.'

What emerges powerfully from the work and from the thinking about it are the primacy of imaginative process, and the connections between seeing and bodily sensation and the 'material ground' of existence (from the subatomic to the depths of the universe). It seems to me that its very power is what currently marginalizes the work, in an art world that thinks and sees in terms of concepts, and therefore of the known (which is the fashionable). A prevailing rhetoric of radicalism and innovation prevents work of this quality from being seen. Emphasis on imaginative process indicates possibilities of freedom. As one's mind solidifies, so process involves fluidity.

26 September

A morning of watery, shadowy light under large cumulus. Walked with Lee up the track. Comma butterfly – vivid orange, 'like a bit of Victorian jewellery' – feeding on rotting blackberries. We were able to watch it as it settled, pulsing, on fruit & bramble leaves, which were almost blue in the sun. Sound of a tractor trimming a hedge. Maize still, or trembling in a breeze. We talked, among other things, about the work one does, or hopes to do, as one gets older; that one should care less about the world's conventions, or one's own. Uniformity belongs to youth!

Clear evening with a chill in the air. Beautiful pink & blue Michaelmas daisies in the rock garden, autumn crocuses leaning on the ground – white-violet, Lee says, he has a prejudice against the word purple! Smell of cut grass, and damp smells of vegetation under trees & by the pond. The red of haws startles me when I come upon it in the shadow of trees. I startle pheasants, which fly off noisily. A hare with tall, black-tipped ears, like antlers, runs away down the ride between maize and trees above the beck, towards Cawston church tower.

As the light fades, we drive to Itteringham and The Walpole Arms, where I treat us all to a meal, and we talk and drink two bottles of red wine.

29 July 2008

Long drive from Wales to Moor Farm, breaking the journey at Roughwood in the Chilterns, where we had lunch with Kate and her mother. What talking journeys these long drives are for us, with Lee as far as the Chilterns, then mainly with Kate!

30 July

Full summer, hot, with cirrus in a pale blue sky, and larger clouds beginning to gather. The most noticeable change in the garden, the addition of a small greenhouse on the former cricket pitch, and garden chairs on the lawn beyond the bramley. Two years since I was last here, yet, arriving, I feel there is something eternal about the place & its surroundings.

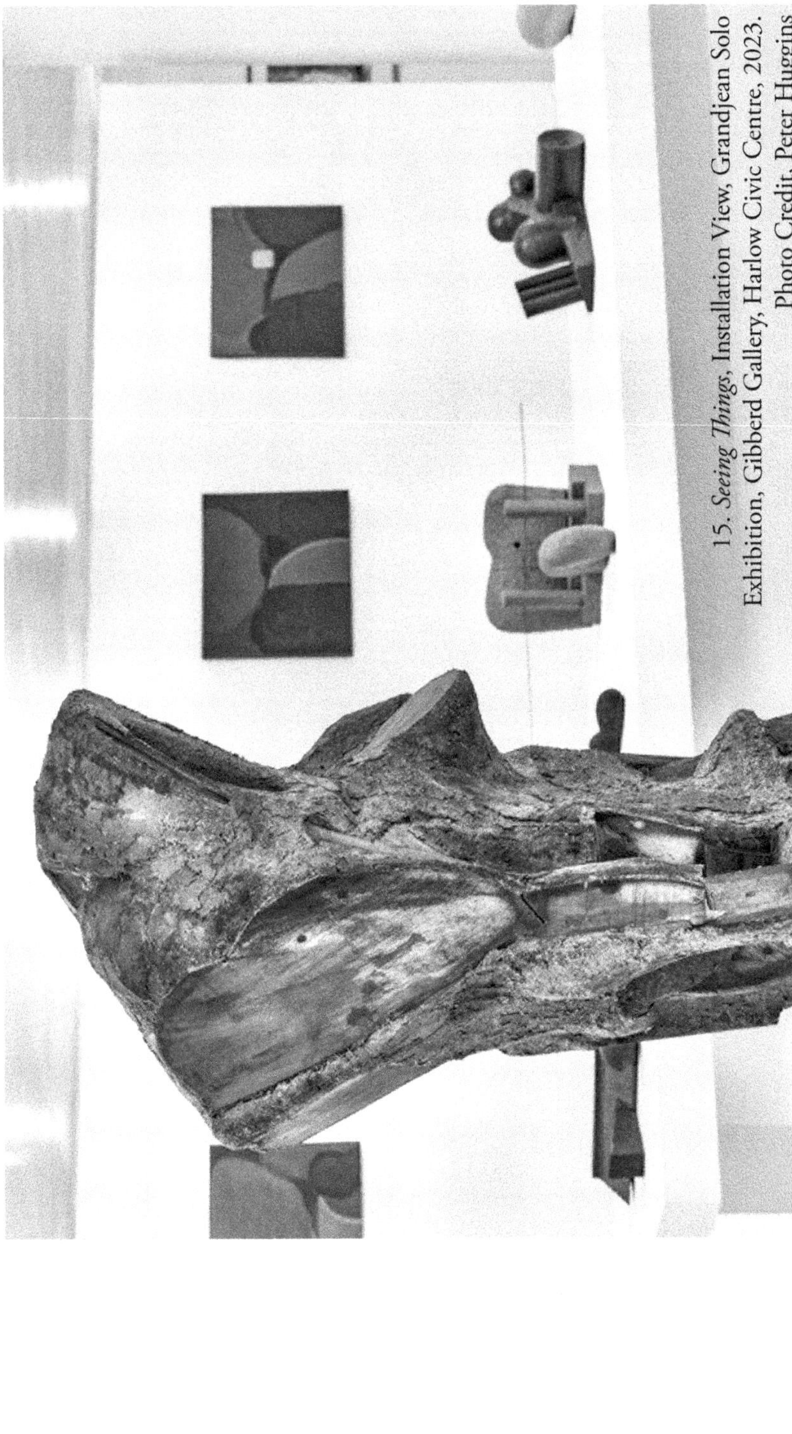

15. *Seeing Things*, Installation View, Grandjean Solo Exhibition, Gibberd Gallery, Harlow Civic Centre, 2023. Photo Credit, Peter Huggins

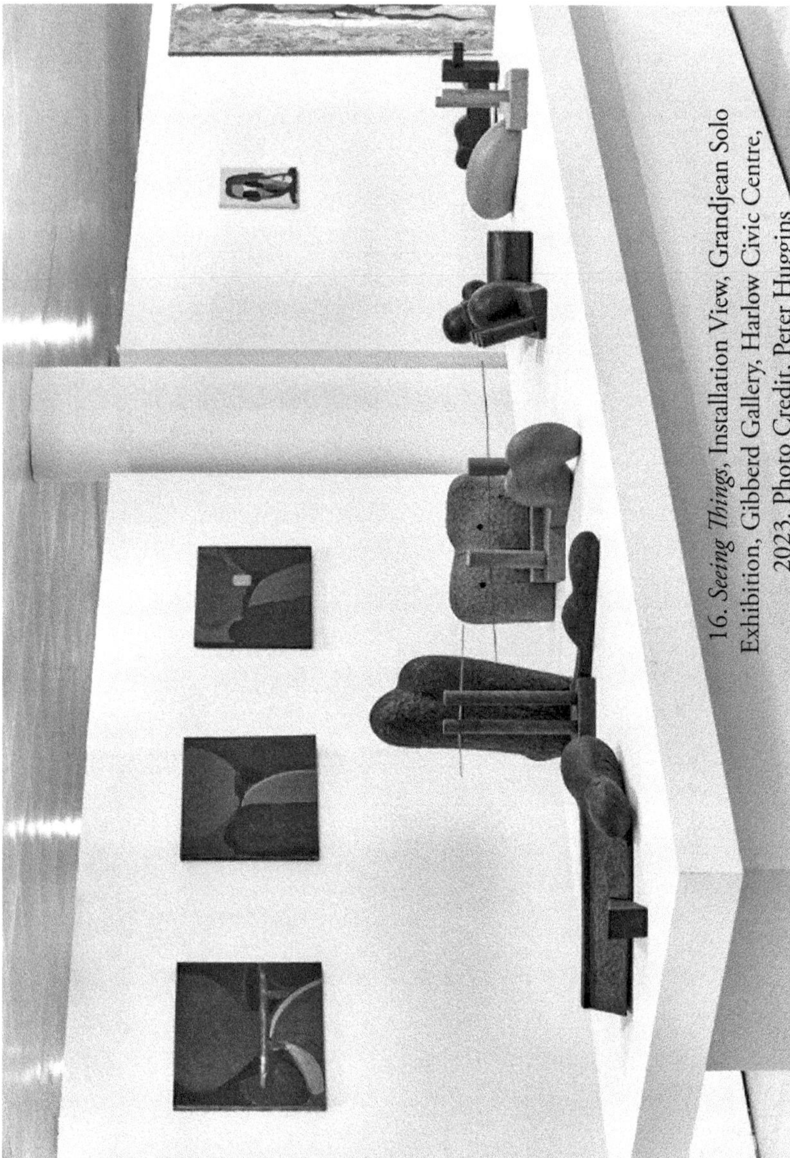

16. *Seeing Things*, Installation View, Grandjean Solo Exhibition, Gibberd Gallery, Harlow Civic Centre, 2023. Photo Credit, Peter Huggins

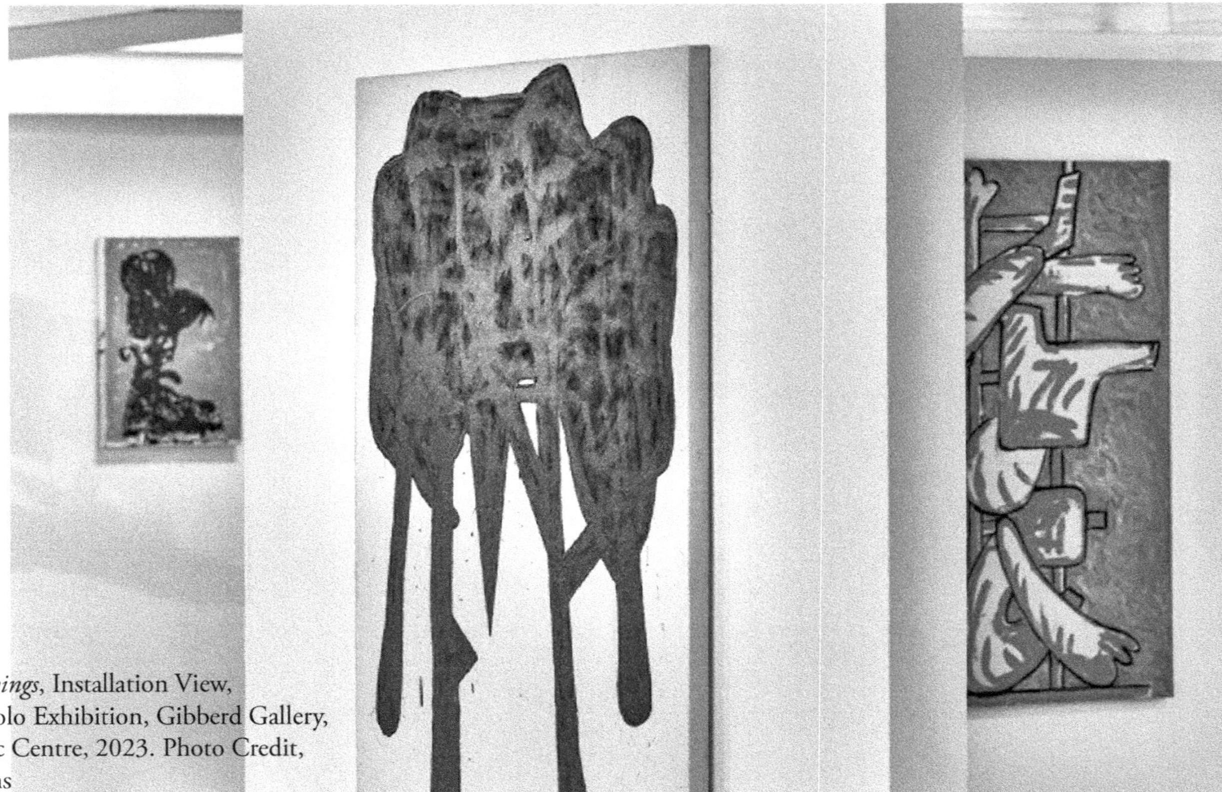

17. *Seeing Things*, Installation View, Grandjean Solo Exhibition, Gibberd Gallery, Harlow Civic Centre, 2023. Photo Credit, Peter Huggins

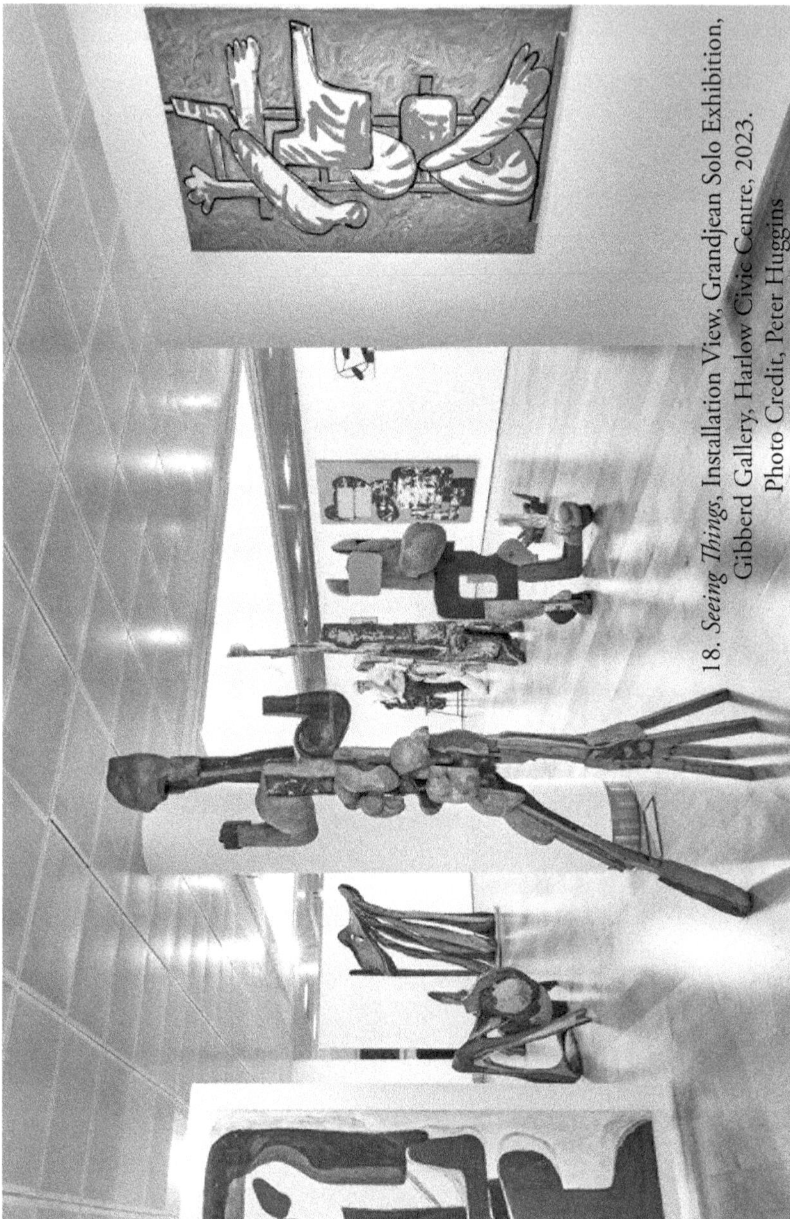

18. *Seeing Things*, Installation View, Grandjean Solo Exhibition, Gibberd Gallery, Harlow Civic Centre, 2023. Photo Credit, Peter Huggins

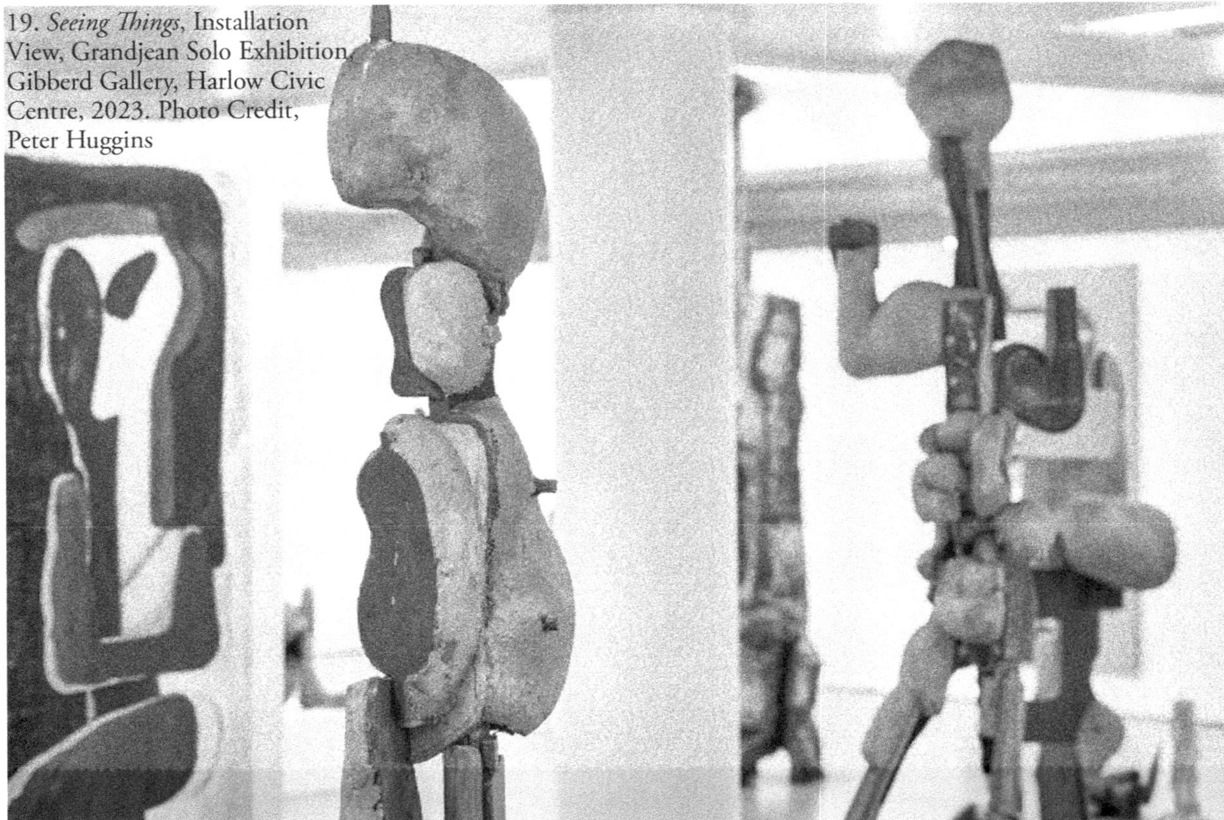

19. *Seeing Things*, Installation View, Grandjean Solo Exhibition, Gibberd Gallery, Harlow Civic Centre, 2023. Photo Credit, Peter Huggins

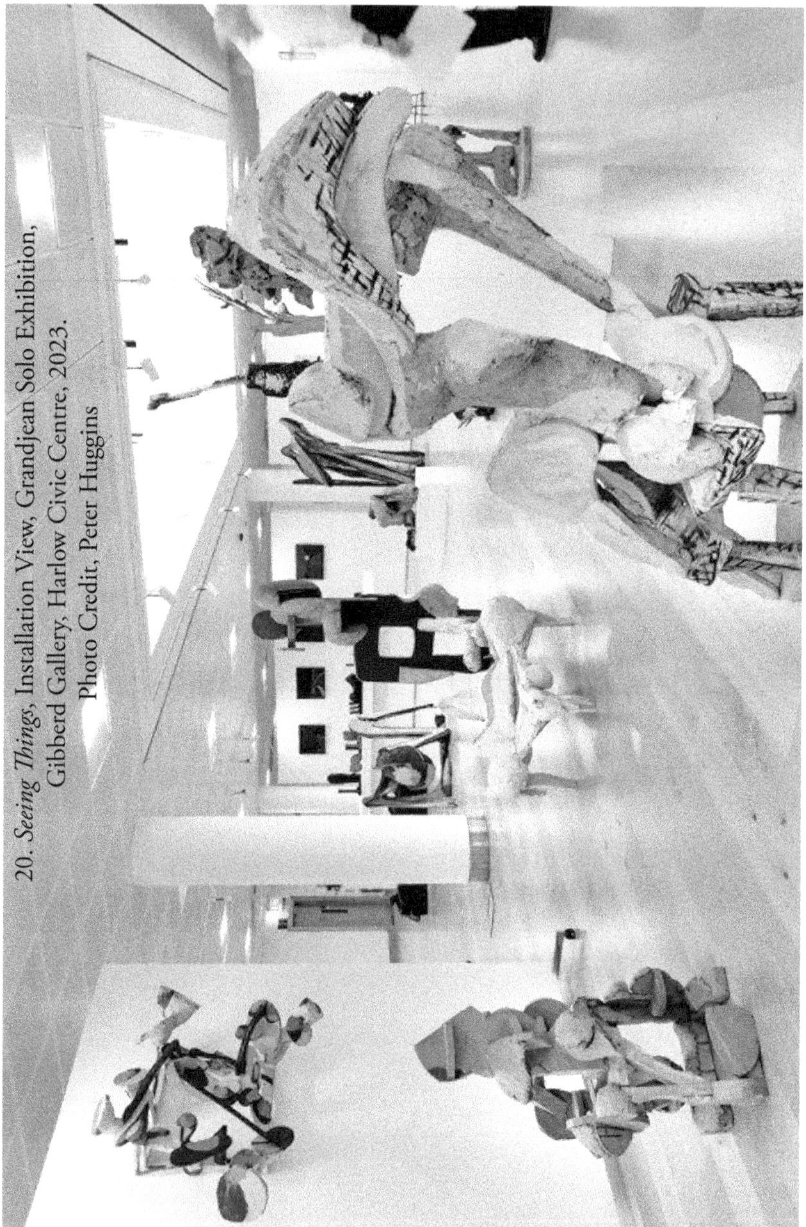

20. *Seeing Things*, Installation View, Grandjean Solo Exhibition, Gibberd Gallery, Harlow Civic Centre, 2023. Photo Credit, Peter Huggins

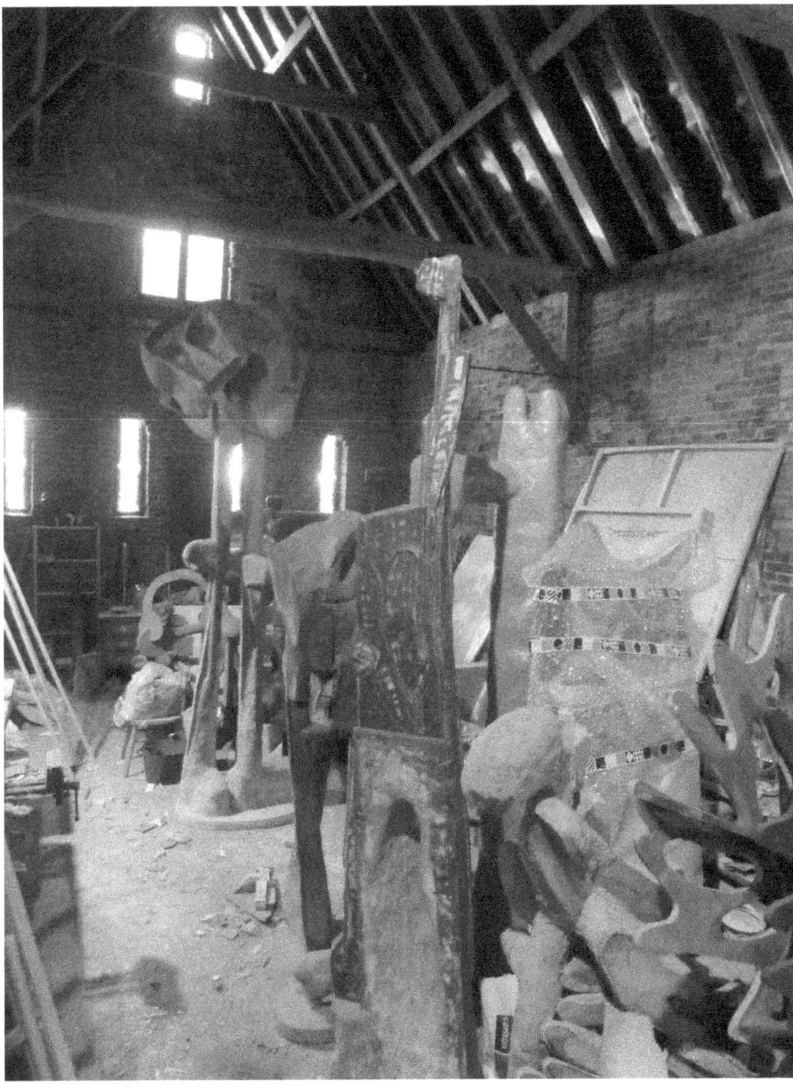

21. Barn studio interior 1

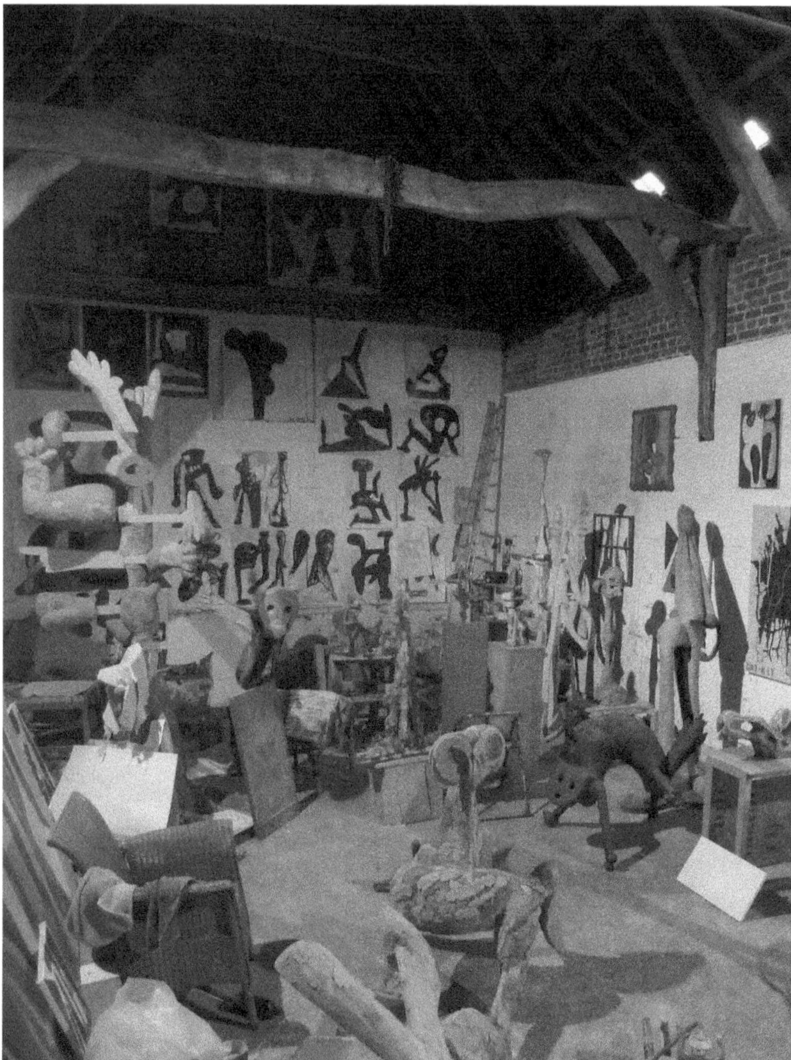

22. Barn studio interior 2

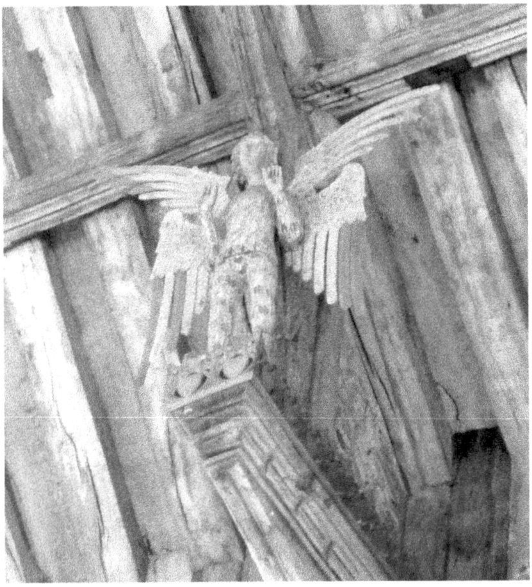

23. Cawston Church, angel
24. Cawston Church, main door figure

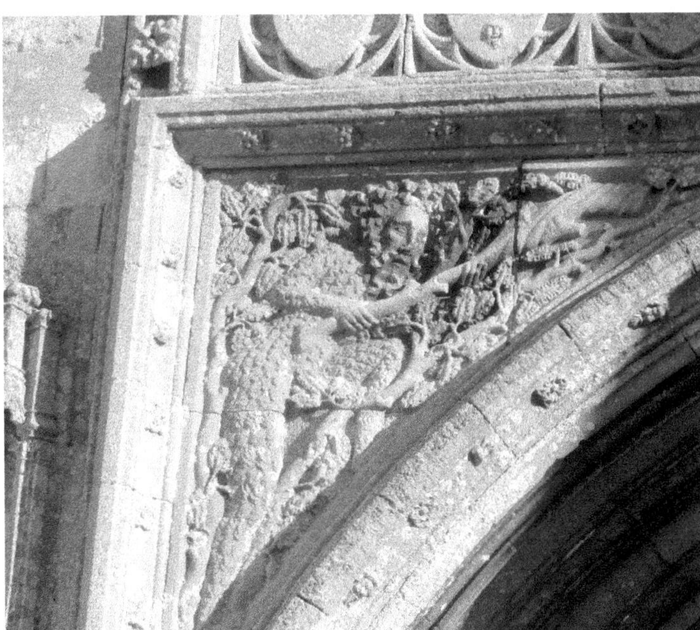

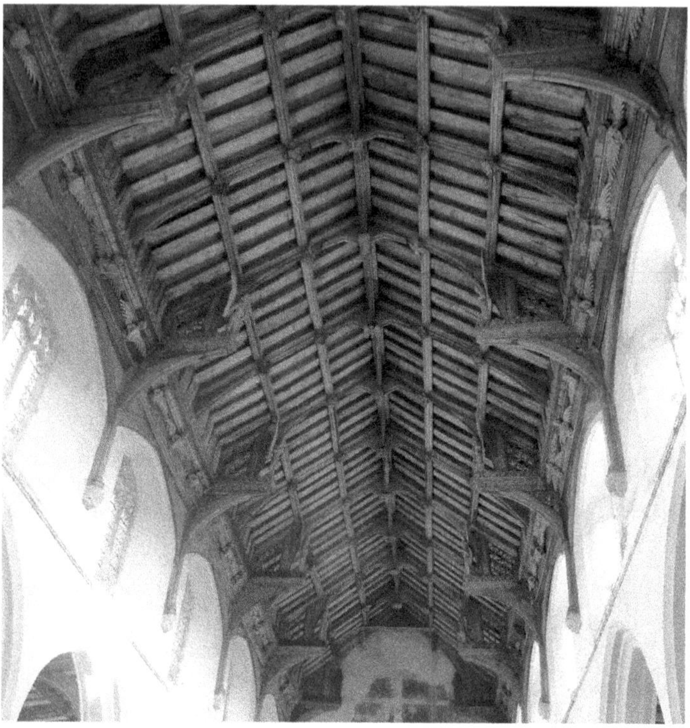

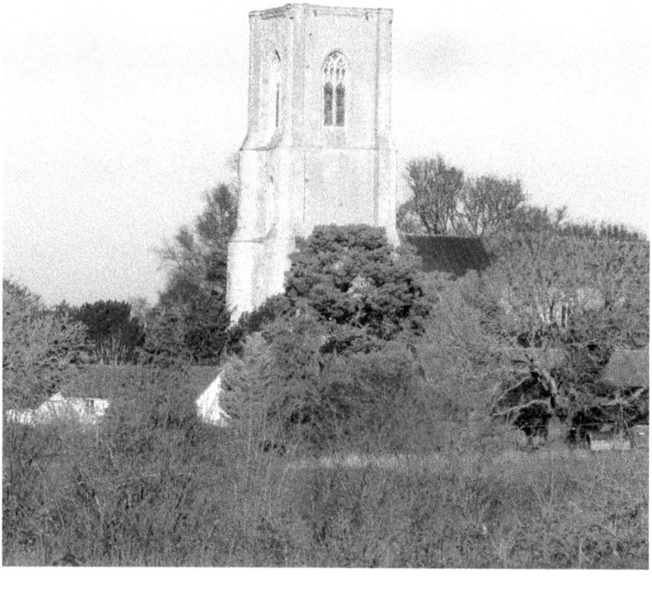

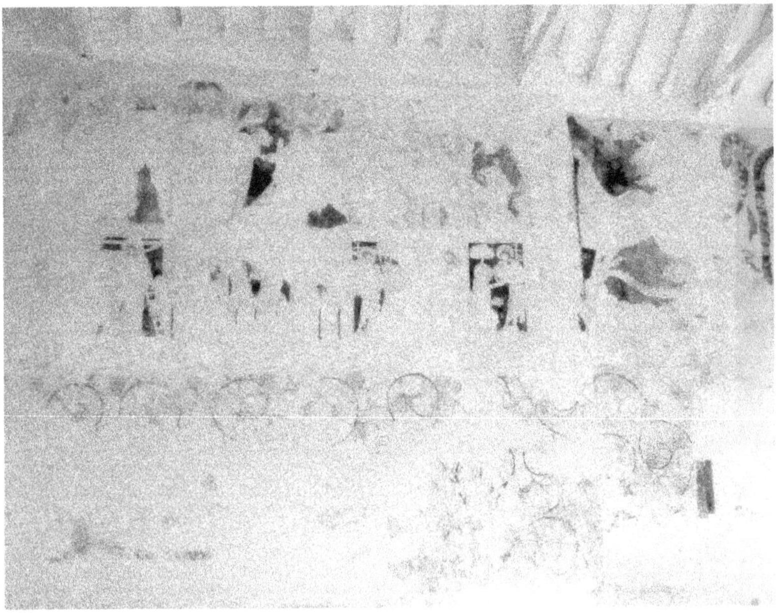

25. *(opposite)* Cawston Church roof
26. *(opposite)* Cawston Church tower
27. *(above)* Little Witchingham church wall paintings

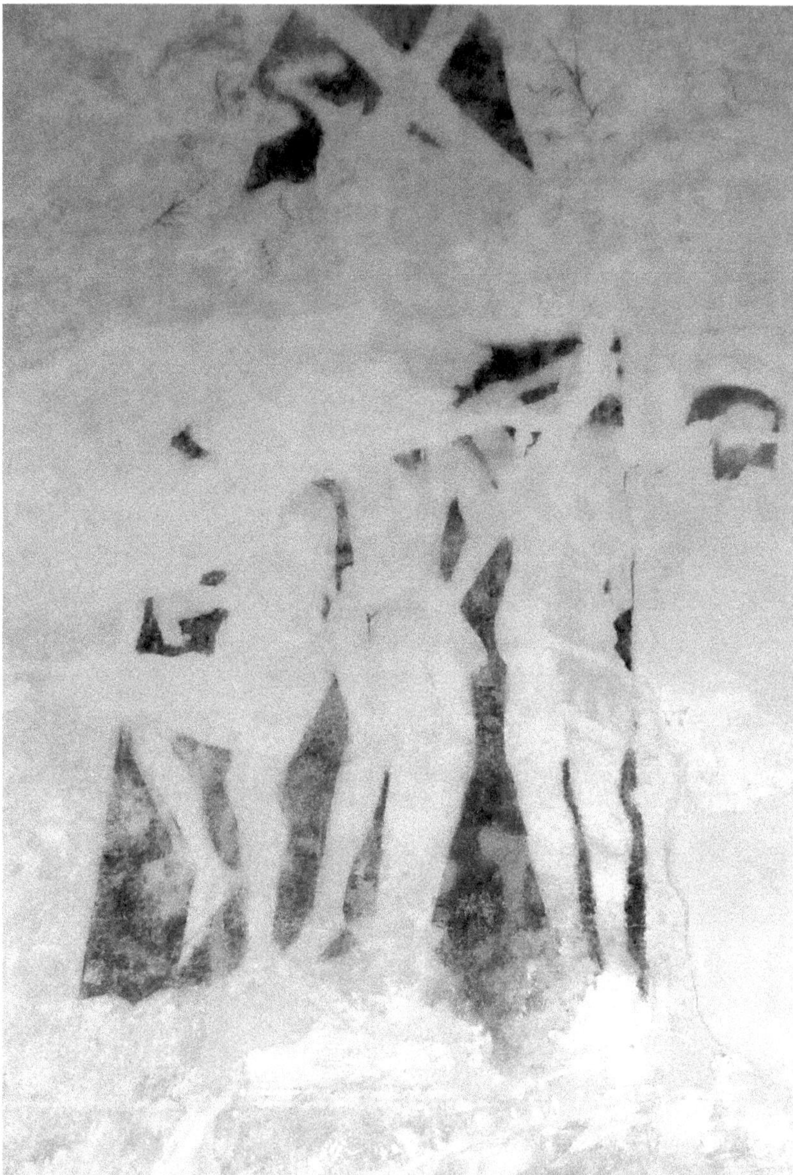

28. Little Witchingham church wall paintings (detail)

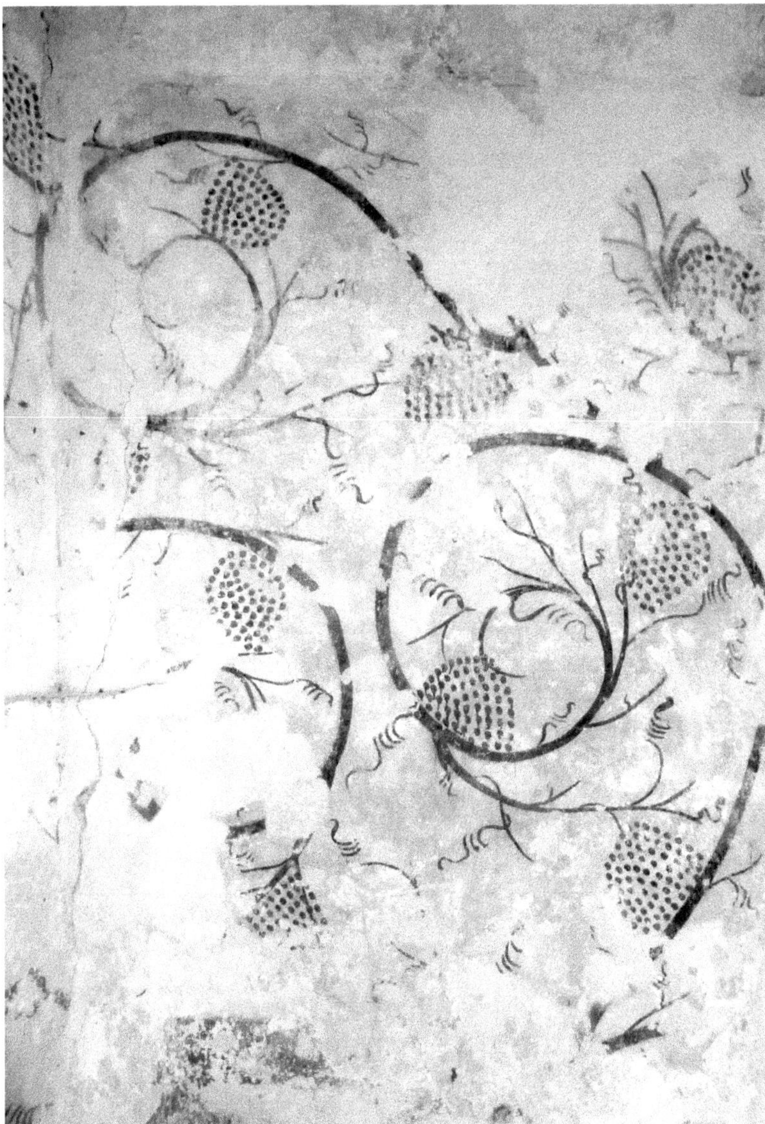

29. Little Witchingham church wall paintings (detail)

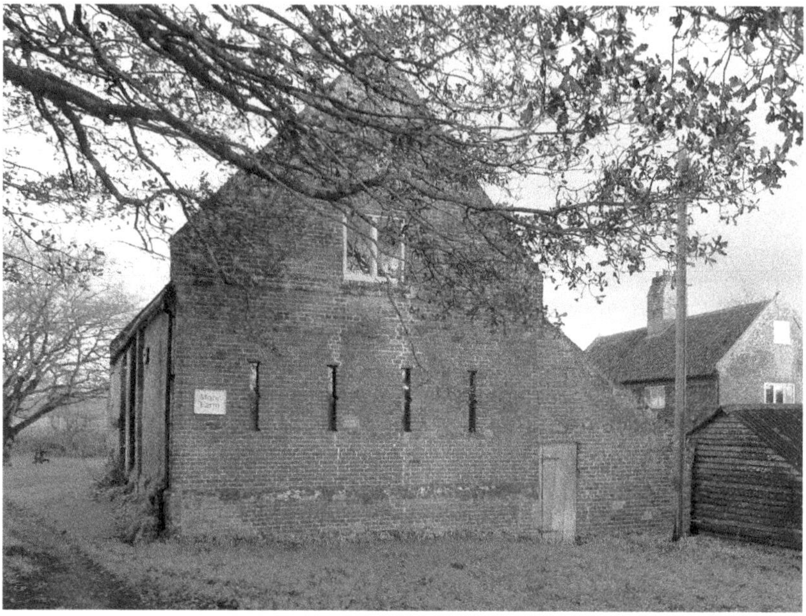

30. *(above)* Moor Farm Barn studio
31. *(opposite, top)* Moor Farm from the pond
32. *(opposite, bottom)* Moor Farm, path to fields

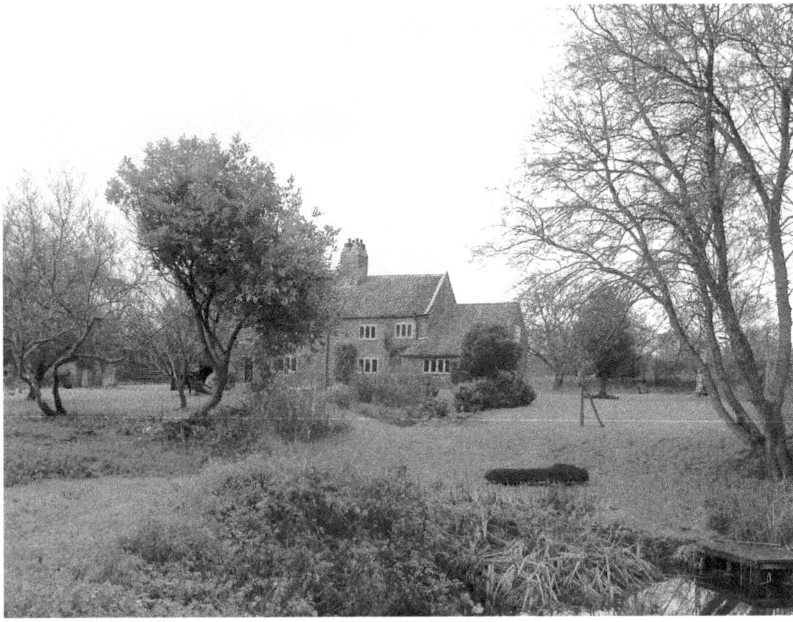

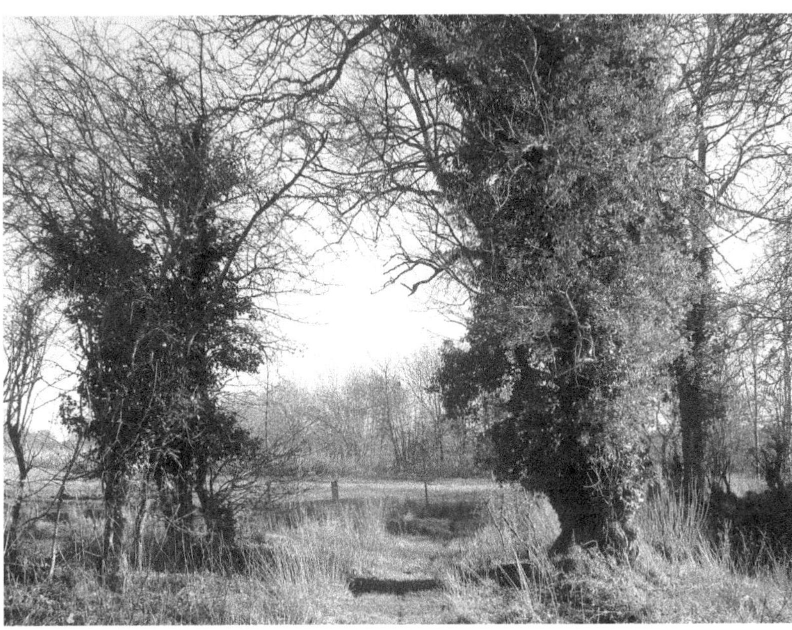

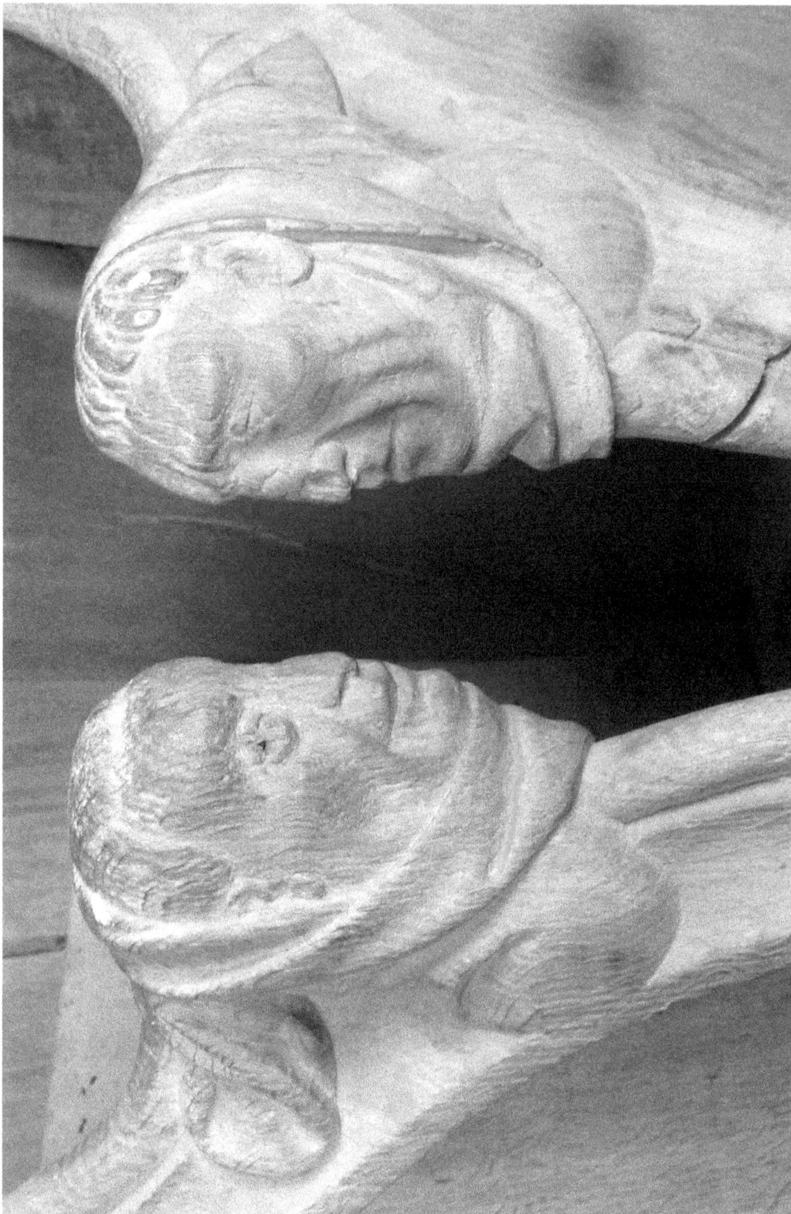

33. Salle Church: carved bench ends

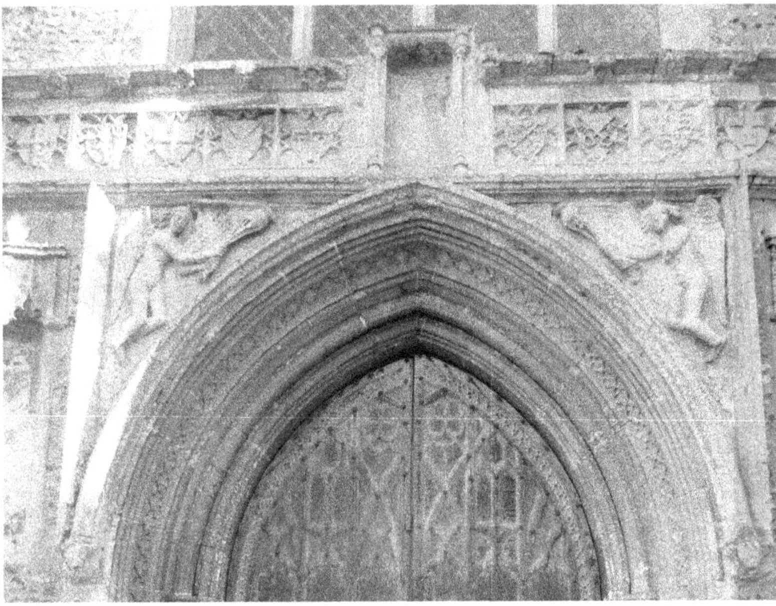

34. *(above)* Salle Church main door
35. *(below)* Salle Church tower

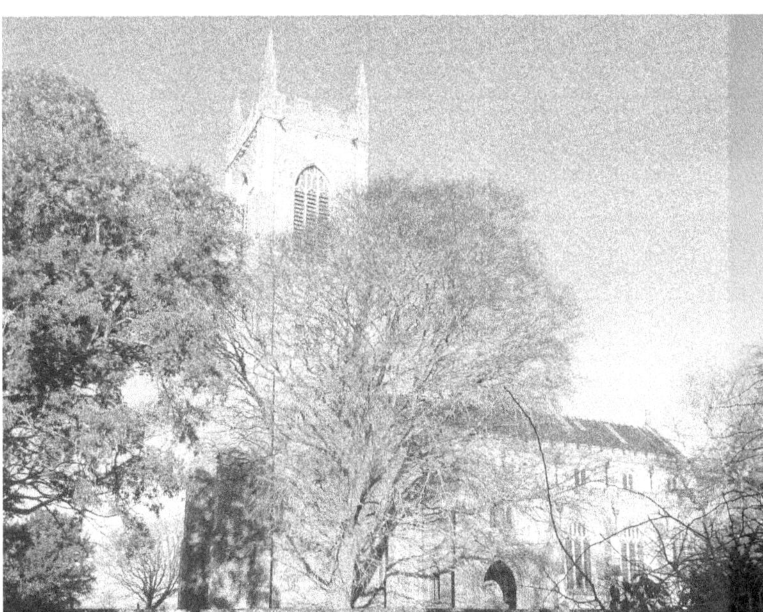

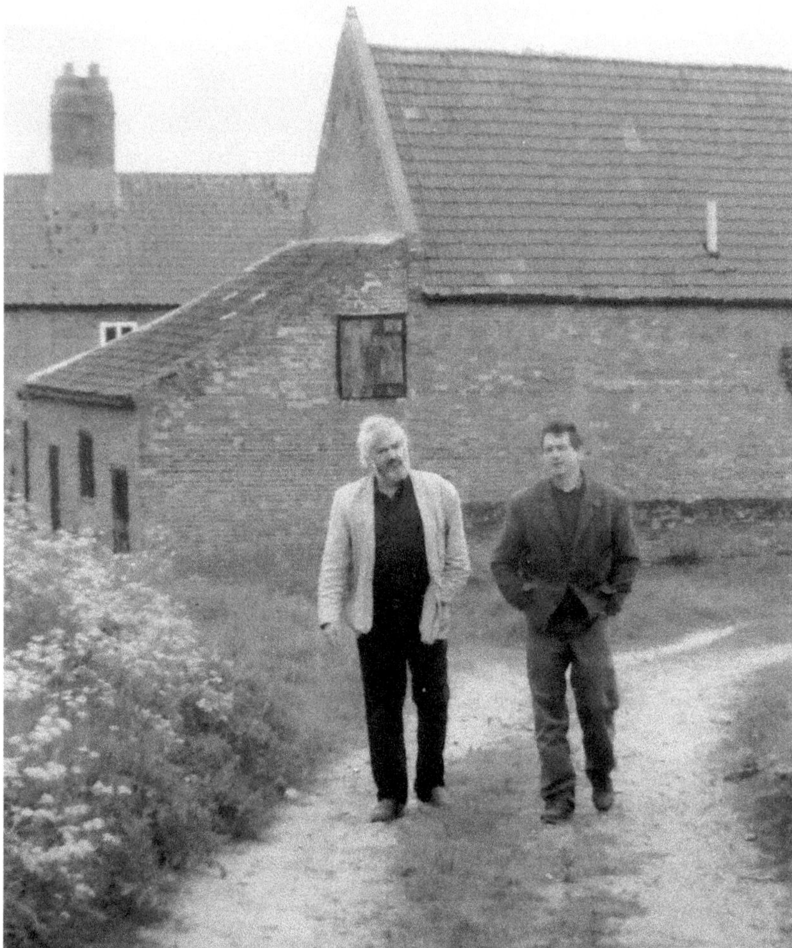

36. Jeremy Hooker (left) & Lee Grandjean, ca. 1987.

But, of course, there are changes. The set-aside field is now a wood of oak & ash & other trees. Hidden beyond it, the beck. This area of open, wild ground with trees here and there is good for wildlife. Cawston church tower visible from beside the horse-pond, where the water is lower than usual. A cornfield stretches away in the direction of Cawston, wheat green at the field edge, in the shadow of trees by the pond, but ochre and glowing almost gold across the field in the sun.

Jay perched on a branch of the bramley pecking at a green apple. Another jay flies up, replacing the other, which makes way for it, and pecks at an apple.

In the barn-studio, which is full of new work, busier than I've ever seen it. An immediate impression of colour! Energy! 'Labyrinth', which I've seen before: first, or one of the first, of the new works. A sculpture based on the conceit that it images the way the brain works. Melted plastic milk containers, consolidated with foam & cement, becoming like complex bones (a Golgotha as I saw it at first glimpse). The surface is fluid, but structured. Lee 'builds with fluidity'. Not in control of detail; material & process has its own life. ('There are as many neurons in the human brain as trees in the Amazon rain forest and as many possible synaptic connections as leaves on the trees in the Amazon rain forest! It is from such fantastic complexity that the miracle of human consciousness emerges and which makes us individual.' Lee's UEA Lecture)

'Celebrity Series'. A group (including 'Hello' and 'OK') which 'celebrates the three classical poses in art: standing, reclining, and sitting and also attempt a parody of a rather grotesque form of the posturing of celebrities in the various magazines' (UEA Lecture). As he says, posed celebrity photographs are an influence here, e.g., 'Posh Spice on a recliner in LA'. These have a satirical element, like gargoyles, an element of the monstrous, both humorous and disturbing: 'Henry Moore meets plastic surgery'. 'Clinic 1, Clinic 2': celebrity surgery; 'gloss of magazines turned into melting stuff'. There's anxiety in them; the self-image modelled, but all is flesh, dying.

'We are all fluid.'

'Celebrity: Pool Side': a startling, glossy, brilliant blue, compelling but almost too bright to look at. Here he uses household gloss paint, poured and dripped: an image of the human form in process of dissolution, or turned inside out, beautiful and disturbing. 'Wicker Chair', 'Valet'. Sculptures made of found things, common domestic objects, with a history – chair, frame for hanging clothes – things he improvises around.

'Valet' is ghostly, like an apparition. 'I think that doubt, openness, chance, improvisation and sensuality are good and creative qualities.' (UEA Lecture, quoting Susan Greenfield)

From the first, I've never doubted Lee's stature as a sculptor. But there are times, and today was one of them, when I'm absolutely certain of his importance. To step into the studio and encounter the sheer inventiveness – no repetition – the intelligence working in plastic form, the tactile & visual qualities, the sheer unclassifiable startling dynamic *life* of the objects. To anyone capable of looking, the objects *speak* for themselves. But, verbally, Lee is his own best interpreter. His misfortune – our misfortune – is that he's working at a time when sculpture criticism is in a poor state, when art criticism generally is conventional, in thrall to the fashions of a mainstream art (self-consciously avant-garde) that's a branch of showbiz. There are hopeful signs – among some young artists, for example – there are always hopeful signs, while talented artists are dedicated to working on, in isolation if necessary. But it isn't only the gifted unfashionable artist who suffers, but the culture, and the language of art.

Towards evening, in the garden, Lee & Kate preparing a barbecue supper. A chaffinch in the apple tree above our heads gathering beakfuls of grubs, for a late brood, perhaps. Breeze moving in the big birch-tree near the house, long pendant twigs swaying, and as if all the small leaves *twinkle*. Soft *coo – coo – coo* of doves, one on the chimney-pot. I walk to the field entrance by the pond, go in past a splendid cuckoo-pint with a lordly knob of red berries, and burdock, when, low over Cawston church, over my head, comes a jet-fighter, screaming, louder and louder, until I think I can't bear it, the sound will knock me over. Then it is gone.

31 July

Time in the studio in the morning, listening and talking against background of radio Test Match commentary. I realize more how Lee incorporates personal experience into his work, or how particular experiences generate images & ideas, e.g., falling off a ladder in 'The Good Shepherd', or an early memory of looking at clothes hanging on a door, which seem to move, becoming frightening, strange, in his 'ghost' or apparition images.

In the afternoon Kate became intent on researching family history, especially my family history, on the net. This turned up some fascinating information, as well as stimulating memories. How near, how far, all those lives of labouring men and women, of which I know only a few fragments, but to which I feel connected. And perhaps it is here, at Moor Farm, where we are surrounded by the work of many unknown, invisible lives – lives present in their handiwork – that I am especially able to feel the connection,

But here we are very much alive in the present, too, chatting over the computer, settling down after supper, on an oppressive evening, rain falling straight down, to watch a DVD of *No Country for Old Men.*

1 August

First day on which I am no longer an employed man.

Morning fresh & breezy after rain, cumulus coming over from the south west. Some days I move more easily than others. Now, with relative ease, I walked with Lee round the field left wild, but in which he mows paths. Yellows among the various long grasses: bird's-foot trefoil, buttercups. A heady smell of meadowsweet as we approach the bottom of the field. Butterflies, and here & there, singly or in groups, wooden sculptures, wood henges, just showing above the grasses. Peacock glowing on one of the 'Strange Attractors' (from *Groundwork*). Skipper on a purple knapweed. A spiderweb covered with grass seed ('map of the cosmos'). Purple vetch under a cherry tree in the field corner. Sea sound of wind rising and falling in grasses & trees. Cloud cover gathering as we return to the house for coffee and continue our talk.

Afternoon of dramatic light & shade. Wind blowing grey & white cloud masses over the orange-tiled, redbrick house. Wind strengthening, clouds turbulent, birch tree thrashing.

I asked Lee to tell me again about a sculpture I think of, from his words, as MAN WITH ELECTRIC HAND. This is 'Cockler' (elmwood with oil paint), 1983.

After first coming to Moor Farm in 1981 he was intent on making sculpture out of immediate experience, from what was in front of him. 'Starting again in a way.' He felt joy in being here and in visiting the coast. 'Very liberating.' At the seaside he was struck by 'the relation to something very direct' in people by the sea, scrabbling for shellfish in the sand, carrying them away in buckets & bulging plastic bags, which were *dripping.* With other sculptors at Wimbledon, Glynn Williams & Ken Turnell, he was trying to reinvent the figure in sculpture; creating appearance of what the body is doing – pressures upon it, tensions, in stretching. (In Rodin's *Burghers of Calais,* how he *animates* the keys to the city.) 'Cockler' stands on a piece of ground, pressing down, with exaggerated foot. Push up of shoulder, pull down of hand: exaggerated. The bucket is animated, swelling in shape. Head bowed, exaggerated, pulled over. The left hand, bigger than the right, is stretched, thumb & fingers elongated. Red colouring intensifies a sense of 'jagged explosion'. The intention is cartoon-like, 'a burst of energy' around the hand. 'Cockler' signals the beginning of a thought *felt in the body*, a connection to a larger whole. Feeling yourself part of the material of everything.

Having met Glynn Williams, he shared a studio with him in Kingsland Road, Shoreditch. He taught with Ken Turnell at Central and they started a 'trialogue of re-invention'. Out of their talk came the ethos of teaching sculpture at Wimbledon School of Art.

Lee spoke of the 'frozen moment of sculpture', the moment that gives us the meaning of the greater story, all the moments, the dynamism of what goes before & what comes after. For Gaudier sculpture was the mountain. For Lee sculpture is the volcano.

In the city he imagined buildings exploding (seeing this as 'a kind of sublime': the released forces of nature in structures made by men. He thought of Oppenheimer's 'I am become God, destroyer of worlds'. He read in Zola's *Germinal* about the awesome beauty of destruction, creating new forms, breaking down old orders. The ambition was to create new forms out of what had gone before.

In 'Cockler' the electric hand is meeting-place, threshold. Travelling between London and Norfolk he became obsessed with the edge between country and city. Our talks about subject-matter in Winchester were part of the development.

Most artists embrace the given time. The Wimbledon sculptors went back to ancient means, to think about image differently. Lee went back to using wood.

Ultimately, he found wood couldn't deal with the complexity of the world. He needed a more fluid material, including 'bits of the world', e.g., plastic, for work fusing modelling and constructing.

2 August

Rain in an almost windless, close atmosphere. During dry intervals, rabbits reappear on the lawn, rounded, soft-bodied shapes, hopping, feeding, sitting up with long ears erect, eyes like dark pebbles, watching. Afternoon drive with Lee in rain to Stratton Strawless. Fields of wet barley & wheat darker, scarlet poppies at the margins. Inside the church,

St Margaret's, with a squat, flint tower, we found an exhibition, 'Indications of Spring'. This marks the tricentenary of Robert Marsham, and describes his family's 'phenological record', which he inaugurated and which lasted until the 1950s. I'd never heard of phenology ('the relations between climate and periodic biological phenomena', such as plant flowering), though it's what, in a small, amateurish way, I like to do. Robert Marsham corresponded with Gilbert White, and his tree-planting influenced Humphry Repton.

We saw in the church, as well as the exhibition, what we had come to see: the black abbess, a medieval stone effigy, painted black, and fragments of stained glass. Most beautiful, in the window above the abbess, the head of an angel, like a young Apollo. This is perhaps one of what the Guide refers to as fragments of Flemish stained glass, 'looted by Napoleon's armies as they marched through Europe and sold at auction in Paris'. The Marsham family chapel, with its alabaster memorials, bespeaks wealth, social distinction, and piety. Among much that represents adult attainments there's a moving pathos about the effigy of an infant in swaddling clothes.

3 August

Warm, muggy after rain. Walked/struggled up the track to where Marriot's Way crosses it. Green & reddening blackberries, some already ripe and edible, in the hedgerows. Small butterflies, skippers, and one wasp among the fruit. Booton & Cawston churches clearly visible, but Salle is now hidden by trees. Avril, 91 and still vigorous, came to lunch. In the evening I took Lee & Kate for an Indian meal in Aylsham.

4 August

Lark singing against background of cumulus as it descended into the wheatfield. This was the last I saw of Moor Farm as we set off to drive to Roughwood and so back to Wales by early evening.

5 August

After breakfast, and after I'd shown him Ceri Thomas's book on Ernest Zobole and we'd talked about the paintings, Lee left for his return journey. Following the visit and after so much good talk I feel rather flat. Lee's work & company are a tremendous inspiration to me; but do I now have the energy to benefit in my own work? I've an idea of the effort required, the courage to take risks. As he once said to me, 'we must break our taste'. That was his refusal of repetition, of facility. True to his aim, he has been consistently inventive, always wanting to make something he has never seen before, and succeeding. The very inventiveness contributes to his invisibility, since acclaimed sculptors are usually identified with a trademark product. It's the same with poets or any kind of artist: a 'name' is identified with a style.

18 October

Lee's 60th birthday. It's strange to think that when I first met him, he was only 32. We were both quite young men then. The strangeness comes from the speed at which the 'middle years' pass. Childhood seems to last forever, and something of that sense of time lingers in young manhood. Afterwards, it all seems helter-skelter. My great regret is that I haven't made more of myself as a poet since my stroke. Laziness, but also lack of resolution, indecisiveness in face of the changes, coinciding with external factors, the stroke wrought in me. I never needed more to make it new – the perennial mantra of someone always beginning again, but now faced with unexpected changes affecting the very sense of life, and depleting my life-energy.

For Lee, it should be different, and I've every confidence that it will be. He has been producing remarkable work, both continuous and ever-new, since I first met him. It isn't a question now of coming into his own, but of going from strength to strength, and finding increasing recognition.

from THOUGHTS ON A STAR-MAP
for Lee on his sixtieth birthday
Time to begin.

A block of wood
lies on the studio floor –
a windthrown trunk
that was feathered with leaves.

New light flashes
through gaps in the roof
where lately swallows flew in,
cutting the air.

Think of the birds
flying away. Imagine the sound
of a human kiss
waved into space.
What will it find?
Who will know what we are?

20 June 2010

From an email from David Annwn, in which he quotes a piece by one of his Open University students recalling his first encounter with a fellow student whom he met on his first day at Art College: 'A dark-haired, popular, talkative and confident young man with a slightly broken nose, who wore a distinctive short camel-coloured jacket and who spoke with a Cockney accent. He seemed a man-of-the-world, popular with women' and was endlessly garrulous in a likeable way'. Lee, of course, to whom I relayed this description of 'the fascinating talker' as a young artist. How good to hear his voice, and to think of them all, including their baby granddaughter, at Moor Farm.

14 August

Driving with Lee in the Black Mountains, blue-black under cloud – mood indigo. At Patrishow, one rowan, a blaze of red, in the graveyard. Sheep in fields below, bracken-covered heights above. Stepped with difficulty down to the holy well by Nant Mair.

15 August

Morning: Mieke by taxi to Cardiff airport. We waited until hearing from Elin that she'd arrived safely at Amsterdam before setting off to drive to Moor Farm, talking all the way.

Evening: at Moor Farm, where Kate greeted us and I met Louis, for the first time in some years, and his beautiful wife, Laura, and their lovely little daughter, Amelie, 14 months old. This was a wonderful meeting: Louis so pleased to see me, the whole family at Moor Farm so lively and thoughtful.

16 August

Excursion in two cars on a clouded day to Warham Camp, a large circular Iron Age (Iceni) settlement near the coast. Here, Lee opened a gate and drove me down a green lane to an area of rough pasture, from which

I was able to walk to the camp. Ragwort & thistles among the rough grass. Yarrow & scabies & yellow lady's bedstraw, and, to my special delight, a solitary harebell. Henry Moore had lived close by, at Wighton. Lee remarked on the pleasure Moore would have taken in the shapely earthworks. Leaning on the gate with Louis, we saw a pair of buzzards circling over distant trees.

From Warham Camp we drove to a tearoom near the sea, on an estate at Wiveton, where we had a cream tea. Outside the tearoom, in the productive grounds, two large Gloucester Old Spots were rooting and a cock strutted among a harem of hens.

17 August

In the barn studio with Lee. There's usually one work that strikes me when I first step in. This time it was 'Pellet', a piece incorporating a large black oval, based on an owl pellet, attached to a slug-like organic shape & a table. In this, like a weird animal, and in other pieces, Lee is juxtaposing the figurative and the fluid, the wild and the human (bourgeois) world. There's humour at the desperate edge, as in Beckett's characters in *Godot*. 'Four Figures', from his work with discarded furniture at Eindhoven, Lee describes as pastiche Cubism, or Cubism seen through digital pixilation, a rearrangement of objects on a wrong scale, a scrambling of visual properties. In all his work one sees the importance of studies of the brain, and ways in which matter creates ideas. The sculpture is a journey making connections between memories & perceptions & ideas, as in the humorous 'Eating Raw Herring with Paultje and Thinking of René Daniels' which incorporates fragments representing the green-white North Sea seen from the airplane, the experience of eating raw herring, and images of Daniels' paintings.

Lee had spoken the previous evening of his dislike of mannerism with its reconfiguring of the already known. Now, he spoke of his preference for an artisan approach. Aged 18, starting at Waltham Forest Technical College and School of Art, in Walthamstow, he walked down a corridor towards three tables, designated: Graphic Design, Fine Art, Industrial Design. It was Design that attracted him, and, from his liking for machines, he chose Industrial Design. He felt an aversion to Fine Art, seeing in his mind 'a posh frame' and thinking of the frame as a bourgeois concept. His studies at Walthamstow were also influenced by his attraction to Celia Birtwell, who taught at the college. An influence that led to his work in Textiles, which he pursued at Winchester School of Art.

The fluidity of Lee's work includes an element of morbidity. This is of course part of the natural cycle, in our degeneration, our passing, in flesh that rots. But it is also present in the culture, in its dominant styles, in celebrity … Aware from the beginning of the strength of his work, I am now more conscious of its combination of the grotesque and the elegant. On a warm afternoon, sun appearing between cloud masses, we walked round the garden & wild field, Lee showing me the changes they have made. These include a vegetable garden, whose produce we've been eating, and Kate's wildflower garden, rich now in blue cornflowers, yellow corn marigolds, poppies, camomile, pansies, both gardens dug at the top of the wild field.

Evening

A family barbecue under the dome of the apple trees. Patches of blue sky among cloud. Still. Distant sound of doves.

Always, here, my sense of the sculptural is enhanced. Shapes of bent & twisted apple tree trunks; roofs of house & barn; scalloped pantiles; rough lawn pitted with rabbit scratchings; cavernous dark under trees & shrubs; leaves, cloud edges & cloud masses; and, of course, actual sculptures, placed about the garden, and sometimes disappearing among vegetation. A world of shapes, but always in the process of moving, changing.

Darkling, an owl hooting in distant woods.

Back indoors, they persuaded me to read poems, some of my own, as, the previous evening, I had read some William Carlos Williams.

18 August

Flight of the green woodpecker, arrow-straight, into the bramley

To Salthouse, where, rather cold in a sea wind, we sat outside at Cookie's Crab Shop and had lunch. Afterwards, following the coast, to Burnham Deepdale and the church with its Saxon round flint tower. Here, Lee was keen to show me the medieval stained-glass windows, mostly rearranged fragments. In one God the Father supports the Son with hands under his arms on the cross, with the Holy Spirit in the form of a dove flying down. A friend had wrongly perceived God pushing the Son's arms down onto the cross.

The Norman font, made of Barnack stone from Rutlandshire, is carved with scenes depicting the farming year:

January: A man drinking from a horn
February: A man sitting in a chair by the fire
March: Digging with a spade
April: Pruning fruit trees or vines
May: A person with a Rogationtide banner
June: Weeding
July: Mowing with a scythe
August: Binding a sheaf of corn
September: Threshing corn with a flail
October: Grinding corn, or filling a wine barrel?
November: Slaughtering a pig
December: Feasting together

19 August
Mellow warmth in the sun, cloud building. Sitting under the apple tree listening to cricket on the radio. Smells of late summer – honeysuckle climbing to the tree top. Leaf shadows moving in a breeze. After the struggle out of bed a great sense of well-being. Lee with a wheelbarrow carrying logs in for the winter. Occasional thistledown with the breeze – butterflies, at will.

Afternoon
Through the opening out of the garden, where the old gate once stood. Hawthorn berries ripening in the hedge above the pond. On the other side a wheatfield, stubble ploughed in. Partridge feather on a rotting log, which is an insect paradise. Down the track, Cawston church tower appearing above trees. In our journeys I have glimpsed majestic pinnacle Salle, no longer visible from the fields, as well as numerous other churches. But it's Cawston which, like the woodpecker, I have to see.

I must work. Time is running out.

20 August
Writing my journal, Lee at the Oval with Louis & Guy to watch the England/Pakistan Test Match. Mieke arrives, having taken a taxi from Norwich airport.

21 August
Moorhen & chicks crossing the lawn.

Morning with Mieke & Lee looking at his work. Afternoon visit to Binham Priory, where a wedding was in progress close by. Bridesmaids with posies on the priory's grassy enclosure when we arrived. I was reminded of my first Shakespeare play in the open air at Beaulieu Abbey cloisters. Here, at Binham, outside the church, fragments of ruined walls tower above. 'There's so much sky.'

Later, sitting in the garden at Moor Farm in a strong wind. Young green woodpecker pecking ants from the ground quite close to me. Evening meal at The Walpole Arms.

22 August
A glorious day in the sun with another barbecue. Wispy cirrus above woolsack cumulus in the beautiful East Anglian skies. Bees & other insects seemingly in waves as they visit the Japanese anemones beside us. Life couldn't be better than at times like this.

23 August
Rain in the night. A damp & blowy morning. One small rabbit on the lawn. The harsh winter killed off many rabbits. After breakfast we set out for the long drive back to South Wales, dropping Kate off in London on the way. Lee says he actually enjoys these drives, in which he finds plenty to look at. I can't say I do, apart from the conversation, and for Mieke the car journey is painful. But it's wonderful that Lee makes the effort.

25 August
The goodness of life at Moor Farm – Lee & Kate & their family, the place itself – is what I most think about afterwards. I'm aware too that I'm more disabled, needing more support, than on my last visit. Lee's practicality & constant good humour are inspiring. His time working in Eindhoven was productive & enjoyable. He has contacts that could have led to his work being shown, if influential people had put it forward, but it isn't the kind of thing they respond to. Too 'wild', perhaps; or, I would suggest, not fashionable. I feel certain, as I have from the beginning, of his power & originality, and of the disgrace that his work is simply not seen, as even Peter Fuller, otherwise an advocate, failed to see it. Lee talking about his work could persuade practically anyone to look at it. His writing, if published, would have that effect. I know no one who thinks so deeply about making objects, with implications for all imaginative processes. I encourage him to write, of course, but with hesitation – which he well

understands – lest writing interfere with his primary work. If this journal survives me, what it shows of Lee & his work may constitute its principal value.

I come back to work, as I would have to anyway, beginning with writing up my paper on 'Marches of the Spirit' for *Scintilla.* But it's also my own spirit I have to work on, practically.

8 May 2011

In the afternoon I was delighted – and relieved – to receive a call from Lee, back from South America, with tales of the Pacific & the Andes & the Amazon. He spoke with wonder of the difference of the world he has seen. Barely imaginable to me here, as I look out on full-leaved trees and white & grey clouds drifting over from the west – a mild & gently fertile scene!

23 August

With Lee, to Brecon, where we met Chris Meredith. The purpose of our visit was an exhibition of art works responding to an area of eroding peat on a hill in the Brecon Beacon National Park: a project for which Chris had written a strong sequence of poems. Afterwards we sat talking with Chris over a meal at The George.

24 August

Mieke left early for Cardiff airport and a week with Elin. Lee and I set out later to drive to Moor Farm, and were held up by an accident on the M4, passing slowly under Liddington Hill, half in cloud shadow, and by apple and pear trees, and hawthorns with red berries, on the verges. Stopping and starting, and between talking, we listened to reports on the car radio of Gaddafi being toppled in Libya.

25 August

Moor Farm. From the bathroom window, a moorhen crossing the lawn, tail jerking up, neck jerkily stretching forward. A tractor in the big field sowing winter wheat, or perhaps sugar beet.

Rain. With Lee in the 'snug', a barn lean-to which he's converted into a painting studio. The new paintings we looked at were drawn partly from surroundings here, and partly from the visit to Peru. The former included 'Track', from drawings looking through an oak tree up the track, and 'Ashes', a diptych comprising tree studies on one panel, facing a blank. Object/ absence of object; complexity /monotonous space. Also 'Night Birch, 'From February to May', and 'Night Road'. From Peru, 'Jungle Town', a series of four paintings (acrylic on canvas, like most of the work). These were inspired by names painted on the outside of houses – spaces hired by candidates in the elections – contrasted with jungle and density of leaves. Blocked abstract language painted in vivid colours, against living green, full of darkness. Again, the diptych form, which has characterized all his work, and is a source of endless invention:

> built/ organic
> order/ chaos
> concept/ unknowing

Evening
Hare on the lawn, dark eyes, long, antenna ears twitching.

26 August
Hare nearer the house, in front of the bramley. A little one close-by, and a moorhen. The peaceable kingdom.

Through more rain, with Lee, to the barn studio. Inside, in the space crowded with figures, an immediate impression of Easter Island. As Lee acknowledges, there's an influence of Philip Guston in this new, powerfully uncomfortable work, which includes large, standing, lumpy figures, 'brutal' cartoon-like forms. In some , use of duck tape gives a fleshy texture, with a result that's ungainly, odd, but retaining elegance. It is too easy to call these works expressionistic. 'Soutine rather than Mondrian, to put it crudely.' Lee is hostile to mannerism, which puts style foremost.

A large blue figure, like a cartoon Epstein 'Lazarus'. 'Sweat', black & grey, a box (like a water tank), lagged & covered in hessian, on pipe legs. 'Antelope', from three bentwood chairs, with hanging leather from old sandals. An image found in the play of lines, and a homage to African and Oceanic sculpture. 'Reclining Figure' (winter buds): oak branches screwed together, paint cans hammered in (like buds), with 'crushed intensity'. 'Keeper', from Guy's old desk, with wicket keeping gloves, like hands on the figure. 'Reclining Figure' (white), a decomposing figure (like the ghastly effigy in Winchester Cathedral), liquid held momentarily.

In statue-like forms Lee captures a moment of fixity in shifting, fluid process, on the way to further reduction. 'We don't live in permanence.'

'We give such weight to culture, but it's all passing, we live in ruins.' As he talks, I become aware of the coalescence in his work of images, often with surprising juxtapositions. His 'diversity of work' is a problem for people who want repetition. I realize that it's much easier to 'read', and appreciate, a kind of sculpture that patents specific forms and images. But what I see in Lee's work is a constantly inventive imagination creating images that neither he nor anyone has seen before, but which continue to explore a profound duality. And what I see throughout is energy.

Later I asked him to go over again what he's told me about the transition between sculpture and painting (granted that he works in both media, with increased emphasis on painting now.)

As a student at Winchester School of Art, studying Textile Design and printing on fabric, he was taught by a colourist, Norman Wyn Griffiths, and discovered painting. Producing an 'arty show' which got low marks it was with the momentum of anger that he moved to London, to an attic room in Holland Park, rented from Griffiths. He saw himself as a painter (his work 'abstract'), and lived by teaching screen printing one day a week at Waltham Forest Technical College and School of Art. So, he started as a painter.

Meeting Richard Rome, he shared a studio with him in Shoreditch. Here he started folding canvases, working with big rolls of brown (craft) paper & drums of acrylic & raw pigment, the painting becoming more and more physical. For Lee, the root is in gesture, in process that came from painting, from belief in imaginative image (not truth to material, or representation of utilitarian objects).

Evening

Rain, drear, dark green, grey. Looking at pictures on the computer of Lima, Iquitos in the Amazon jungle, Cusco in the Andes, Machu Picchu. Inca buildings of huge, rugged stone. How I wish I'd travelled more when I was able to. There's so much of the world I'll never see, so much of a different nature, such magnificent human works.

27 August

At last, a day of sunshine, patchy cloud. To Wiveton with Lee & Kate, and Guy & Claire, who arrived from London for the weekend last night. Lunch was the Grandjean's treat: a splendid meal of crab, my second in two days! Along the coast: Blakeney, Stiffkey (with effigies beside the road), Wells-next-to-the-sea, where I went to sleep in the car, after cider for lunch, while they went walking. Binham priory, thunderstorm approaching, heavy water on the roads back to Reepham, but we missed the storm.

26 August

In the study writing up the last, very full week, while the Grandjeans are canoeing on the Bure. Another sunny day, broken white cloud passing over slowly, a breeze moving leaves on the bramley and trees round the lawn. When I come here now, all Is so familiar I feel as though I've never been away. Yet I miss home too, though only away for a short time. It's partly, I think, that I feel my clumsiness more, the disability that prevents me from venturing up the track, or going into the field beyond the pond where I could get a view of Cawston church tower. Returning from our visit to the coast yesterday, Salle appeared over trees, the pinnacle tower tall and graceful, almost like a cathedral. How I love these Norfolk churches in the landscape! More than picturesque, if meaning only for few what they once meant.

29 August

Morning walk with Lee round garden & wild meadow. Fresh wind gusting from north-west. Warm in patches of sun. Part of the meadow purple with knapweed. Cornflowers, yarrow, pansies, corn cockle, a few poppies in the wild flower garden. Ladybirds on thistles. Few butterflies: speckled wood, a green-veined white.

30 August

Up track on grass verge, to a high place from which we can see the undulating land all round. Below us, Moor Farm, an ancient settlement, originally farming cattle & sheep in marshland, barn like an upturned boat. Cumulus with cirrus above, a vapour trail like a unicorn, or 'cartoon narwhal'. Tiny grasshoppers jump under our feet. The sandy, flinty, sowed field looks as though it has been combed.

Lee talks about his forthcoming exhibition, 'Banter', with Desmond Brett in a former maltings at Halesworth in Suffolk. I broach the subject of a book about his work drawing on visits over the years recorded in my journal. A personal book, which would include material from our collaborations. He responds enthusiastically. We discuss the practicalities – mainly, finding a publisher for an illustrated book – which looks daunting.

It is hot in the sun when we sit outside but cool in shadows and a breeze, as a cloud mass comes over.

When Lee first came to live at Moor Farm he asked himself: 'where is the edge between country and city?'. He wanted to be part of something bigger than city culture. Art schools teach that the artist now can only be ironic, cynical. He is still trying to make original work, and stresses the importance of raw, authentic energy. It pleased him when speaking to two men from Goldsmith's, they looked at each other and said: 'This guy's a romantic'.

> 'Do you work from nature?' (Hans Hofmann)
> 'I am nature' (Jackson Pollock)

Something I've learnt from Lee – though increasingly coming to it on my own – is openness. For example: to take in what is going on, and being lauded, in the contemporary 'art world' in its own terms, without wasting energy with anger. To be aware of what is happening in one's own time without losing focus on one's own work. It doesn't mean being less critical – how could one value good work without being critical? It means being more aware, and readier to be surprised, and to detach from the meretricious, 'placing' it, if necessary, but not hurting oneself with negative feelings. Appreciation of good but neglected work is my way, which helps to make a way in for others.

24 May 2012

At Moor Farm. 'Beginning of summer,' Lee said, as we stepped outside. Immediately, a honey scent of rapeseed from surrounding fields & a shock of colours – yellow, blue sky, reds of barn, greens, white may in hedge. Two swallows on the barn roof. Cow parsley beginning to flower, red campion, hedge mustard, ramsons in a wild patch beside the lawn; bird's eye, scarlet pimpernel, wild strawberry on gravelly margins. A few last primroses. Bluebells gathering.

In the snug Lee showed me his Lima studies, some paintings made at Miraflores, where Louis and Laura have their apartment, looking over high cliffs on which the city is partly built. Studies of block 'objects', including pebbles from the beach. 'Like living in a Morandi.'

'Foreshore': bits and their background, detritus, objects that have lost their use, at the point of transition (by the Pacific but also alongside the Thames), starting to transmute into something else. Objects from the crumbling city, being reconfigured, and becoming other in the painting. 'Pack': an acrylic influenced by the tsunami, stuff from modern life washed down the river. The beginning of an image, the 'place' sculpture might come from; a creation myth, stuff floating, like a pack of ice, like a face.

In the barn. Like entering a cave of magic objects, and walking into a strong smell of oil paint. Two big canvases: grounds from which things and figures emerge. Dualities, dichotomies: built/dynamic, growing: the centre from which all Lee's work comes. He is working from cartoon-like studies. As he says, influence from Philip Guston is strong in his later work. A work-in-progress, untitled, but might be called 'Crowd', struck me as being, potentially, an iconic image for our time. Inspired by the riots in London last year: a wall of faces emerging, dissolving, 'drawn with grey & white undercoat paint, images emerging from drips.

As we sat talking a swallow became trapped in the roof space above us, and Lee, by turning off the lights, managed to get it to fly out to the light outside.

Afternoon

Sitting out on the lawn in sun & breeze, talking. A surround of bird song, twittering, lyric snatches or syllables, a robin close by, a blackbird farther off, harsh cry of a pheasant from the woods.

Later, sitting on the sofa beside Lee looking at his pictures of Peru, I couldn't get up without help, and felt what a lump I am!

Evening: a lesser spotted woodpecker on Guy's oak. As twilight darkened, we watched from the house for the barn owl, and were unexpectedly rewarded by two hares appearing, and running round each other by the two old apple trees. And the owl did appear, entering the box in the sycamore, made precisely with this hope in mind, and then flying out. Presumably the male, with food for his mate within.

23 May

My second visit with Lee to St Faith's, Little Witchingham. Outside, within a semi-circle of leafy lime trees, a graveyard of leaning or fallen stones, ground elder, red campion, nettles, grass and parsley growing towards the windows. Inside, a familiar musty smell, and an empty interior lit by sunlight through the windows, but not the emptiness I have felt in other churches and cathedrals, for this one, though no longer in 'use', is alive with the paintings on the walls: fragmentary images from the

Passion story, in red ochre. It isn't 'art' only that makes the place alive, but masterly brushwork, the superb freehand drawing, calligraphy, 'as good as any Chinese painting'. 'Incredibly sophisticated, Mantegna, Giotto, that kind of quality.' And of course, it's the story, rendered delicately, gently, with loving attention, and to us, perhaps, more moving because fragmentary, as if emerging from, or struggling to survive obliteration.

Lunch in the garden on a perfect early summer afternoon, reminiscing. Sky apparently cloudless but with a little cirrus. Less breeze today. A bath of warmth.

Early evening. Swallows overhead, hawking. Sun on the field maple by the pond – luminous, almost fluorescent.

Later, Lee showed me a DVD of Philip Guston. What I took from it was a sense of raw energy, the courage to approach the real anew, and make out of life as one experiences it, not an idea or ideal, but raw experience, the 'thickness' of things, making one's own story, accepting more that is given, trusting instincts.

Always here, at Moor Farm, I have a sense of creative possibility, of what I might, and should, write.

24 May

The wall paintings at Little Witchingham sent us to see the painting at All Saints, Weston Longville, ascribed also to the East Anglian school. This is a large church, in use; empty, except for the female Church Warden with whom we had a friendly chat. In the Tree of Jesse interlacing vine stems form roundels containing figures, rather like illuminated initials in medieval bibles. Again, the details are moving – heads, faces, feet, medieval dress. What moved me most, however, is something easy to miss – a Saxon Calvary, set in a step of the font, and worn down to its bare shape. Lettered slate slabs, many of them black, partly cover the floor. Some are 17th and early 18th century. Parson Woodforde, for whom this church is famous, would have stepped on them. I would guess he was a man who lived as completely in his world as any man ever has.

Early evening, in the barn with a cold beer, looking with Lee at 'From Nature', a work in progress. A painting split into two parts, mainly in different shades of green. On the smaller left side, a movement of blobs and drips, like cellular forms; on the right a *thicket* (based on the plantation beside the beck, which was rough open ground when I first came here): a tangle of branches and leaves with spaces among them. We sat talking, sun circles on walls and paintings through gaps in the roof.

Lee is working on paintings as 'ground', from which sculptural figures emerge, for example, survivors from a building, or monsters from a wood. He conceives paintings as scenes, worlds that figures relate to, from which they come. Animate figures, pulling themselves together out of debris. The result in the sculptures – 'Blue Legs', for example – is grotesque, vitally expressive, larger than life, but (as I see them) an enlargement and mirroring of human attributes, as monsters and cartoon figures are, but with sculptural shaping and energy. 'Parts can be a whole,' Lee says.

25 May

Sun, breeze stronger, blowing blossom off the old apple trees. Just glimpsed, passing over the lawn, a yaffle, identified by its looping flight. No one lives in paradise, but if they did, in England, this would be one place. Walked alone through the gap where the gate had been, between the pond, sheltered by trees and a flowering hawthorn, and the field edge. Here the field is a newly ploughed area of rhythmic, curved lines of reddish-brown clods, alongside the rapeseed. Over the field and beyond a copse, a view of Cawston church tower. The old tree stump where I've sat before, has been hollowed out, crumbled down to soil, by beetles, fungi, woodlice, insects. I know, in the church roof, the gaze of wooden angels, primitives of another age, faces set towards another world.

An afternoon lazing on the lawn listening to the Test Match on the radio. Wasps taking fibres from the wooden chairs to make their nest. Buttercups and bird's eye at the edge, clusters of daisies across the lawn – flowers my mother taught me to see and love.

26 May

Sat in the garden with Lee talking about earlier days – his parents' separation, when he lived in Harlow with his mother and visited his father in London, his 'Mod' and my 'Beat' period in the '50s and early '60s. Walking round part of the garden by myself, I was able to take long strides, moving better than usual, when I could feel sure of my footing. At lunch we drank chilled wine under the apple trees and I ate a Cromer crab which Kate had ordered specially for me. Three buzzards circled high over the plantation and the field beyond.

27 May

What a world of difference there is between East Anglia and South Wales – the landscapes, with the histories whose imprint they bear. Differences also in the places in-between, the great flat spaces of Cambridgeshire, London and the country of the M25, the skies near Heathrow, Wiltshire downland, the Severn… What I notice particularly are the Norfolk lanes and fields, and the hills and former mining villages of Glamorgan. And Moor Farm is present to my mind. I can see the place, and feel as if I could reach out and touch the bricks with my fingers, and walk from room to room and up the crooked wooden stairs. I know it isn't mine, but belongs to Lee and Kate and their lives, and I'm only a visitor. But the meanings to me – the friendship it represents, the example of imaginative energy and invention – are part of my life. No one inspires me like Lee. Without neglecting anyone or anything that is important to him, his work is the centre of his life, the thing that makes him who he is. It is a constant inventiveness, in the mind, and in practice, without which mental concepts are nothing. He holds together a feeling for tradition with a keen sense of our own times, the world as it now is. In consequence his work is *of now, and simultaneously a development from artistic traditions.* In many ways it is an affront to the contemporary art world, appearing crude, 'out of order', too full of life, I'd say, dynamic, energetic, bold and humorous. I've watched it over thirty years as an astonishing growth, a process of evolving forms, with constant, unpredictable inventiveness drawing upon a central dichotomy of the natural and the built, nature's creative energy and human constructions. I came away with the gift of a painting which I'd admired on my last visit: a diptych, 'Night Birch 11', the winter tree illuminated, like lightning, against its absence, the dark void.

8 October

From Lee's 'Stuff Becomes', UEA Talk 2012:

'I used to burn old sculptures when they were made of more flammable materials. I felt that there was a moment when I might rescue the work from the flames and it would emerge as a better piece. The older reality would be gone, a more authentic totality would be in its place, a never-before-seen thing, from which nothing could be taken away or added. …

In my processing of material into sculpture I would like my engagement to be as impartial yet as aggressive as the fire.

I am interested in ruins. My sculptural imagination is drawn to answer questions like: What is left standing? What survives? What is the core body? Such are the stuff of the sculptor's dreams.

Destruction is central to creativity and making. Everything changes, process is throughout the cosmos and I want my art making to be of that nature.

...

Doubt will be a part of great making, asking continual questions, daring to fail. Meaning cannot be illustrated, it has to be embodied in every part of the work.'

The last sentence I've quoted follows Lee's words about Michelangelo's Rondanini Pietà: 'A restless searching vision is material evidence'.

He talks of work often starting 'with a feeling that demands visualisation' and says: 'There is in my work a mixture of humour and fear'.

'I have never been interested in any orthodox idea of beauty, but rather I find beauty in something having a convincing energy within itself and often this authenticity of character could be perceived as ugly to someone else.'

On a grey day here in Wales, low cloud over the valley, some yellow and brown leaves among trees, his words and the new images he has sent me take me back to Moor Farm and our conversations. Always, he reminds me, creativity isn't thought alone. Words, like sculpture, have to have the body behind them, in feeling, with its roots in physical sensation, if not in the vigour of a walking poet. Any *body* of work has a life behind it. Any real poem is material evidence.

26 June, 2013

In 1972, Lee saw the reproduction of a Philip Guston painting: "Ever since I have been interested in a form of 'anti-aesthetic' which would never be the prevalent taste. It's about recognising that feeling when confronted by genuine visual invention. There is a particular kind of presence about a work of art that immediately meets the viewer with a certain discomfort, strange and awkward, but then the image stays in the memory, refuses to go away". 'Conversation with David Webb'

'Destruction is central to creativity and making. Everything changes, process is throughout the cosmos and I want my art making to be of that nature.'

'A restless, searching questioning vision (that goes on to the end)...' 'I am trying perhaps to build a body of work that constitutes a whole other place.'

Void Symposium Talk, June 7, 2013

Again, Lee is his own best commentator, in our culture where it seems very few 'in the know' about contemporary art have any interest in looking at and responding to such work. How much I've learnt from him! If we'd never met, I suspect my taste in sculpture would have been fairly conventional, if not for 'usual woodcraft clichés, beauties and sentimentalities'. It hasn't always been easy for me to follow him, as new work has broken my taste. But I have appreciated the energy, and understood the constant inventiveness. At the same time, my feeling of imminent breakthrough – of Lee being recognised as one of the important artists of our time – has receded. And he will go on working, inventing, whether recognized or not.

I suppose the message to me as a poet, as always, is energy: the life in the work that breaks old forms and makes new ones. What I require is courage.

12 July

Lee arrived in the afternoon for a four-day visit. He & Joe prepared a barbecue in the patio, where we sat out under fruit trees in the garden, with oak & ash trees towering over the park wall. Walking from the car in the heat to see the practise nurse in the afternoon I felt wobbly.

14 July

Lee cutting back bamboos & trees in our wild garden, letting more light into the yard. A pair of buzzards mewing, circling higher & higher on a thermal over park & quarry woods.

We watched the exciting Test match on TV. Later I looked with him at his images on his iPad and listened while he talked.

He's now making what he calls 'a group of characters', 'animate beings'. 'They stand.' He is 'imagining a place in the future'. For this he uses old furniture, bits & pieces of discarded structure. 'Debris' is an important word: e.g., wrecked stuff left by a tsunami, and the Thames foreshore at low tide, city fabric crumbling. Lima too was an influence, ancient city of the Incas, and modern city, often surrounded by mist, on cliff edge. His 'characters' are 'shanty figures' cobbled together from what is to hand, discarded furniture, etc., their histories reused. He uses plaster, cement in liquid form, so that his figures are like something that has emerged from mud.

Lee doesn't deny – or encourage – my perception of a post-nuclear world. He's after characters that are sensate, with consciousness other than the human. He's thinking through making, producing objects that can be envisioned but not read. They're not conceptual. He's against conceptualism, but not against thinking!

He spoke again about Philip Guston ('my generation's Cézanne'). Guston was a great teacher. Late in his career, he abandoned one style and adopted another which was against the grain, painting ugly, difficult images. Lee mentioned the German new expressionists (e.g. Kiefer, Baselitz) and the work of Rose Wylie currently occupying one room at the Tate. The interest in popular culture ('which is in us') isn't literal, as it is with so many fashionable contemporary British artists. Lee wants to get at something more fundamental, biological, underlying culture (being, standing, sex, blood, earth: not superficial appearances of pop culture, but 'being in the world'). The characters and their 'place' are new images. They're also a development of the built/ grown dichotomy that Lee has been exploring for many years.

Late in the afternoon we drove up onto the moors above Bedlinog where there was a breeze. Beacons in haze, scraggy sheep, ponies that may be descended from pit ponies; in the distance open-cast mines, grassed slag heaps, quarries, and, alas, evidence of fly tipping. Here, started off by a good article about history teaching in *The Guardian Review*, we talked about ancestry. Lee feels himself to be a Londoner & a European, not English. He does however have an Orwellian kind of patriotism in his love of the land. As a young boy, his father took him to Shoreham in Kent on Communist Party social weekends. Later too he went there, when his father was Secretary for the Society for Friendship with Bulgaria. Lee spoke of his feeling for the downs (where Glynn Williams now lives, near Amesbury) and I know he feels the same about Norfolk. He says that in Winchester I brought him to a sense of the importance of subject as 'opening to the world'.

Back on the road through Gelligaer, a red kite over the moors, foxgloves, elder flowers & purple thistles by dry-stone walls.

'Keep working in a way that is true to yourself.'

We talked several times about 'our book'. Next year – God willing – I'll search my journals for all the passages about Lee & his work. These, edited, will be part of the book, together with a selection of his images over the years, extracts from his writings, and from my Ipswich pamphlet, and selections from *Their Silence a Language*. It will also include a short memoir of Lee's early (London) years.

23 November 2014

Lee has sent me images of his show, *The Way Things Are 2014,* an installation of new Sculpture and Painting, at Clifford Chance, Canary Wharf. A room of brightly coloured, animate figures, strange beings, reminiscent of cartoons. He is 'very engaged in present work, using a process that brings painting together with sculpture, moves from drawing shape to building form'. He speaks of the objects as 'survivors from the ruins of things, built of fragments but achieving some presence of that nobility that survivors have'. These, 'in a certain sense,' could be said to 'emerge from the ruins of modernism. One rebuilds in one's own way that which one loves'.

Always, with Lee, this sense of connection with the past, while aiming to make something that he's never seen before. What I perceive is his striking originality. While he's aware, as I am, of the influence of Philip Guston, what he's making are distinctive Grandjeans – a further instance of the 'constant inventiveness' Kate spoke of.

How good it would be to see them now. Moor Farm is one of the places I can walk through in my mind – the house, the garden, the studio, the lanes & paths & fields, with, here, a view of Cawston church tower, and, there, trees hiding Salle. There will probably be a green woodpecker on the lawn. As the light fades, a barn owl will hunt along the beck. Indoors, we'll sit by the log fire, and talk.

11 June 2015

Excursion with Lee (who arrived yesterday evening) to Llantwit Major. At the beach on the Bristol Channel, sea changing colours of blue, grey, green, the Somerset coast a darker blue. Wash wash of waves on smooth blue-grey stones under the Jurassic cliffs. Cloud shadow, white waves, big gulls patrolling or riding the waves. This ancient seaway which bore the blue stones from Preseli to Wiltshire. Smell of fish & chips from the beach café where we had lunch. Lee gave me a fine cuttlebone, which reminded me of my first shore, at Warsash in wartime, when we picked them up and took them home for the chickens,

From the beach we drove to St Illtyd's Church and looked at the Celtic stones in the restored Galilee Chapel. The Samson Cross ('Samson erected this cross for his soul') & Samson Pillar & The Howell Cross, with interlaced so-called 'decoration', which surely represents a spiritual maze. The sacred stones in the restored church are an impressive sight, but also, inevitably, like museum pieces so that it's hard now to imagine the world they belonged to, which was that of divine learning, *peregrini*, & fierce *men such as Gildas.*

Travelling on, past St Donat's, we descended to Southerndown, the Jurassic cliffs & the sea.

12 June

This morning Lee showed me pictures of his new work, much of it from the space of the international law firm (Clifford Chance), & paintings & sculptures involving monoprinting. These were mainly hybrid, humanoid forms, strange, comic, yet also noble 'beings', surviving the collapse of all things, and made from 'debris' (a favourite word for Lee). Later I asked him about his sense of apocalypse, which I've seen in his work of recent years. One meaning arises from his reconstruction of modernism, building from fragments, seeking possibilities of new forms. He's 'always a Cubist'. Guston is important for his work in the cartoon tradition with its complete remaking of reality. There's a link here to African sculpture with new equivalents for eyes & mouths. In this sense, apocalypse relates to art, the beginnings & ends of artistic traditions. But Lee is also acutely aware that for some people it is always the end of the world, as in Syria & Iran & parts of Nigeria today. The artist needs to *make* in the face of ending, which is not an imagined future, but here and now.

In art, nightmare can be beautiful, as in Philip Guston's work, and in Picasso's. Lee has also been influenced by reading Samuel Beckett & Primo Levi. What I've been slower to understand is his use of energy & humour drawn from imagery of popular culture & fashion, as in the vulgarity of 'Lips on Sticks', and in 'Fashion' itself (raucous, dressed up on red carpet, Hello magazine imagery). There's lyricism also in works which respond to his granddaughter, such as 'O Girl'. He's seeking to make, from everything he sees, a coherent 'presence', in the form of 'complex things, not easily read'.

I was touched also by the pictures of Moor Farm & surroundings which Lee brought me, since he knows I'm unable to visit this year.

Later we went to Senghenydd and the Gardens which memorialize the victims of the two terrible pit disasters of the early years of the last century. Here, 'The Rescue' is a very different sort of work from Lee's modernist sculptures and it brought tears to my eyes, while he was moved by looking at the names of all the men and boys who had died in the explosions. Another sculpture represents a young girl holding her sister in her arms, carved from a living sycamore on the site. While in the Gardens we were joined by two old miners who are employed to keep it tidy. Lee talked with one of the men, as I talked with the other, who told me the following story. In the crowd on the day when the Memorial Garden was opened to the public, he was approached by a woman who addressed him by name: 'Hello, David'. He responded by asking her how she knew him. 'I'm your sister,' she said. And she was. She had emigrated to Canada many years ago.

13 June

At last, after attempts yesterday & several wrong turnings today, we found our way, by narrow, winding, rough lanes uphill, to Eglwysilan, on the hill across the valley. This is out of sight over the ridge of the mynydd which I look out of now, from my study window, but difficult to find. And what is there is a large pub, The Rose and Crown, and a big church, within a graveyard where a number of men killed in the Senghenydd pit disasters are buried. But today there was no sign of anyone and it was hard to imagine a congregation, or customers at a pub apparently so difficult of access. Church & pub are very much in use, however. The mystery of the place, as we experienced it, is compounded by the name of the Saint to whom the church is dedicated. Saint Llan may have been an early Celtic saint, or the name may be a corruption of Helen (Mother of Constantine), or of Elen, or Elian, or no person at all, but 'llan', the place of a church & religious community. As we drove back down, the white buildings of the university appeared folded in the land below, and I remembered often looking up from them to the mountain, but from neither side can the church between the Aber and Taff valleys be seen.

14 June

Lee left for his long drive home after tea yesterday. For three days we had talked and enjoyed each other's company, at home, in the car, at The Bunch of Grapes in Pontypridd, where we'd had lunch every day. For me, it was a release from tension. I can't say how much this means to me; he I so steady, with such ready understanding. What I learn from him, as always, is about work, and the need to avoid culture snobbery, and to be open to the energy of our prevailing culture. His life has a whole urban dimension that mine lacks, and in consequence he is more open, and not prone to nostalgia & narrow natural vision, which tempt me.

His mother, at 98, is sinking. She no longer recognises Lee and he is preparing himself for her funeral and the words he will speak. Given her love of nature, he asked my advice, and I responded by showing him Dorothy Wordsworth's description of coming upon the daffodils which inspired her brother's poem. This was what he wanted.

22 June

Lee's post-catastrophe figures attract me more and more. I realise that he's responding to our time as a whole, not isolating one part of it, as artists and poets tend to do, whether to celebrate a contemporary spirit or to escape into an imagined past. His earlier work, in wood or stone, was closer to my primitivism. As always, what he does challenges me. To break my taste. To be less narrow.

15 February 2016

Last night I spoke on the phone to Lee & Kate, who were waiting to hear of the birth of Guy's second child. Lee, full of work as ever, with exhibitions this year in Norwich & Manningtree & a visit to Berlin to make sculpture. In Norwich he will show his group of figures called 'Speakers', because recordings inside them will give them a kind of voice. In my mind's eye I can imagine something of this – an art responding to Philip Guston & Samuel Beckett, and post-apocalyptic. Far on from the sculpture I first saw Lee at work on, in Winchester and then at Moor Farm. First & last, though, *invention.* Work in a great tradition, but always new, responding to our time. How well I can visualize Lee & Kate by the log fire in the sitting room, a little snow on the dark garden, the night fields spreading far around, tawny owls calling in the woods. I can be there in my mind, and wonder whether I shall ever be there bodily again.

18 October

Lee rang in the evening, on his 68th birthday. We discussed him taking me to Norfolk for a week in November, to stay at Moor Farm and visit three shows that he will have on then. He spoke of my *Diary of a Stroke* with love. He has a special liking for the fragmentary form of my journals. So do I! He finds a sadness, a melancholy, in the book, and speculates that it is due to my Christian upbringing, and continuing preoccupation with religion. I suppose this does colour my kind of seriousness, and the questions that press on me. His intelligence is more *robust* – as befits a sculptor, one might say. He was brought up with a materialism that underpins his thinking, though what he has made of it – constantly makes with it – is far more subtle & flexible than his father's dogmatism. It may be that I look out more, wondering about death & personal survival, & the 'question of God'. I wouldn't expect Lee to take much interest in Kierkegaard or contemporary theology! But he's far from being a man imprisoned by a glass-walled universe.

If I do express a sadness, it's because it's part of me, integral to my sense of things. I've never found the given world enough, in the sense of a self-revelation of what is. It's always had a margin of mystery for me. More than a margin; the world is mysterious through & through. And this sense draws me to the languages of religions, and the speculations of theologians. I feel the Church as a reality that I'm outside of, not as a groundless idea. In that feeling, that not belonging, there is, I suppose, a sense of loss, however much I enjoy the pleasure of living.

3 November

In the evening I phoned Lee to tell him I wouldn't be able to come to Norfolk with him later in the month. I have been feeling insecure & lacking in confidence since my fall, and my worry isn't about the journey but about Moor Farm & the surroundings, for here, with special hand rails, I can get around the house without much danger of falling, but the conditions there would be risky for me. I need help with dressing now, and although Lee & Kate would have arranged everything for my comfort, there would have been difficulties. Lee understood completely, he had half expected it; but we are both disappointed.

I shall probably see Lee again – he will come here – but I'm unlikely to be able to visit Moor Farm again. It seemed doubtful on the last one or two occasions, but now it seems certain. I can see it all so clearly in my mind – the beloved place, the old house, the rooms, the barn studio, the garden with the horse pond – rabbits & moorhens on the lawn, a green woodpecker – the fields around, Cawston church tower, the pinnacles of Salle …. Often walking around by myself, I've wondered about the absence of the generations that lived there, builders & farmers, names & tallies scratched in brick. … Yet it is so much Lee & Kate's, and the place of his work: one of the great good places, I believe. I may not go again, but Moor Farm will live in my mind & heart as long as I live.

13 November

'Wanting to get to the raw core of things, I had this vision some time ago, an imaginative narrative, that when everything collapses, there will be a compost of all things, of all structural and organic things mixed up in the mud of cities, concrete dust and so on, and that out of this general debris, hybrids of being might emerge. That's a sort of creation myth …'

Lee, in conversation with Nell Croose, Outpost Gallery

In his text to The Outpost exhibition, Lee speaks of the inspiration for his groups of figures (and the title of the exhibition) in the last line & final stage direction of *Waiting for Godot* ("'Let's go [They do not move]": 'It is the condition I celebrate in sculpture: all the energy is implicit and potential, all possibility in one moment, going on in a frozen forever'.

His later work – the groups of figures – could easily be seen as a dire apocalyptic warning: 'Mashups: human, animal, insect. What distorted combinations inhabit the last dreams? But in them, also, is 'humour and perhaps a noble survival, is at the heart of it'.

The Beckett influence and the influence of Philip Guston are strong in these figures, which are also quintessential Grandjeans. The figures may be unsettling – he rejects the smooth & beautiful; he's more interested in the ugly, but his 'objects of survival, from the debris and ruin' don't depress. They're not made in a spirit of failure, either personal or end-of-the-world. The maker's energy is in them, and his joy in work. As he says at the end of the interview: 'I love doing this, I run to the studio!'

That is what Lee has given me over the years: energy, the joy in work that is energy. It's what he has helped to release in me, against the downward drag of lazy & depressive inclinations, and as a balancing counter-force to my concentration on thinking. I don't undervalue the latter. but, exercised at the expense of making, it is harmful. This journal, I think, is partly helpful, and partly injurious. It damages when totally abstracted from work, and when dwelling on negative feelings. It helps when working to push through, to move on; when it *quickens.* It belongs, then, with the body of work that I live to make.

21 September 2017

Lee arrived before lunch today, having stayed overnight in London. He brought images of his four granddaughters, and of Moor Farm & new work. His latest sculptures (cement over wire mesh) show his fascination with the image of martyrs, especially paintings of St Sebastian. This relates to his thinking about the difference between sculpture and painting. In painting the martyr or saint is idealized, symbol of spirit. Sculpture is the physical event.

Later I introduced Lee to the thinking of Alfred North Whitehead, the philosopher who confirms one's sense of process & flux, of being ***in*** the work. For Lee, a little information is suggestive.

22 September

In rain & mist, we drove on the road to Brecon, stopping for lunch at Ty-Newydd Country Hotel. We could see, when visible, bronze patches of dying bracken on the mountainsides. The sky lightened but did not clear. A faint rainbow appeared in front of us.

23 September

Lee talked to me about *Meeting*, a sculpture in our *Groundwork* exhibition. He explained how he had travelled on the train from Norwich into London at night, coming into the city past the backs of houses with glimpses of lit rooms & fragments of lives. Walking in London among trees & buildings he was aware of destructive & creative forces all in process, and buildings blown up, becoming cloud. I had thought of his earlier work in relation to 9/11. Now he spoke of the Grenfell disaster and of his sculpture as 'monument of events that happened after its making'. There's no claim to prophecy in this, and no aesthetic satisfaction at a human tragedy. I would explain it by saying he is close to the pulse of events in our time, aware of destruction & creation, and of culture & nature & their interactions. He is sensitive to cataclysmic change, and to complexity and chaos, as integral to order in nature. He sees and feels sculpturally, in material processes – growing, building, breaking, dissolving, growing and making anew. Biological processes operate below culture; they are centred in the body, which is our vehicle of perception. 'The mind is physical', material but fully animated, transcending materiality. Transformation is at the core.

What is the root difference between us? Lee is more pagan than Christian. He has a strong sense of myth which he owes to his mother. She was a storyteller; his father was more the doctrinaire Marxist. Lee talks to nature; he can play with the idea of gods & goddesses.; trees give him comfort as living things. I cannot speak for Christianity, but Christianity, with belief in the personal God-man, is part of my imaginative world. He has found his way, using ideas, not being used by them, as we must.

In the afternoon, we drove in sunshine into Caerphilly for Lee to buy key rings and dragon soft toys for his granddaughters (four little girls that 'Gramps' adores). On the way he started to talk about death, the strange idea of not being. He has no belief, and no interest in, ideas of life after death. We agree that living and working in the here and now is what matters. We hope our work will matter to those who come after. As I sat in the car waiting for him to make his purchases four or five seagulls flew over, their cries bringing me a sense of the sea. Afterwards we drove again on the mountain road, seeing the mountains that mist had hidden.

In the evening I questioned Lee further about the work he has shown over the past year, especially *Home Truths* at North House Gallery, Manningtree. All representations of the body, including cartoons (boyhood comics, Philip Guston) interest him. He makes objects that are wholly artefacts, embracing many things that bodies have (torsos, noses, hands, etc.). He celebrates the misshapen; figures in Beckett's late plays are a particular influence. He admires Paolozzi: debris, hybrids of the grown & built. His material is out of ruins, e.g., plywood, cement. He finds cement good to use, it is alive to him, from first touch as a child. He is drawn to stuff of the building site and everyday urban surfaces. His figures/characters have humour & dignity, like figures in Beckett. When life is reduced, humanity is revealed in small things (Primo Levi).

With carving, Lee was starting again. But he found the materials, especially wood, too laden with history. (I remember what Peter Fuller wrote about his wooden sculptures in relation to East Anglian medieval sacred art.). Lee is working out of the debris of modernism, trying to rebuild. He has said this or something like it to me before, and it has struck me as being the sort of thematic statement critics could understand, which might help them to *see* his work. But it's too simple – all words are. Ideally, one would be in the presence of his sculptures, while he talks about them. Anything else, including my notes, risks falsifying the sculptural imaginative process and the thinking it engenders.

There's a theatrical quality to his 'characters'. The space of the Manningtree living rooms made for interactions among them. In another show, in a former shoe shop in Norwich, two years ago, he collaborated with a sound artist who placed speakers inside the sculptures to make grunts (more like Beckett). The figures included *Blue Legs & Gob*: things in 'chattering' relationships.

And where, I ask, were the critics to see and write about these exhibitions? Where, indeed! It enrages me to think about such neglect. Lee takes it quite calmly: doing the work is the thing.

He spoke to me of his interest in Caro's earliest *Man Taking Off His Shirt*, which shows what it's like being in a body. (An ambition Caro abandoned for a more forma, aesthetic, 'outer' arrangement of parts.) With body we feel the form. He admires Rodin's *Earth.* Using odd bits of material left lying about Moor Farm – old Xmas trees & carpentry – with paint, helps him to beat 'the cliché of driftwood'. Bright colours characterise his later sculptures, which at times have to my eyes a harlequin effect. He has recently been using roots to make root form images, but isn't satisfied with them.

When I think back over the years that I've been looking at Lee's work and recognising his 'constant invention', I realize that I've acquired some sense of his sculptural imagination and how it works in the process of making. But the sculptures have to be looked at all round, touched, lived with, and no words can adequately describe their being.

Later

The sense I gain from talking with Lee about his work is that we are embedded in the world. We aren't, as some theorists of the brain think, complex systems of wires. Mind & imagination work through the body, through the whole organism with its senses, and mind embeds us all in our relationships with the world. Sculpture and language are different ways of exploring the deep experience of connectedness. This may help to explain my sense of working not so much with, as *within* language, and not just thinking about words, but sensing them. None of this is entirely clear to me; nor could it be. I work as a poet, not a theorist.

For Lee, mind is fully incarnate. This is a radically different idea from mind as an epiphenomenon of the brain as mechanism, even computer. I see that for him there is no need of God; the question of God's existence simply doesn't arise. I am more needy; neediness has defined me since I was a boy. This is a statement of fact, not a criticism, however much I have suffered from feeling incomplete. It isn't only childish, I think, to seek in the spirit world an invisible friend. From childhood, reaching out has been my way. It has its negative and positive poles, and I swing restlessly between them. In shaping a poem, I find temporary rest.

Lee makes reference to parts of the body, drawing the viewer's mind to their body feeling – they feel i*nto* these things/forms. As he says, 'I make to be more complete or feel more whole and connected'.

31 January 2018

Lee has come out as a poet:

Out of the corner of my eye,
Outside the window a change of light,
Rooks dropping into the ash trees.

This isn't news to me. In his care of words & vividness of expression he has always been a poet. Only he is first a shaper of physical objects, but ever an image-maker. He speaks of working energetically 'on several fronts, large figures/characters, drawings and small stone carvings of ruins. Still have ambition for canvases as background to the figures'. His message takes me to Moor Farm, where he is 'gathering wood, feeding the fire hearth. Trimming hedges, feeding the birds. ... Snowdrops up and massing. ... Winter work anticipating a purple moon Pink blue mornings frost set'. What a book he could write if he could spare time from his sculpture & painting! His words are, in any case, an integral part of his work as an artist: expressions of his whole imaginative life.

27 October 2018
'Ghosts and Things Almost Human': Lee's work in an exhibition, shared with five other artists, 'An Appetite for Risk', at The Cut, Halesworth, 4 Sept–10 Oct. Amanda Geitner, following an interview with Lee conducted in his studio, writes with sensitive understanding of his work. She describes a large canvas on which he has traced 'the detail of a bombed building in Aleppo, Syria', and speaks of his objects functioning 'as evidence of survival in the face of ruin'. 'From the Fields', a large standing figure, 'is only part human'. 'The title refers to Francis Bacon's 1950s series of paintings based on Van Gogh.'

"This creature is certainly sentient, caught in motion, and yet strangely weightless and fragile. Grandjean describes making objects that are 'more like the objects in a painting than objects in the real world.' ... This perhaps explains their otherworldly quality, as if the artist were trying to conjure for us a creature that lingers in his mind's eye after a particularly vivid dream."

The dream from which Lee's 'creatures' emerge is also our common dream, drawn from the daylight atrocities of the wars of our time, and the fear of a catastrophe – immediate or brought about by gradual change – that will destroy life as we know it. He is an artist of mutating human images, of humankind becoming monstrous. And if there were no universal threat? "Grandjean's interest is in our encounter with the 'lumpen fact of a thing', the biological basis of being in the world, be it insect or animal".

As I read these notes, I can almost hear Lee talking to Amanda Geitner, the figures & canvases around them in the studio creating a strangely attractive, magical and alarming world. In my mind's eye, too, I can see Mieke and me during our first visit to Moor Farm, both fit, and very much in love.

30 November

Talking with Lee, who arrived for a few days' stay this afternoon.

His fascination with 'the act of becoming a thing' (Homer: a reference to dying – the Gaul becoming thing). When you lose yourself in making an object. Body language: we know the world through body – human, animal, insect. This is an inexhaustible language to speak in. He has been having 'a rich time since finishing teaching'. For him, retirement was a release. He has never enjoyed work more. Using a phrase Kate rightly used of him, he speaks of his admiration of Picasso's 'constant invention' and 'plastic imagination', and speaking of energy – his key value – praised David Smith. Pollock's 'I am nature' speaks to him, if not interpreted egotistically. Imagination is a human thing: *making* a painting, not representing, but transforming, as in Cézanne. If the source is yourself, how do you get past ego? As a conduit, working with process. You make 'the thing that stands outside you'. He speaks of Morandi painting objects (pots, bottles on a shelf), creating not just descriptions, or symbols, but *life-forms*: paintings that shimmer, shake with vitality.

1 December

Further conversations on another day too wet & foggy to tempt us to go out.

Lee showed me pictures of his latest work using 'kits', based on an analogy with collage. I call these 'figures'; he calls them 'characters' – for example, 'Nomad', 'Stepping Out', 'Oh Ma, Oh Pa', 'History: The Hill', 'From the Fields'. These brightly coloured sculptural objects have a 'frozen dynamic'. They are still, but charged with energy. The influence of cartoons continues. As well as admiring Philip Guston, he loved *The Beano*, as I did. What's newer is his use of kits, which involves arranging shapes cut out of plywood. I understood this process better when he showed me pictures of Etruscan tombs: modelled surfaces showing the objects of a person's life.

Driving to Dan-y-Lan, Lee had felt some misgiving about arriving at this place closely associated with Mieke in his mind and finding her not here. But in a way she is here, and not only because we talked about her. I know how she would have enjoyed the conversation, listening to Lee and looking at pictures of his work, and joining in when we talked about politics, speaking mockingly & angrily of Brexit, Trump, etc.

2 December

On another foggy day, feeling tired, I went over Moor Farm in my mind, and talked with Lee about the place. He then spoke to me about his memories of boyhood in Bucharest. How cold it was in snow in the Carpathians, where he heard wolves. He had a nanny who took him to a German-speaking village in the mountains. He remembered vividly a blacksmith there, and a massive stone sharpening wheel, with a man astride it sharpening all the tools. He roamed streets of Bucharest barefoot; witnessed a pig-killing in the mountain village called Cincul; accompanied a shepherd boy working in the hills. He went on then to talk about his first home in Peckham Rye. All this was vivid, detailed: material that he intends to write in a memoir for his grandchildren. Others too should find it a fascinating book. Lee is a good storyteller and also, as I've long known, potentially a powerful writer.

In the evening we watched several Humphrey Jennings films, including *The Silent Village,* which I hadn't heard of, let alone seen, before. In this film, Jennings uses Cwmgiedd, a mining community in the Upper Swansea Valley, in 1943, for a documentary drama reconstructing the Lidice massacre. How this must have brought the tragedy home at the time. And now there is the additional tragic sense that the way of life of those good people, the miners & their families, with their compassionate internationalism and communal values, has gone: not just naturally, one generation following another, but betrayed, the industry that sustained it dismantled, and nothing provided to replace it. We talked about the film and about Jennings. Today too we discussed Zola, including his time in England.

3 December

'Lumpen' is an important word for Lee and his sense of bodily being in the world. (I suspect that it also carries early associations from his parents' work as communist activists.) He is interested in the inner made outer, and in fusion, painting, drawing and sculpture working together. He seeks freshness, to make an artefact that has life. For him, this also means oddness, as in his 'characters', which to my eye are both non-human and touchingly human. He spoke of his inability to draw accurately. This, I think, is a strength, since his real interest is in instresses, as in depicting the inner rhythm of trees. The particular: 'the thing that draws you to the thing'. He would rather see Cézanne's transformations of Mont St Victoire than the mountain itself. In Lee's own work, there is violence, and anxiety, and out of it, nobility. The reference here is especially to the characters, which one viewer described 'ennobling the disabled' – a phrase with special meaning for me.

Lee spoke of his great-grandfather, Louis Grandjean (whose Christian name he learnt only after his son, Louis, was christened), who, to avoid conscription, escaped to Britain from the siege of Paris during the Franco-Prussian war, rowing across the Channel. He became a boot maker in Soho. As a boy, Lee was fascinated by a model boot, made to represent the firm, which was in the possession of an aunt. Also, by the picture of a model hansom cab. As he spoke of this, I remembered the model wagon, or Hay Wain, 'ship of the harvest', which had been part of my family inheritance as a boy. Lee's sense of made object had clearly been very strong since boyhood. With me, something similar had influenced my feeling for words. Different as our backgrounds are, there are also deep affinities.

19 December

Lee is preparing with two young artists for an exhibition called 'Becoming Thing', in the new year. Also, another show later in the year, for which he asks me to write a piece.

'Becoming Thing'

"Emphasis on process and giving one's ego and presumption up to truly follow what is emergent from that process. Homer talks about dying as our being 'becoming thing' but one can perhaps think of the phrase as describing the artist giving certain aspects of self up (phenomenological bracketing is relevant here) to wholly accept what is discovered in the process of making. Yes, breaking one's taste to renew vision using physical process and improvisation in it, as an engagement with all of one's consciousness." (Lee Grandjean, 19/11/18)

What Lee always calls me back to is our physical (human) being, the embodied experience we share with all living creatures. While obviously applicable to sculpture, this also relates to modernist poetry and the 'poetic' novel (e.g., *Ulysses*). In Eliot, as well as Pound, the poem reaches for roots below 19th century idealism, and experience of spirit without body, floating free of the clay we are. Eliot was a great sensuous poet who was uncomfortable with body, and ultimately more at ease with the mysticism of *Four Quartets.* I think a contemporary religious poetry should be at once spiritual and enfleshed. Of course, Lee isn't a Christian artist. But he has, I think, a greater sense of the sacred than most.

9 March 2019

Figures in Lee's forthcoming show include ''The Dutch' (For M)', which he describes as follows:

'The Dutch Girl just emerged out of the process of making becoming more and more Dutch as it went on. Recognising the wooden clog foot was the start of it, had to search out what traditional Dutch costume hats looked like. This is that particular Delft blue as well and the pink rosy glow of it. Was thinking of Mieke all the while.'

It will be in a show now called 'The Dutch (For M)' and will be sited downstairs in proximity to Moore's Family Group. It's not a representative work. I doubt that Mieke's daughters would like it, if I were daring enough to show them a photo of it. But Mieke would have been amused and touched. She would have understood Lee's modernist form and image-making with its exaggeration and dismantling and reconstruction of the human body. He isn't cruel in his treatment of the human image, like Francis Bacon, or sexually violent, as Picasso was. Lee appreciates the human form. In 'The Dutch Girl' there's humour, beginning with the yellow, wooden clog. But this and the costume hat imply more than a token Dutchness. Thinking of Mieke, he says, and in this sculpture I can see her womanly shapeliness, and her solid substantiality (like the sea-clay of her land), while the colours hint at her magical being, like a Vermeer woman, absolutely *there*, and a mystery.

1 April

From Lee's 'Notes on Exhibition, Becoming Thing', which he shares with artists Alex Crocker and Laura Bygrave living near him in Reepham:

"What seems evident is an ambition: to let material and process 'speak' through image, and that the evolution of that image is 'made through the improvisation of material process which starts with an engagement with subject, and by transformative process a final image, derived from the subject, is discovered.'"

'Discovering new images is still possible. Style emerges out of the ambition to have clarity of expression in the final work, the result is the outcome of an adventure in critical process, what happens, happens, what survives, survives.'

'Art reflects complex fragmentary life, or rather what it feels like.'

'Do we remember in clear sequences or clear outlines? Recalled experience is a cubist construction of disjointed parts, emphasis shifts.'

This piece is characteristically generous. It also reflects the feeling of collaboration Lee enjoys with some younger artists. What I also notice is how he has achieved clarity through thinking *with* and *through* the process of making. He was always a thinking artist, highly individual in his mode of imagining and making, but in his ability to explain his work to himself, and to us, he has definitely become stronger and more lucid over the years.

Lee once told me that I had made him aware of the importance of subject. That was during our early talks at Winchester School of Art. In those days I was rather a slave to subject, as if certain elemental words would bring things before us, so that we could see and handle them. I risked literalism, which is a hazard of my sense of language, and the relation of word to thing. This, in turn, reflects a rather passive cast of mind. From Lee, I learnt more about process, about *working* the materials (language, imagery) and finding meaning – the shape of meaning – in the process.

4 August

In his message, Lee calls my new book of poems, *Word and Stone,* "a true 'refreshment'", and writes:

'I physically felt a truth, that poetry is an antidote, an anti-venom more literally, against the swirling unreason that surrounds us on all sides. … it was the very act of reading your words that pushed away shadow. To look at things with care, give proper attention, to love the truth that comes from deep looking at things.'

How good to think that my work 'pushes away shadow'. There is never any standing still. Like Lee, I live to work. And work is a constant making, a reassembling of oneself, and a pursuit. One's very being is process, with no end in one's lifetime.

27 September

Lee, in interview with Laura Bygrave:

'I think the things I make step out of painting in some ways; they occupy that world of the imagination. I want to make new forms, things that I haven't seen before, that perhaps don't exist in the world; about something that has been felt or that acts as some kind of embodied revelation.
'The studio is a space where everything is possible. …One loses oneself in process, just thinking through making. I'm trying to get at a certain kind of energy that is true to what emerges in the work …things are to be discovered … destination is a creative thing. It's a part of sculptural practice.'

Lee Grandjean, Thoughts on Making Sculpture and Painting, July 2020

In making my work I am as much interested in form as content, judging the work to be successful when there is a satisfactory balance between form and content. I am as engaged with image as I am with the fullest development of formal language, whether in sculpture or painting. In sculpture I have developed a process that takes me right through from drawing to final three-dimensional form. The work is discovered through process, there is no pre-design. Improvisation is at the heart of it. I draw on plywood, cut out the 'kit' of shapes, build with these as sections joined together with other structural timber and then partially fill out this 'armature'. I prefer to use readily available general building materials, sourced from the nearest DIY shop or builders' merchant, only paint do I get from a specialist art store.

I am creating bodies, beings in the world, characters, energies, animations. I don't pursue beauty, I am as interested in what is ugly. Truth to material is limiting. I USE stuff, transform it, animate it, want it to be wholly of the imaginative world of the sculpture. Improvisation within process is discovering my nature. I want to BE nature when I am working, fulfilling the visual logic that emerges during the process. The works 'grow' into their final form. Being true to that emergent image structure is the point, what it looks like is always a discovery. The content is visual and manifests wholly within the experience of the work. In sculpture I fuse drawing and painting with the physical object. I celebrate the word HYBRID.

I love the parallel activity of painting. I see my sculptures within the atmospheres set out in some paintings. Otherwise I might explore collections of shapes, laid out before they become locked into any fixed interrelationship. I draw and paint on paper to discover the images that float up from my conscious and unconscious memories. The distinctions of abstract, figurative, conceptual, are not relevant to me. Making art is a way of living life in the fullest possible way.

4 July 2022

Received in hospital, a card inscribed 'With love from Kate and Lee', displaying images of his 'Small Fires I–VI 2022, 'Carved redwood with alkyd paint'. Of this work, Lee writes:

'Here they are. Some primeval heat to place between other sculpture in the Harlow show. Probably be about eight. These aren't quite finished, might be touches of colour in final finish. I don't envisage them on plinths but on the floor, flickering energy. Here and there. A survival motif perhaps. The wood is Redwood'. (This derived from eight chunks from a tree that crashed in a friend's garden.).

'An early memory, seen from the busy Rye Lane to Tower Bridge, meths drinkers around a fire on the Elephant and Castle bomb-site. Also a small lead model of a camp fire in a book on toy soldiers.

Always wanted to make fire as thing. Here we are.'

'Fire made thing.' I remember the occasion when Lee made a fire of rejected or damaged wooden sculptures in the dark. Somehow, the energy of sculptures blazing up into the night sky was part of the sculptural experience. These redwood works on their plinths are spiky with a kind of arrested life. They might also be abstract images of deer caught in a moment of quivering attention – wooden, but charged with sensitive life.

The Harlow show has been postponed due to the Covid pandemic. It will now open 15 April through to June 2023

Printed in the card: *Keep the fires burning!*

www.ingramcontent.com/pod-product-compliance
Ingram Content Group UK Ltd.
Pitfield, Milton Keynes, MK11 3LW, UK
UKHW041931170425
457600UK00001B/38

9 781848 619715